Cost
Accounting
FOR
DUMMIES®

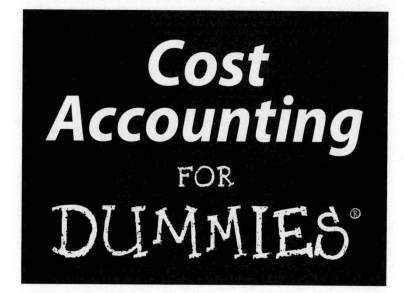

Cost Accounting FOR DUMMIES®

by Ken Boyd

WILEY

John Wiley & Sons, Inc.

Cost Accounting For Dummies®

Published by
John Wiley & Sons, Inc.
111 River St.
Hoboken, NJ 07030-5774
www.wiley.com

Copyright © 2013 by John Wiley & Sons, Inc., Hoboken, New Jersey

Published by John Wiley & Sons, Inc., Hoboken, New Jersey

Published simultaneously in Canada

For general information on our other products and services, please contact our Customer Care
Department within the U.S. at 877-762-2974, outside the U.S. at 317-572-3993, or fax 317-572-4002.

For technical support, please visit www.wiley.com/techsupport.

Wiley publishes in a variety of print and electronic formats and by print-on-demand. Some material
included with standard print versions of this book may not be included in e-books or in print-on-demand.
If this book refers to media such as a CD or DVD that is not included in the version you purchased, you
may download this material at http://booksupport.wiley.com. For more information about Wiley
products, visit www.wiley.com.

Library of Congress Control Number: 2012956409

ISBN 978-1-118-45380-3 (pbk); ISBN 978-1-118-45381-0 (ebk); ISBN 978-1-118-45382-7 (ebk);
ISBN 978-1-118-45383-4 (ebk)

Manufactured in the United States of America

10 9 8 7 6 5 4 3 2 1

WILEY

About the Author

Ken Boyd, a former CPA, has over 28 years of experience in accounting, education, and financial services. Ken is the owner of St. Louis Test Preparation (www.stltest.net). He provides online tutoring in accounting and finance to both graduate and undergraduate students. His YouTube channel (kenboydstl) has hundreds of videos on accounting and finance.

In recent years, Ken has served as an adjunct professor of accounting at the Cook School of Business at St. Louis University (SLU). Ken also worked as an instructor for Dearborn Financial, a division of Kaplan, Inc. In that role, he taught test preparation courses for the National Association of Security Dealers (NASD) Series 7, 6, and 63 exams. Ken taught over 1,000 students for Dearborn.

Ken has written test questions for the Certified Public Accountant (CPA) Exam for ACT, Inc. Ken is married and lives in St. Louis, Missouri, with his wife Patty and his three children, Kaitlin, Connor, and Meaghan.

Dedication

I dedicate this book to my father, Bill Boyd, who is a hero to me. I would also like to dedicate this book to my wife and closest friend, Patty, and our children. Finally, this book is dedicated to the faculty and staff of three St. Louis schools: Chaminade College Preparatory School, St. Peter Catholic School in Kirkwood, and Visitation Academy. Thank you for your devotion and for educating our children.

Author's Acknowledgments

I want to thank Erin Calligan Mooney, acquisitions editor, for the opportunity to write this book. Thanks also to Matt Wagner of Fresh Books Literary Agency, who presented me to Wiley. I owe a huge debt of thanks to Barry Schoenborn, who served as the technical writer for this book. His wit, wisdom, and work ethic helped me become a writer.

Many thanks to the Wiley team: Alissa Schwipps, senior project editor; Susan Hobbs, copy editor; and Anna K. Jensen and John T. Caldwell, the technical editors. They worked very hard to make this book more accurate and easier to read. Without them, there wouldn't be a book.

Publisher's Acknowledgments

We're proud of this book; please send us your comments at `http://dummies.custhelp.com`. For other comments, please contact our Customer Care Department within the U.S. at 877-762-2974, outside the U.S. at 317-572-3993, or fax 317-572-4002.

Some of the people who helped bring this book to market include the following:

Acquisitions, Editorial, and Vertical Websites

Senior Project Editor: Alissa Schwipps

Acquisitions Editor: Erin Calligan Mooney

Copy Editor: Susan Hobbs

Assistant Editor: David Lutton

Editorial Program Coordinator: Joe Niesen

Technical Editors: John T. Caldwell, CPA, MST, CGMA, Anna K. Jensen, MBA, CPA, CMA, CGMA

Editorial Manager: Christine Meloy Beck

Editorial Assistants: Rachelle S. Amick, Alexa Koschier

Cover Photo: © Dmitriy Shironosov / iStockphoto.com

Cartoons: Rich Tennant (`www.the5thwave.com`)

Composition Services

Project Coordinator: Sheree Montgomery

Layout and Graphics: Joyce Haughey

Proofreaders: Lindsay Amones, Kathy Simpson

Indexer: Valerie Haynes Perry

Special Help: Barry Schoenborn

Publishing and Editorial for Consumer Dummies

    Kathleen Nebenhaus, Vice President and Executive Publisher

    David Palmer, Associate Publisher

    Kristin Ferguson-Wagstaffe, Product Development Director

Publishing for Technology Dummies

    Andy Cummings, Vice President and Publisher

Composition Services

    Debbie Stailey, Director of Composition Services

Contents at a Glance

Table of Contents

Introduction

T he world needs accountants. People who know how to do accounting make the business world go round. Accountants analyze and report on every aspect of a business.

Cost accounting can be the most difficult accounting topic to grasp. This area has a unique language — a set of terms that differ quite a bit from other areas of accounting. Students and business owners may find cost accounting more challenging than other areas of accounting.

I wrote *Cost Accounting For Dummies* because your ability to understand this material has a huge payoff. Every business can be improved using cost accounting. The concepts help you to lower costs and increase profits. I'm passionate about helping you learn more about these critical topics.

About This Book

Some cost accounting books overwhelm you with dozens of complex topics. Not *Cost Accounting For Dummies*. Here, I focus on the really important topics that are used the most often. Accounting knowledge is meaningful when you can *use* it to solve a problem.

As a friend of mine once said, "It's hard to drink out of a fire hose," so I present the material in this book in an easy-to-read reference format. The book is logically divided into parts. Each part contains several chapters that are divided into readable "chunks" or sections. This system avoids blasting you with information. Instead, topics are introduced at a steady (but not overwhelming) rate, with concepts building on one another, making the reading (and understanding) easier.

The great thing about the book is that you decide where to start and what to read. It's a reference book. You can locate a topic in the table of contents or the index, read about it, and move on. Accountants love organization (most accountants place their pencils in order from shortest to longest). This book is organized to be a quick reference.

Conventions Used in This Book

I use the following conventions throughout the text to make information consistent and easy to understand:

- ✔ All web addresses appear in monofont.
- ✔ New terms appear in *italic type* and are closely followed by an easy-to-understand definition.
- ✔ **Bold** is used to highlight the action parts of numbered steps.

In accounting, sometimes two terms can mean the same thing. Here are some of those terms that you find in this book:

- ✔ *Cost of sales* has the same meaning as *cost of goods sold.*
- ✔ *Sales* and *revenue* mean the same.
- ✔ *Indirect costs* has the same meaning as *overhead costs.*
- ✔ *Predetermined, budgeted,* and *planned* all have the same meaning.
- ✔ *Net income* is also *profit,* for the purposes of this book.

This book discusses three of the four basic financial statements. The fourth statement, statement of retained earnings, isn't covered. Three components of the statement — retained earnings, dividends, and net income — are addressed using the other three financial statements. So the fourth statement wasn't needed. I cover financial statements in Chapter 6.

When numbers appear, I use numerals, not words. This is common in accounting books.

Finally, keep in mind that companies sell both products and services. Some companies are manufacturers, and some are retailers. You see examples from both perspectives throughout the book.

What You're Not to Read

I've written this book so that you can find information easily as well as effortlessly understand what you find. And though it'd be great if you read every word, I've set off some text from the main information, text you can live without if you're just after the reference material.

The stuff set off from the main text is interesting. It's meant to be funny and sometimes thought-provoking. But if you're just after the nuts and bolts, you can come back to these items later:

- ✔ **Text in sidebars:** Sidebars are shaded boxes that usually give detailed examples or flesh out historical perspectives on the topic at hand.

- ✔ **Anything with a Technical Stuff icon:** This icon indicates information that's interesting but that you can probably live without. Read these tidbits later if you're pressed for time.

Foolish Assumptions

I had to make some assumptions about you, the reader. As I wrote the book, here's what I assumed:

- ✔ You're someone who needs an easy-to-read overview of cost accounting. Also, you want to investigate the topics that are used the most often to solve problems. You may be reading this book while taking a cost accounting course, but a business owner who needs more cost accounting knowledge should also find value in reading it.

- ✔ You're able to follow basic arithmetic and algebra. Many of items you need to calculate appear in the form of equations. Accountants love to create an x or y variable and then solve for that variable, using an equation.

- ✔ You have a beginner's-level knowledge of how a business works. You understand that sales less expenses equals profit. You're aware that a business needs to have capital (cash, equipment, and so forth) to operate.

- ✔ You're willing to read, pause, and assess what you've read. Learning cost accounting takes some effort. It's not the sort of thing you can rush through. Whereas the text makes it easy to find information, it takes some effort to understand what you read. After you get it, you can use cost accounting to improve your business for years to come.

How This Book Is Organized

This book is divided into parts that focus on the thought process of cost accounting. When an accountant is considering an issue related to costs, the parts broadly represent the steps he or she uses to resolve the issue — to plan (budget), make decisions, allocate resources, and ensure that a quality product or service is created.

Part I: Understanding the Fundamentals of Costs

So what exactly is cost accounting — and why should you care? Chapter 1 explains how cost accounting relates to other areas of accounting, but you still need to know basic terms, which you find in Chapter 2. You also learn about the types of costs and which are costs are most important. Chapter 3 is all about cost-volume profit (CVP) analysis, the starting point for planning your costs. Hey, accountants love to plan. You then learn about job costing and process costing in the next chapter. And Part I wraps up with Chapter 5 and activity-based costing (ABC). ABC teaches you how to dig deeper into your costs to find cost savings.

Part II: Planning and Control

Part II starts with Chapter 6 and a stroll through the budgeting process. Budgets are great if they are realistic and something you take seriously. You analyze the differences between your budget and actual results using variances — that's in Chapter 7. Moving on to Chapter 8, you get into overhead costs, which are often neglected in accounting, but these costs have a big impact on profit. If you're not careful, increasing overhead costs can cut into your profit. You go over inventory costs in Chapter 9, because inventory is often the most expensive cost in a business.

Part III: Making Decisions

You planned your business in Part II; now Part III helps you make good decisions in running your business. Cost drivers connect your business activities (sales and production, for example) to the costs you incur. You'll find cost drivers in Chapter 10. Chapter 11 explains how your business decisions need to be relevant. Relevant decisions are the important decisions — an area that you should focus on. And because you use costs to determine your product price, pricing decisions are discussed in Chapter 12.

Part IV: Allocating Costs and Resources

Ready, aim, fire. After you make decisions, you really should take action. Part IV covers allocating resources. Chapter 13 analyzes the profitability of your business. Most businesses have departments that share resources. The cost of using those resources is defined as a *support cost* — see Chapter 14 for more. Chapter 15 addresses joint costs. These costs occur when you use the same production to produce multiple products. Everyone in your organization needs to understand how costs are shared. That process can prevent employee complaints down the road. Process costing is presented in detail in Chapter 16.

Part V: Considering Quality Issues

Successful businesses must deliver a quality product. I don't go back and buy from companies that don't sell a quality product. Chapter 17 deals with spoilage and rework. Spoiled products are defective products and can't be sold to a customer. Rework refers to fixing a defective product. When you order product, you should consider how to minimize your ordering costs, so Chapter 18 addresses that topic. Chapter 19 looks at quality issues related to production and product delivery, and also covers the critical issue of customer satisfaction. This section can make the difference between good companies and great ones.

Part VI: The Part of Tens

Every *For Dummies* book includes a Part of Tens. It's a great tool to have when you start using cost accounting. Sometimes you win, sometimes you lose, and sometimes it rains. Chapter 20 lists ten costing mistakes. Mistakes always cause you to incur more costs — and possibly end up with a net loss for the year. Improvements are covered in Chapter 21. This chapter is the payoff for the effort you've made to read this book. The concepts in Chapter 21 help you reduce costs and improve profits. Keep these points in the back of your mind as you manage your business. If someone asks you what's in this book, you might mention the Part of Tens.

Icons Used in This Book

To make this book easier to read and simpler to use, I include some icons that can help you find and fathom key ideas and information.

This icon appears whenever an idea or item can help reinforce your understanding of a concept. A tip might make it easier to remember a topic.

Any time you see this icon, you know the information that follows is so important that it's worth reading more than once.

This icon flags information that's a big concern. Warnings critical to your business are tagged with this type of icon.

This icon appears next to information that's interesting but not essential. Don't be afraid to skip these paragraphs. But come back at a later date and check them out. They'll be waiting for you.

Where to Go from Here

This book is organized so that you can go wherever you want to find complete information. Want to know about product pricing, for example? Head to Chapter 12. If you've taken an accounting course or two, start at Chapter 3 with cost-volume-profit. You can use the table of contents to find broad categories of information or use the index to look up more specific topics.

If you're not sure where you want to go, you may want to start with Part I. It gives you all the basic info you need to understand cost accounting and points to places where you can find more detailed information.

Part I
Understanding the Fundamentals of Costs

The 5th Wave   By Rich Tennant

"I'm not familiar with cost accounting terms.
What do you think that means?"

In this part . . .

So you're ready to learn all there is to know about cost accounting. You've come to the right place! Part I introduces cost accounting terms as well as some basic methods of analysis. You compare cost accounting to other accounting methods and learn four important cost terms: direct costs, indirect costs, fixed costs, and variable costs. You also find out about product and period costs, cost-volume-profit (CVP) analysis, and job costing. Process costing and the flow of manufacturing is also looked at.

Chapter 1

So You Want to Know about Cost Accounting

*I*n a nutshell, *cost accounting* is the process of analyzing and planning what it costs to produce or supply a product or service. The analysis helps reduce costs — and possibly eliminate them. Lower costs, of course, allow for increased profits.

Business folks use cost accounting to determine the profitability of a product. The rule is simple: The price should cover the product cost and generate a profit. Competition may dictate the price charged for a product. In other instances, a profit is added to a product cost to create a unique price.

This chapter introduces cost accounting and how to compare and contrast cost accounting with other accounting methods. The chapter also explains how cost accounting can help you improve your business, such as by using pricing, budgeting, and other tools that can help you become more profitable.

Comparing Accounting Methods

Accounting is the process of recording, reporting, and analyzing business transactions. It's the written record of a business. *Cost accounting* is the process of capturing all of the costs of "production," whether a business manufactures products, delivers services, or sells retail items. Cost accounting is used for all types of businesses.

Often, cost accounting overlaps with other types of accounting, such as financial accounting and management accounting. If you have some knowledge about these other areas of accounting, that background can help you understand cost accounting. If not, no big deal. This section helps clarify what cost accounting is, how it's used, and how these accounting methods relate.

Financial accounting is a reporting process. An accountant reports on the financial position of a firm and the firm's performance by creating financial statements. The statements are used by external (outside) parties to show how the company is doing. External parties include *shareholders, creditors,* and *regulators.*

The external parties may not have an accounting background, so there are many rules of the road (and they are very specific) for creating financial statements. The rules exist so that each set of financial statements is standardized. If all companies follow the same set of rules to create financial statements, the information is usually comparable.

Financial accounting looks backward. It's *retrospective.* The accountant is creating financial statements for transactions that have already happened. So unlike cost accounting, financial accounting doesn't provide any planning or forecasting.

Your external users want financial statements on a periodic basis. Companies typically issue financial statements on a monthly, quarterly, or annual basis. External users want to know how you're doing — for a variety of reasons.

Considering your shareholders

If you own a business, *shareholders* own shares of your company in the form of common stock. That also means that shareholders own *equity* in your business. You may pay them a share of company earnings as a *dividend.*

Shareholders are interested in seeing the value of the business increase. As your sales and earnings grow, your company is seen as more valuable. A shareholder reviews your financial statements to see if sales and earnings are increasing. If they are, your shareholder is happy — she may even buy more of your common stock.

As sales and earnings grow, other investors may be willing to pay a higher price for your common stock. An existing shareholder might then sell his or her investment in common stock for a gain.

Mulling over creditors

Creditors are lenders. They lend your company money so you can purchase assets, which help your business operate. Assets are defined as items you use to make money in your business, like machinery and equipment. You sign a loan agreement with a lender, and that agreement states the interest rate for the loan and when the loan payments are due. You pay *interest* on the loan and also repay the original amount borrowed — the *principal* amount.

Instead of a bank loan, you can issue debt directly to the public by selling *bonds.* The bond certificate states the terms of the bond. That document lists the interest rate and the *maturity date.* The bond investor is repaid on the maturity date.

A creditor is interested in your ability to pay the interest and repay the loan. Like a shareholder, a creditor wants to see a company that generates earnings and an increasing level of sales. If you create earnings, you eventually collect more cash than you spend. That additional cash pays the principal and interest on the loan.

Addressing concerns of regulators

Nearly every business falls under some sort of regulation. *Regulators* protect the public by enforcing laws and regulations. Part of that process involves reviewing your financial statements.

In addition to the "standard" set of financial reports (covered later in the book), regulators may require extra information from you. This specialized reporting is required to address a specific regulation or law. For example, if you're a food manufacturer, the Food and Drug Administration (FDA) requires you to disclose food ingredients on a food label. That's a form of specialized reporting for a regulator.

Using management accounting

Management accounting is the process of creating accurate and timely reports for managers. Managers use the reports to make decisions. There are many theories and accepted practices in management accounting for developing reports. Ultimately, management accounting uses the "whatever works" method to create reports. Any report that provides the best possible information to solve a problem is a good one.

Management accounting is an internal reporting process. The information you create isn't shared with the outside world. So you can put together any type of report that's helpful to you.

 As an accountant, you may be in a situation in which management asks you to create lots of reports but doesn't *use* them all. Ask management how a report you're asked to create will be used. The manager might conclude that the report really isn't necessary — which saves you time and energy.

Financial accounting looks backward. You report on past events. Management accounting is *forward-looking.* It's *prospective.* You're using the reports to make decisions about the future. For example, a decision whether to manufacture a product component or buy it from someone else is a typical management decision based on management accounting.

Every manager has a preferred set of management reports, the ones he or she considers the most useful. I had a conversation with the retired chief financial officer (CFO) of a worldwide defense contractor. Engineers, including all of senior management, dominated the company. The former CFO told me that he was successful because he figured out which financial management reports the engineers wanted. In fact, that set of reports was standardized and used in every senior management meeting.

Fitting in cost accounting

Cost accounting is closer to management accounting than financial accounting. Cost accountants gather information to make decisions about the *future*. Also, cost reports are considered to be internal reports. Both of those traits apply to management accounting.

You see overlap between cost and management accounting. A good example is special orders. A *special order* is an order you take on when you have excess production capacity. A customer approaches you about producing an "extra" order — an order you weren't expecting. You need to decide what price you will accept for the special order.

Management accounting instructs you to consider only the cost and revenues that *change,* based on your decision, called *differential* costs and revenues. That makes sense, because the method is forward-looking. Old, unchanging stuff generally doesn't count.

Your price for the special order depends on the costs. Reports you generate about costs help you make the decision to accept or reject the special order. If your producing cost reporting, that sounds like cost accounting to me. So you see how cost and management accounting can overlap. There's more on special orders later.

Cost accounting sometimes uses historical information to start the analytical process. For example, when you plan your costs for next year, you take a look at spending in past years. Spending in prior year provides a starting point for planning costs — a baseline. The baseline is adjusted for all the foreseeable changes that might occur in the new year. That helps you decide whether your budgeted costs should be higher or lower.

Using Cost Accounting to Your Advantage

Cost accounting runs through your entire business process. To begin, you decide whether the cost of obtaining the information is worth the benefit you receive from it. If you decide that it is, you use cost accounting to analyze your costs, make decisions, and look for cost reductions in your business.

Starting with cost-benefit analysis

The cost of obtaining information should be lower than the benefit you receive from your analysis. The cost includes labor hours and technology costs. For example, you need someone to search for the information. You also may need to create new cost reports in using your technology. The benefit of performing the analysis is the cost savings you're able to implement.

Say you manufacture dining room tables; you make five different models of tables. At one point in production, your staff sands the wooden tabletops by hand.

Until now, you haven't calculated the time required to sand each type of table. You take the total labor costs for sanding and trace them to each table, regardless of the model. Maybe you should do a cost analysis and assign the sanding cost to each table model.

You incur some costs to do the analysis. Someone on your staff will go through the employee time cards (used for payroll). The workers record the time they spend on all tasks, including sanding. They also record the table models they worked on during production. Your accountant can compute the total sanding time per table model, based on the time cards.

Consider what you might gain. You assign the sanding cost more precisely. As a result, each table model's total cost is more accurate. Because your profit is the sale price less the total costs, the updated cost allows you to calculate a more precise profit. Sounds like the cost of the analysis might be worth it, especially if the competition is high in your furniture-making industry.

Planning your work: Budgeting

Cost accounting plays a role in your budgeting process. You might think of budgeting as just forecasting sales and planning expenses. If you own a flower shop, you budget by forecasting sales of each type of flower or arrangement. You also plan expenses, such as utility costs for the shop and your lease payment.

Your work with cost accounting takes budgeting to a new level of detail. Until now, you looked at costs by *type* (utilities, lease expense). Now, you analyze cost by type and by *product* (for example, those roses need to be kept in a cooler, which requires electricity). Based on the product's costs and sale price, you can compute a profit.

So start off with an analysis of each product's cost, price, and profit. Build on that information. You could then put together a budget for each department. Finish up by combining all of your smaller budgets into a company-wide budget. That company-wide budget will give you all of the company's costs by type and your revenue total. You build your company-wide budget based on cost accounting by product.

By starting your budget at the product level, your budget is a lot more specific. When you compare your actual results to your budget, you'll see the differences in more detail. The detail lets you make more precise changes in your business going forward.

Controlling your costs

Cost accounting helps you stay on top of your costs — and make changes along the way. You should analyze costs frequently. Most companies perform this analysis on at least a monthly basis . . . and sometimes weekly or even daily. The more specific you make your analysis, the better. As always, the benefits you gain from your analysis should outweigh the costs.

If you analyze costs frequently, you find areas where you can reduce costs immediately. There's nothing worse than discovering a problem after it's too late to fix, so don't create a budget and shove it in a drawer. Review your actual results, and compare those results to your budget. If you find large differences, dig deeper. Consider reviewing more detail to find out what caused the difference.

Here are some tools you can use to control costs. Each tool is explained in detail in this book:

- **Cost-volume profit (CVP) analysis:** CVP is a simple tool to analyze costs, sale price, and units sold. There's a user-friendly formula — the kind of tool you can play around with on a notepad or spreadsheet. Check out Chapter 3 for more on CVP.

- **Variance analysis:** A *variance* is the difference between your planned costs and actual costs. A large variance is a red flag — a number that gets your attention. You investigate variances to find ways to reduce your costs. Chapter 7 tells you more.

- **Activity-based costing (ABC):** This analysis allows you to assign costs using the activities put into making your product or service. ABC assigns costs to products based on levels of activity: labor hours incurred, machine hours used, and so forth. See Chapter 5 for an in-depth look.

- **Support costs:** Nearly every business incurs *support costs*. These are areas of your business that support your production and sales efforts. Accounting and legal costs are good examples of support costs.

- **Joint costing:** Your business may use the same process to produce several different products. This situation is called *joint production*. The products will share common costs of this production, or *joint costs*. Now, it's likely that each product has its own unique costs *after* joint production; however, you need a tool to allocate the joint costs when the products are produced together.

Setting a price

After you've nailed down your product's full cost (all costs, both fixed and variable), you can price your product effectively. The difference between your price and full product cost is your profit (see Chapter 12).

Pricing and competition

Consider how pricing comes into play. Your product's price may be limited, based on competition. Say you sell baseball gloves. To compete and maintain you current level of sales, you can't price your glove any higher than $100.

To meet your profit goal, you start at the top and work your way down. The top is your $100 price; you can't go any higher without losing sales. Your profit is sale price less cost. The only way to increase your profit is to lower your costs.

Increasing a price

Assume that you make a product that's unique. You don't have many competitors. As a result, customers are willing to pay more because they can't get the same product somewhere else.

To meet your profit goal, you start at the bottom and work your way up. You compute your full costs first. Then you calculate a sale price, based on your profit goal. You have the ability to push the top (the price) higher because you believe that customers are willing to pay a higher price.

Changing prices after more analysis

In the section "Controlling your costs," you see a list of tools to analyze costs. You use the tools to assign costs to your products more precisely. When you change the costs assigned, you can consider changing the product's price. That's because a change in the product's cost changes the level of profit.

Say that you sell hiking boots. In planning, you budget a sale price of $80 per pair. During the year, you start performing cost analysis. You determine that $5 more in machine production cost should be assigned to each pair of hiking boots.

That $5 increase in cost lowers your profit. So you have a few choices to make to maintain the same level of profit. You could decide to raise your price. If you face heavy competition, a higher price may hurt your sales. The other choice is to find ways to lower other costs.

Keep in mind that pricing your product isn't a one-time event. As you analyze costs, you may need to adjust prices more than once during the year.

Improving going forward

Successful businesses constantly make improvements. This approach is the only way companies can survive and thrive over the long term. That's because competitors eventually take business away from you if you're not willing to change.

One type of improvement is analyzing your business to lower costs. You can lower your costs in several ways. Maybe you remove an activity that isn't necessary. When you eliminate the activity, you get rid of the related costs. Here are some other possible improvements.

Using the accrual method of accounting

You decide to use the accrual method of accounting. This method matches your revenue with the expenses you incur to generate the revenue. Using this method, rather than the cash basis of accounting, gives you a more realistic picture of your profitability. That better view helps you make more informed decisions.

Deciding on relevance

Make a judgment about what you believe to be relevant. Relevant means "important enough" to consider in a decision (see Chapter 11). Your threshold for considering relevance might be expressed as a dollar amount. Maybe any amount over $10,000 is relevant to you. Relevance can also be expressed as a percentage. You might consider a change of 10 percent or more to be relevant.

When you decide what amount or percentage is relevant, you use it as a filter for decision-making. Anything over the threshold needs to be analyzed and considered in your decision-making. Below the threshold, you "pass further analysis" — a term my old CPA firm used to mean "not important enough to investigate."

Demanding quality

Demand is a strong word, but it should be applied to quality. You will not succeed as a business without a constant focus on quality. It's simply too easy for customers to use technology to find the product or service somewhere else.

Quality means more than making a product or service that the client wants. The term also means fixing your product, if it doesn't work.

Finally, quality means asking customers what changes they want in your product or what new products they would like to see. Ask your customers, and they'll gladly tell you.

Chapter 2

Brushing Up on Cost Accounting Basics

*T*his chapter provides the rules of the road for cost accounting. Use these basic terms and ideas to understand more complex topics later in the book. If you read another chapter and start to get lost, head back here and take a look at these concepts again.

Understanding the Big Four Terms

Direct costs, indirect costs, fixed costs, and *variable costs* are the four most important cost accounting terms . . . and these four terms can be confusing. The following sections outline a process for understanding the differences among these words. If you follow this process, you should be able to keep these important terms straight in your mind.

Comparing direct and indirect costs

Direct costs are costs you can *trace* (or tie) to your product or service. *Indirect costs* can't be traced directly to the product or service. Instead, indirect costs are *allocated.* (Indirect costs are also referred to as *overhead costs.*)

Material and labor costs are good examples of direct costs. Say you manufacture cotton gloves. You buy cotton, yarn, and leather to make the gloves. You can trace the materials directly to the gloves; for example, you can take a glove apart and see the materials that were used to create it. Cotton, yarn, and leather are considered *direct material costs,* because they can be directly tied to one unit of product.

You pay workers to cut, sew, and dye the materials. Because you can trace the hourly labor cost directly to the gloves, these costs are *direct labor costs.* You can review each employee time sheet and determine how many hours each employee worked, and how many gloves he or she moved through production.

Indirect costs can't be *traced* directly to a product or service. So instead, they have to be *allocated.* You typically allocate costs by assigning a cost per unit. The per unit rate attaches all of the indirect costs to your products. The term *overhead* is also used to describe indirect costs.

Allocating indirect costs

To allocate overhead, you need to *compute* a rate or amount of cost per product. Assume you lease the building where you manufacture the cotton gloves. Obviously, the reason you're leasing the building is to make gloves.

You can't trace the cost of the lease to any particular pair of gloves. The cost belongs to all of the gloves, yet the cost does need to be included in the cost of a *single unit of your product.* That way, you can determine the price and profit for one unit (one glove).

One way to allocate overhead is to base it on some level of activity. As you see later in Chapter 5, activities in your business cause you to incur costs. Assume you run a machine for 1,000 hours a year and pay $2,000 for the repair and maintenance on the machine. You could allocate the repair cost to each hour of machine time as $2,000 ÷ 1,000 hours, or $2 per machine hour.

Deciding on direct versus indirect costs

As a business owner, you need to analyze all of your costs and decide which ones are direct and which ones are indirect. One way to do that is to visualize your product. Look at that pair of gloves one more time. You can certainly picture the materials (cotton, yarn, and leather) used in a pair of gloves. Also, you can visualize a worker cutting the cotton and sewing it together.

That exercise should convince you that material and labor are direct costs. You can imagine those costs "traveling along" with the gloves as they are produced, packaged, and shipped to a customer. Okay, direct costs. Got it.

Working with direct costs in cost planning is preferable because direct costs are *known*. In the previous example, you defined material and labor costs as direct, because you can attach the costs directly to the product. If the costs are known, your planning is more precise. Actual costs are likely close to your planned amounts. Because indirect costs are based on estimates, your budgeted costs are less precise.

Next, you review your checkbook to find other costs. You find checks for vehicle insurance for a truck. Consider what you just read in the previous section. Insurance costs can't be traced directly to the gloves, so you need to decide on an activity level to allocate the costs.

The truck's insurance cost can be allocated based on the number of miles you drive the truck. Assume you compute an insurance allocation of $0.10 per mile. You now need to get the cost allocated to your product.

Instead of allocating the cost to individual pairs of gloves, you allocate costs to each *shipment* of gloves. When a customer orders gloves, they are packed up and shipped, using the truck. Based on the number of miles driven to a client, you can allocate the truck insurance cost.

Indirect costs can be allocated using many levels and kinds of activity. You've seen how costs can be allocated by product and by shipment. As you see later in the book, you can allocate costs by company department or product line. As long as the cost is eventually allocated to a product or service, you can justify many methods of indirect cost allocation.

Mulling over fixed and variable costs

Total *fixed costs* don't change when your level of production or sales changes. On the other hand, total *variable costs* do change with your level of production or sales.

Kicking around fixed costs

Consider a lease payment for a piece of equipment. Whether your production increases or decreases, the check you write for the lease stays the same. The cost is fixed in your lease agreement.

Say the lease payment is $500 per month. Assume you manufacture office desks. You can't directly *trace* the lease payment to the product you produce — the cost is indirect. So you *allocate* the lease payment cost to each desk you produce. In March you produce 1,000 desks. The equipment lease is $500 ÷ 1,000 desks, or $0.50 per desk.

In April, you make 800 desks. The April equipment lease is $500 ÷ 800 desks, or $0.63 per desk. Because you produce fewer desks in April but the lease payment doesn't change, you allocate a larger *cost per unit* (desk).

There's a difference between *total* fixed costs and the fixed costs *per unit*. The total fixed costs don't change with your activity level. Fixed costs per unit do change as your production level goes up or down. As a strategy, businesses aim to produce and sell as much as they can for the same amount of fixed costs. That strategy generates the lowest possible per unit fixed cost.

Computing variable costs

Total variable costs change in total with your level of production. Say you use plywood to make each office desk. Each desk requires $4 of plywood. The $4 cost per desk *does not change* with production.

If you produced 1,000 desks in March, your total variable plywood cost is 1,000 desks × $4, or $4,000. The 800 desks produced in April generate $3,200 in variable plywood costs. The total variable costs *do* change, but the $4 variable cost per unit stays the same.

Table 2-1 summarizes fixed and variable costs.

Table 2-1	Fixed and Variable Costs
Change with Level of Production?	
Fixed Costs	
Total fixed costs	no
Fixed cost per unit	yes
Variable costs	
Total variable costs	yes
Variable cost per unit	no

Fitting the costs together

This section explains how direct costs, indirect costs, fixed costs, and variable costs all fit together. One simple way to explain the relationship is to go over some examples. Table 2-2 shows you an example of four types of costs.

Table 2-2	Fixed and Variable Costs, Direct and Indirect Costs — Examples	
	Direct Cost	*Indirect Cost*
Fixed costs	Hourly union wages	Equipment lease
Variable costs	Material and labor cost	Factory utility costs

Table 2-2 is new territory. Each cost can be classified as either direct or indirect and either fixed or variable. Go through the examples one at a time.

Say you manage a factory. You pay wages to hourly workers based on a union contract. The contract states the number of hours each employee works and his or her pay rate per hour. The total wages paid is a fixed cost. The cost is also a direct cost. That's because the only reason to have hourly workers is because you're producing a product. No production, no hourly workers — and no cost.

In the section "Kicking around fixed costs," you work with an equipment lease. Because the equipment is used to make a product, the lease is a fixed, indirect cost. You allocate the indirect cost based on the number of units (desks) created.

Material and direct labor costs are addressed in the section "Comparing direct and indirect costs." Those are variable costs that change (in total) with your level of production.

If you manage a factory, you incur utility costs to heat, cool, and provide power to the factory. The more product you produce, the more utility costs you incur. So utility costs can vary with the level of activity.

Utility costs are also indirect costs. Because you can't trace the costs directly to a product, you have to allocate them. Utility costs are often allocated using labor hours for a particular time period.

Covering Costs in Different Industries

In the Introduction, I note that this book covers both products and services. A *product* is a physical item that your customer can touch, see, and feel. When a customer pays you for *doing* something — such as cleaning an office or driving a product from point A to point B — that's a *service*.

Reviewing manufacturing costs

Manufacturers make products. They incur material and labor costs, as well as overhead.

No manufacturer can produce a product instantly. When you close the factory doors for the night, you have partially completed goods on hand. Those products are called *work-in-process* (*WIP*).

Assume you make blue jeans. The jean production moves from one department to another. Say that the denim material has been cut for 100 pairs of jeans. The next step is to sew the denim and then dye the material. You close your factory doors before the jeans move to the sewing department.

Consider the cost you've incurred on the jeans. You purchased the denim, a material cost. You paid your workers to run machines to cut the denim (labor costs). So the work-in-process jeans have incurred costs.

When work-in-process goods are completed, they are defined as *finished goods*. Finished goods are ready for sale to a customer. They incurred all manufacturing costs.

Considering costs for retailers

A *retailer* doesn't make a product. Instead, it buys inventory and sells it to customers. The largest cost for most retailers is inventory. (See Chapter 9 for more on inventory.) Retailers don't create work-in-process or finished goods. Those terms apply only to manufacturers.

Retailers incur ordering costs to order inventory and carrying costs to *store* inventory. Check out Chapter 18 for the details. The risk for a retailer is carrying too much inventory — or running out of inventory when a customer wants to buy more product.

This is a delicate balance. The more inventory you own, the more cash you *spend* (and that gives you less cash to use for other things). You don't recover the cash until the customer pays for the product. Likewise, if you run out of inventory, and there's more demand for your product, you lose sales.

Finding costs most companies incur

Most companies incur costs for human resources, marketing, lawyers, accountants (hey, that's good!), and other experts. The costs might be salary and benefits for experts inside your company. You also might pay outside experts to perform the work.

Most companies incur costs for insurance, utilities, supplies, and depreciation expense on assets. So keep in mind that there are costs that apply to companies of all types. These costs are indirect costs. You can't trace them directly to a product or service.

Salespeople are often paid a salary plus a commission based on sales. The cost of a salesperson's commission is normally traced to the product as a direct cost.

Why Are You Spending?: Cost Drivers

A *cost object* is the product, service, or company department where you incur costs. Picture the cost object as a sponge that sucks up money. A *cost driver* is an item that *changes* costs. If the cost object is a sponge full of costs, the cost driver changes the size of the sponge.

If you manufacture leather baseball gloves, leather material is a cost driver. If you manage the human resources department, an increase in job interviews is a cost driver. More interviews require more time from your staff, and that labor time has a cost.

This section covers two related concepts: relevant range and inventoriable costs.

Pushing equipment too hard and relevant range

Relevant range is the area in which a set of assumptions about your costs hold true. By *area,* I mean a minimum and maximum level of use of an asset. As long as your use of the asset stays in that range, the cost assumptions apply. If you use the asset too much (out of the relevant range), it eventually breaks down. Breakdowns occur when you try to operate beyond your asset's maximum capacity.

The bottom of a range is the minimum. For this book, you focus on the maximum.

At this point, you need to know about assets. An *asset* is anything you use to make money in your business (anything that provides your company with some benefit in the future). Essentially, you use up assets to make money.

An asset may be a *tangible asset* — a factory, a vehicle, or a piece of equipment. An asset can be *intangible,* such as a brand name or a patent. For example, the brand names Coca-Cola, McDonald's, and Nike are assets. Those names drive business to those companies.

Assume you're a plumber. You have a truck that you use to carry equipment to homes to work on plumbing. The truck is an asset. As you drive the truck, two things happen. First, you're doing plumbing work and making money. At the same time, the value of the asset is declining. The decline in value of a tangible asset is called *depreciation.*

Now, here's where relevant range comes in. There's a limit to how much you can use the asset. The truck can be driven only so many miles before it needs maintenance or a repair.

Say you're planning your plumbing business for the month. Based on your experience, you know that your truck needs maintenance every 4,000 miles. The maintenance means the truck can't be used for one day.

Because you perform plumbing work seven days a week, the day maintenance is performed is a day when you don't earn revenue. The relevant range for your truck is up to 4,000 miles. Beyond that point, you need to take it out of service for a day. To work seven days a week, you may need to have another truck — another asset.

There's relevant range for many assets. Maybe you can run your sewing machines for 10,000 hours before they need repairs. You might find that your commercial printing press has a maximum number of print jobs it can perform without breaking down. If you need production capacity above the relevant range, you need to invest in another asset. That investment is a cost.

Relevant range isn't just about breakdowns and maintenance. Even if your machinery works as expected, there's only so much capacity you can handle. Say you have machine capacity to produce 1,000,000 gloves a year. If you want increase production to 1,200,000 gloves, you need more machines. That means an investment in more fixed assets.

Previewing inventoriable costs

Inventoriable costs are costs that can be traced to your inventory. That includes the purchase price of the inventory item. However, there are other costs that should be added to the asset's cost. You refer to these costs as inventoriable.

Assume you own a furniture store that sells lamps. You carry an expensive model of lamp in your store. Parts of the lamp can break easily. As a result, it's expensive to ship the lamps. When the lamps arrive, they're stored carefully to prevent breakage.

Your inventory value for the lamp obviously includes the purchase price. It should also include all costs to *prepare the asset for sale,* such as the shipping cost and any extra costs you incur to store and display the lamp.

Now consider the impact of including more costs in inventory. Inventory costs aren't posted as expenses *(expensed)* until the asset is sold. All of the lamp costs remain in inventory until a lamp is sold. At that point, the lamp cost is posted to *cost of sales* (also called *cost of goods sold*).

Other costs are expensed as soon as they are incurred. A good example is marketing costs. Marketing costs are immediately expensed, because it's difficult to know if and when the costs generated a sale.

If you run a million-dollar ad during the Super Bowl for running shoes, it's not possible to know how many shoes were sold as a result of running the ad. So you expense it sooner than later. This is the *principle of conservatism,* which is explained in the next section.

Following the Rules of the Cost Accounting Road

Accountants are big on rules and guidelines. When you have to make a decision as an accountant, you first check for rules and guidelines. Some rules are regulations or laws. This section talks about some critical guidelines you should use in accounting.

Deciding on accrual basis or cash basis

The *cash basis of accounting* recognizes revenue when cash is received and posts expenses when they are paid in cash. This method means that you post your accounting activity based on when cash moves in or out of your business. It's accounting by "using your checkbook."

Recognizing revenue or expenses refers to the timing of when you post the amounts to your accounting records.

Installing the cash basis

There's a problem with the cash basis of accounting — it doesn't follow the *matching principle*. This principle requires accountants post revenue when it's *earned* and expenses when they are *incurred*.

The matching principle is a two-step process. Your first step is to determine when revenue is earned. You earn revenue when you deliver your product or complete a service you perform for a customer. You may receive payment in advance of the delivery or a few weeks after the delivery. When you earn, the revenue may be different from when you receive the cash payment.

For a retailer, revenue is earned when the customer walks out of the store with, say, a new baseball glove. If you're a tax preparer, you earn revenue when you deliver a completed tax return to your client.

After you determine when revenue is earned, you match the revenue to the expenses that are related to the product or service. The retailer would match the inventory cost of the glove with the baseball glove's revenue. The tax preparer would match the labor cost paid to the staff with the revenue from the tax return.

Because the cash basis doesn't follow the matching principle, the method is used only by very small businesses. Everyone else uses the *accrual method* of accounting.

Moving to the accrual method

The *accrual method of accounting* recognizes revenue when it's earned and expenses when they are incurred. Accrual accounting is more complicated than the cash basis you just read about (but only a little bit). That's because your cash may not move in the same period when revenue or expense is recognized.

Say you ship a good to your client in late January. The customer pays for the order in February. You completed everything that the customer required in January, so you should *recognize revenue* in January. But the *cash moves* (you get paid) in February.

Accrual accounting requires you to make an entry to *accounts receivable* and to sales revenue in January. The entry shows that you earned the revenue, even though you haven't been paid yet. Accounts receivable means that you are owed money for a sale that was posted to revenue in January. When the cash is received in February, you reduce accounts receivable and increase cash.

Assume an employee works in your store during the last week of May. Your next payroll is paid in the first week of June. (You probably worked for a company that paid you every two weeks — regardless of the month of payment).

Your store has sales in May. You should include the salary expense for the employee's work during May with the May revenue. That's how the matching principle works. The process matches the effort (costs) with the reward (revenue). However, the cash doesn't move until June.

Using accrual accounting, you make an entry to *accounts payable* and salary expense in May. Accounts payable represents an amount you owe as a business expense. So you post the salary expense in May. When you pay the employee in June, you reduce accounts payable and you reduce cash.

Finishing with conservatism

The *principle of conservatism* relates to decisions you make as an accountant (or as a business owner doing some accounting). By conservative, accountants mean the less-attractive decision. Your goal is to avoid creating accounting records that are overly optimistic.

Consider revenue. If you need to make a judgment on when to recognize revenue, choose to delay recognition. Delay posting the revenue until you're sure the revenue has been earned. That decision is considered the conservative one. It's conservative because it makes your financial statements less attractive to a reader.

Okay, now consider expenses. You should recognize expenses sooner than later. In the section "Previewing inventoriable costs," marketing costs are recognized immediately. That's because the accountant can't justify delaying the expenses to a later period. Posting more expenses sooner makes your financial statements less attractive.

Chapter 3

Using Cost-Volume-Profit Analysis to Plan Your Business Results

*C*ost-volume-profit analysis (CVP) is a tool you can use to analyze your costs and plan for a reasonable profit. The CVP formula is simple, and using it is as easy as plugging in numbers as assumptions and seeing where your profit ends up.

Cost-volume-profit works for enterprises of all sizes. Take the neighborhood lemonade stand as an example. To set up a lemonade stand on the sidewalk, you'll have costs. ("It takes money to make money.") Those costs include lemons, sugar, water, stand construction, advertising, and so on.

Assume your lemonade stand startup costs total $30. You decide to sell each glass of lemonade for $1. How many glasses do you need to sell to recover all your costs? At what point would each lemonade sale create a profit? If your goal were to earn $20 in an afternoon, how many glasses would you need to sell? You can answer these questions using cost-volume-profit.

Understanding How Cost-Volume-Profit Analysis Works

A little comprehension goes a long way. I work with many small-business clients who use cost-volume-profit analysis, but they don't know the terminology or how it really works. To illustrate, one client, Barb, owned an advertising premium company, producing and selling promotional items. She made items such as T-shirts, water bottles, bumper stickers, and anything with a company logo that would help promote a company's product or service.

Barb knew the company's total fixed costs. In fact, she could recite the cost of her lease, insurance, and loan interest off the top of her head. She also knew the variable cost she would incur for every item she produced. Finally, she had a sales amount in mind every month that she hoped to achieve. Barb knew how much profit she would generate if she hit that sales number.

Barb's problem was that all of these facts and numbers were swimming around in her head and not organized on paper. She needed a simple tool to analyze costs, sales (volume), and profit in one place. That's the value of cost-volume-profit analysis. An owner or manager can have all three calculations in one formula and understand how they affect one another. So when you understand cost-volume-profit, you've added a powerful analytical tool to your arsenal.

Calculating the breakeven point

Cost-volume-profit analysis starts with the *breakeven point*. Breakeven answers this question: "What's the amount I need to sell to cover all of my costs?" When you open the front door of your business on the first day of a new month, your first concern is likely to be how much you have to sell to at least cover all costs for that month. At a minimum, you don't want to lose money.

It doesn't matter whether you're selling a few glasses of lemonade or manufacturing automobiles. Either way, the breakeven point has three simple elements:

✔ It includes fixed costs and variable costs.

✔ It includes sales, either units of product sold, or the total dollar amount of sales (revenue). The term volume refers to the level of sales.

✔ It assumes profit of zero.

The reason for the name *breakeven point* is pretty obvious. It's the point where you neither make nor lose money. It's the point where you break even.

Examine the elements required to find the breakeven point: Fixed costs remain constant, regardless of the volume of products or services you provide. Variable costs increase or decrease proportionately with the amount of products you sell or services you deliver. The total variable costs, of course, increase as you produce more products or provide more services, and vice versa if fewer items, products, or services are provided. Sales is the total dollar amount received for your product or service. Finally, profit represents sales less all of your costs.

Okay, if you want to split hairs, there's an exception about fixed costs that is important in analyzing cost-volume-profit: relevant range (see Chapter 1). But in most cases, the level of activity stays within the relevant range for fixed costs.

What makes the breakeven point so important is that every sale above your breakeven point generates a profit. If your breakeven point is 100 units, you make a small profit when you sell the 101st unit. That's good! After you know your breakeven point, you can plan the level of sales you need to generate a specific amount of profit.

What goes up can come down. If you sell only 99 units, you have a small loss. That's not good! The fewer units you sell, the larger your loss.

The breakpoint formula

Before you start selling a product, you need to know the fixed costs, the variable costs, and the sale price. See Chapter 2 for more on cost terms. You can use the cost and price information to determine how many units you need to sell to recover all of your costs — your breakeven point. The formula is

Profit ($0) = sales – variable costs – fixed costs

Failing to get a grip on profit, loss, and breakeven point can be funny, at least on TV. *Saturday Night Live* did a skit years ago about "The Change Bank." Its only business was to make change, and its tag line was "We can meet all of your change needs." The owner was asked: "How do you make money just making change?" "Volume!" says the owner.

The joke in the Change Bank skit is that regardless of how much business you do, there's no profit in making change for people.

A case in point (breakeven point, that is)

You own a software company, and you're thinking about buying a booth at a technology trade show. You hope to sell your product to trade-show visitors. Before deciding to attend, you benefit from a little breakeven analysis.

You might say to yourself, "I'm not getting on a plane unless I can at least cover all of my expenses. How many units do I need to sell to cover all expenses?"

That number is the *unit sales* needed to reach your goal. Say your application sells for $40 per unit, and you have variable costs of $20 per unit. Fixed costs amount to $1,000. Plug those numbers into the formula:

Profit ($0) = sales – variable costs – fixed costs

Profit ($0) = (units × $40) – (units × $20) – $1,000

Profit ($0) = units × ($40 – $20) – $1,000

Profit ($0) = units × $20 – $1,000

To finish this little piece of algebra, add $1,000 to both sides of the equation. Then divide both sides by 20: X = 50, or 50 units.

$1,000 = units × $20

$1,000 / $20 = units

50 = units

You need to sell 50 units at $40 per unit. If you don't think you can sell at least 50 units of software, don't get on the plane for the trade show.

Financial losses: The crash of your cash

When your unit sales are less than breakeven, you're operating at a loss. And that could affect the cash you need to operate each month. You likely will need cash to pay expenses (such as rent, utilities, and salaries) before you collect cash from sales.

Every time you incur a loss, it's likely your available cash balance will decline. Generally, losses reduce your cash balance; conversely, profits increase them. Assume your loss for the month is $1,000. After you collect cash on all of your sales and pay cash for all the bills, your ending cash balance will be $1,000 lower than where you started.

Losses are the curse of business. After all, the business exists to generate profits. Maybe the only good news about a loss is that it gets you analyzing and fixing problems.

Contribution margin: Covering fixed costs

Variable costs probably won't keep you up at night. It's the fixed costs that may cause insomnia, whether you're talking about trade show cost, the monthly rent, or salaries you need to pay your employees each month.

You focus on covering fixed costs using the *contribution margin* (that is, sales less variable costs):

Contribution margin = sales – variable costs

Contribution margin is the money derived from sales after you have covered variable costs, which is used to cover fixed costs and keep for your profit:

Profit = contribution margin – fixed costs

You also can use contribution margin to compute your breakeven point in terms of units. Remember that the breakeven point is the sales needed to cover all of your costs and to create $0 profit). Consider this formula:

Breakeven point in units = Fixed costs ÷ contribution margin per unit

If you sell a software application for $40, and variable costs are $20 (which just happens to be the same as in the trade show example), each unit has a contribution margin of $20. If you have $1,000 in fixed costs, the formula looks like this:

Breakeven point in units = $1,000 ÷ $20

Breakeven point in units = 50

If you sell 50 units, you've covered your fixed costs. Any sales over 50 units are all gravy and put you in Profit Land.

Lowering the breakeven point to reach profitability sooner

The lower the breakeven point, the easier it is to achieve your sales goal. It takes less effort to break even if you can lower the number of units you need to sell. Would you rather have to sell 100 units or 500 units just to break even? There's a big difference in time, effort, and financial risk between 100 and 500 units. Think of *less effort* as taking less risk.

You reduce your breakeven point by changing any one of its components, if you can (and that's sometimes a big *if*). Here are some techniques, using the well-worn software application as an example.

If you can change the costs or sales, you can reduce your breakeven point. To do so, make some changes to the earlier formula:

- ✔ Increasing the sale price to $45 per unit:

    Contribution margin per unit = $45 – $20

    Contribution margin per unit = $25

    Breakeven point in units = $1,000 ÷ $25

    Breakeven point in units = 40

- ✔ Reducing the variable cost to $15 per unit:

    Contribution margin per unit = $40 – $15

    Contribution margin per unit = $25

    Breakeven point in units = $1,000 ÷ $25

    Breakeven point in units = 40

- ✔ Reducing the fixed cost to $800 per unit:

    Contribution margin per unit = $40 – $20

    Contribution margin per unit = $20

    Breakeven point in units = $800 ÷ $20

    Breakeven point in units = 40

In each case, you lowered the breakeven point in units to 40 units instead of 50. The result? It takes less selling effort — and requires less financial risk.

Target net income: Setting the profit goal

Target net income is the profit goal you set. (I use *net income* and *profit* to mean the same thing.)

You compute target net income by plugging the figure into the breakeven formula — with one change. The profit changes from $0 to the target net income amount. Here's the new formula:

Target net income = sales – variable costs – fixed costs

If you're going to take that trip to the trade show, how much profit would make your trip worthwhile? How much profit could you produce if you decided not to go? Maybe that's how you should answer the question. Assume your profit goal/target net income here is $2,000.

Using the original information for sales, variable costs, and fixed costs, you can compute the sales you need to reach target net income:

Target net income = sales – variable costs – fixed costs

$2,000 = $40 × (units) – $20 × (units) – $1,000

$3,000 = $20 × units)

150 = $3,000 ÷ $20

You'll meet target net income by selling 150 units.

You need to sell 100 more units (150 units – 50 units) to increase your profit from breakeven to $2,000. You can think about your target net income in units or dollars.

If you attend the trade show for three days, you need to average 50 sales per day to sell 150 units. If your booth is open for ten hours a day, you need to sell an average of five units per hour. Determine whether that's reasonable. Is there enough interest in your product to reach that level of sales? That's the real purpose of thinking through target net income.

Lower profits and margin of safety

The *margin of safety* is a cushion. If things don't go as planned — if sales are lower than your budget — you need to know how low your total sales can go before you hit the breakeven point. The word *margin,* in this case, refers to the amount (in dollars or units) above the breakeven point.

Consider this example: You're getting ready to book your tickets for the trade show. You computed a breakeven point of 50 units. To reach your target net income, you need to sell 150 units. Target net income uses your budgeted sales level. The difference between your budgeted level of sales (150 units) and your breakeven sales (50 units) is your *margin of safety.*

If actual sales were 30 units below your budget, your units sold would be 120 (150 – 30). You're still way above your breakeven point of 50 units. The question always is if you don't budget correctly, how far off can you be before your unit sales are below breakeven?

Contribution margin versus gross margin

Contribution margin represents the amount of money you have left after variable costs to cover fixed costs and keep for your profit. *Gross margin* explains how much of your sales proceeds are left after paying cost of sales.

Cost of sales is the direct costs of creating your product. (See the direct and indirect cost section of Chapter 2.) If you were manufacturing denim jeans, you would have material costs for the denim and thread (and maybe a zipper), as well as the labor costs to sew the jeans. Your gross margin per pair of jeans sold might look like this:

Gross margin = sale price − cost of sales (material and labor)

Gross margin = $60 − $25

Gross margin = $35

Contribution margin (sales less variable costs) is part of the target net income formula. Try to avoid confusing the gross margin with contribution margin. The terms look similar, and both are thrown around in accounting conversations. Contribution margin is sales less variable costs. Gross margin, on the other hand, is sales less cost of sales.

Using operating leverage

The *degree of operating leverage* is a formula that shows how well you're using your fixed costs to generate a profit. The more profit you can generate from the same amount of fixed cost, the higher your degree of operating leverage.

Here's the formula:

Degree of operating leverage = contribution margin ÷ profit

Profit = contribution margin − fixed costs

You already covered the component parts that make up this formula. To refresh your memory, see the section "Calculating the breakeven point" and the section "Contribution margin: Covering fixed costs."

First, calculate the contribution margin. Use the number of units from the target net income discussion above:

Contribution margin = sales − variable costs

Contribution margin = $40 × (150 units) − $20 × (150 units)

Contribution margin = $20 × (150 units)

Contribution margin = $3,000

Use the degree of operating leverage formula to compute the degree of operating leverage:

Degree of operating leverage = contribution margin ÷ (contribution margin − fixed costs)

Degree of operating leverage = $3,000 ÷ ($3,000 − $1,000)

Degree of operating leverage = $3,000 ÷ $2,000

Degree of operating leverage = 1.5

Degree of operating leverage can also be defined as contribution margin divided by profit. It's saying the same thing. All the calculations simply amount to this statement: "At sales of 150 units, contribution margin is 1.5 times profit."

You also can use the degree of operating leverage formula to assess the relationship between costs and profit. If you minimize your fixed costs, you increase your profit. Even better, you can earn more profit without changing your sale price, contribution margin, or units sold.

Here is how the degree of operating leverage looks if fixed costs were only $500:

Degree of operating leverage = $3,000 ÷ ($3,000 − $500)

Degree of operating leverage = $3,000 ÷ $2,500

Degree of operating leverage = 1.2

The ratio went down from 1.5 to 1.2. Now contribution margin ($3,000) is 1.2 times profit ($2,500). Contribution margin did not change. Because fixed costs went down, profit increased.

What if fixed costs went down to zero? Contribution margin/profit would be 1, and *that's* a trophy position! Your entire contribution margin goes toward profit.

Timing is everything when it comes to costs

Costs are part of almost all of the CVP formulas you use. But (shock and amazement!) some costs are not part of your decision-making.

Sunk costs (*past costs* or *retrospective costs*) aren't relevant when you make decisions about the future. By contrast, fixed costs are relevant if they aren't sunk.

When an airline sells you a ticket a few days in advance of your departure, you can be sure most of the costs of the flight have already been incurred (sunk). Costs include the plane's maintenance and fuel, salaries for the crew, and the fee paid for the gate at the airport. In fact, the cost of those tasty peanuts they serve has been factored in, too. Nearly all of the costs for the flight aren't fixed costs but are past or sunk costs. The airline can't change them.

The timing of your ticket purchase is perfect for the airline. Most of the ticket price goes toward profit. That's because most of the costs have already been incurred.

But something different happens when you buy a ticket six months in advance. The timing might be good for you but dicey for the airline. Whereas you may buy a discounted ticket, many costs for the flight can change. For example, the airline might have to pay more for fuel or have to increase flight attendant salaries. Of course, there's a chance (slim) that fuel prices will down, flight attendants will work for lower wages, or the airline will negotiate lower gate fees with the airport.

The rule of thumb is the more time you have before providing a product or service, the more control you have over costs. If you can take action to change costs, they aren't past or sunk costs. As you get closer to delivering your product or service, more costs become sunk costs.

Using Cost-Volume-Profit Analysis to Make Savvy Business Decisions

Your business decisions have consequences. That's why you get the big bucks! Use CVP to avoid problems (or at least to see them coming).

Deciding to make a product or offer a service is a big decision. You incur costs, and if you don't meet the level of sales needed to cover costs, you incur a loss. Incurring a loss might also reduce your cash to operate going forward. Finally, a decision to make product A may mean there are no resources to make product B. (After all, you don't have unlimited resources to produce everything!) Sometimes this is called *opportunity cost,* giving up the second-best choice to do the first choice.

Use cost-volume-profit analysis for several common decisions, such as deciding whether or not to advertise, deciding on prices for your products, and deciding how to work with the sales mix to improve profits.

You can also use CVP to calculate the impact of taxes on profit. See the section "The Tax Man Cometh, the Profits Goeth."

Pitching the product: Deciding to advertise

When you advertise, you obviously spend company resources. You need to know if the additional cost will generate higher profits.

A marketing executive I know used to tell potential clients, "If you don't advertise, nothing happens." I know he was trying to sell advertising, but he had a point. You need to consider the financial impact of your decision to advertise. Specifically, will your sales increase to "make up" for the advertising expense and result higher profits? Cost-volume-profit is the perfect tool to assess advertising decisions.

The old saying is, "It pays to advertise." But it costs, too. Did you ever hear the old not-so-funny costing joke? CFO: "And further, ladies and gentlemen of the board, think of the money we'll save by *not* advertising!" That guy is now a hobo, roasting weenies under a railroad bridge somewhere.

Assume your business sells books online, and your sales total 5,000 units. Your sale price is $25 per unit, variable costs are $15 per unit, and fixed costs total $10,000.

Use the formula for the breakeven point, and solve the formula for profit:

Profit = $25 × (5,000) − $15 × (5,000) − $10,000

Profit = $125,000 − $75,000 − $10,000

Profit = $40,000

So far, so good. Next, you decide to spend $7,000 on advertising. The cost is fixed, regardless of how many books you sell. Total fixed costs increase from $10,000 to $17,000.

You expect the advertising to increase your book sales by 10 percent. The new total would be 5,500 units (5,000 units × 110%). What is your new profit level?

Profit = $25 × (5,500) − $15 × (5,500) − $17,000

Profit = $137,500 − $82,500 − $17,000

Profit = $38,000

In this case, you're actually worse off. Your profit is $2,000 lower than before. For this product, at this time, the advertising didn't work. The correct decision here is not to advertise, because your profit will decrease.

What if sales increase 20 percent? Plugging your new sales number of 6,000 into the formula, you'll see a $43,000 profit. In this case, you're better off with the advertising expense. Your profit is $3,000 higher. The cost of advertising is the same, so it's possible you spent the advertising dollars in a better way.

If people buy your products whether or not you advertise, there isn't much sense in advertising.

Pricing magic: Lowering your price without losing your profit

Just about everyone has shopped at the big discount stores that advertise low prices. Competitive pricing is a tool they use to get customers into the store. As a business owner, you can attract more sales by lowering prices, too. At what point would a price cut be too much — the point where you don't generate a profit? Cost-volume-profit answers this question.

Imagine that you own a small chain of pizza parlors. You're analyzing sales and costs for one type of pizza: a 16-inch pizza that has always sold well. Sales have increased in the past when you've offered a price cut, so you decide to do it again. Also, you're moving into a big holiday weekend, and you don't want to lose sales to competitors.

You pizza price is $20 per unit. Your variable costs are $8 per unit. Fixed costs total $20,000. You forecast 10,000 pizza sales. Here's how your profit looks before you reduce your prices:

Profit = $20 × (10,000) − $8 × (10,000) − $20,000

Profit = $200,000 − $80,000 − $20,000

Profit = $100,000

You estimate that sales will increase by 25 percent if you cut the price to $16. Your fixed costs won't change. Here's the impact of the price cut on profits.

The new sales in units is 10,000 × 125% = 12,500 units. Here's the new profit level:

Profit = $16 × (12,500) − $8 × (12,500) − $20,000

Profit = $200,000 − $100,000 − $20,000

Profit = $80,000

Oops! Your profit's lower by $20,000. You may have cut the price too much. Trouble is, the increased number of units sold sent the total variable cost up. Use this analysis *before* you cut the price — before you make a decision that would reduce your profit!

If your business is family-owned, you have a spouse who might be upset with a $20,000 reduction in profit. He or she might have warned you, so look before you leap. Otherwise, you may hear the four worst words in the English language: "I told you so."

Now you're aware that a $4 price cut (from $20 to $16) would be too much. How would your profit look with a price of $18? As a bonus, you negotiate a lower lease payment on your store space. Assume the same level of sales (12,500 pizzas) and $15,000 in fixed costs:

Profit = $18 × (12,500) − $8 × (12,500) − $15,000

Profit = $225,000 − $100,000 − $15,000

Profit = $110,000

Trouble is, the increased number of units sold sent the total variable cost up, but variable cost is better covered by the moderate increase in sales and a big reduction in fixed costs.

Sales mix: Combining the results of two products

The *sales mix* is the relative proportion in which a company's products are sold. Most companies sell more than one type of the same product. For example, say you sell shirts. Forty percent of your sales are long-sleeve dress shirts, and 60 percent of your sales are short-sleeve golf shirts. The sales mix is 40 percent long-sleeve and 60 percent short-sleeve.

To use cost-volume-profit analysis effectively, apply the methodology to more than one product at a time. You want to see how multiple products are contributing to your profit goal. Strictly speaking, these are *product types.* You don't have to know the numbers for every color, size, and style of shirt.

Good news! If one product produces less profit (because of low sales), the other product could potentially make up for it. Ideally, you can adjust your sales between products to maintain the total profit you want. If dress shirt sales are lagging, you can sell more golf shirts.

Applying breakeven point to two products

To plan your sales and profits, it's ideal for you to know the breakeven point for every product type you sell. So if you have a store that sells just two product types, compute the breakeven points for both of them.

Say you manage a lumberyard that sells two types of wood to furniture makers: Pristine wood and Sturdy wood. A unit is one board of wood. (If you're selling first-class hardwoods, the sample prices are pretty close to reality. There's some serious money in a board $\frac{13}{16}$ of an inch thick, 10 inches wide, and 40 inches long.)

Pristine wood is used to make beautiful tabletops and sells for $50 per unit. Variable costs are $30 per unit, and fixed costs total $30,000. The breakeven formula is

> Profit ($0) = sales – variable costs – fixed costs
>
> Profit ($0) = (units × $50) – (units × $30) – $30,000
>
> Profit ($0) = units × ($50 – $30) – $30,000
>
> Profit ($0) = units × $20 – $30,000

To finish the calculation, add $30,000 to both sides of the equation. Then divide both sides by $20:

> $30,000 = units × $20
>
> $30,000 / $20 = units
>
> 1,500 = units

You sell 1,500 units of Pristine wood to break even.

Sturdy wood is used to make pretty good tabletops and sells for $25 per unit. Variable costs are $18 per unit, and fixed costs total $25,000. Here's the breakeven formula:

Profit ($0) = sales – variable costs – fixed costs

Profit ($0) = (units × $25) – (units × $18) – $25,000

Profit ($0) = units × ($25 – $18) – $25,000

Profit ($0) = units × $7 – $25,000

To finish the calculation, add $25,000 to both sides of the equation. Then divide both sides by $7:

$25,000 = units × $7

$25,000 / $7 = units

3,572 = units

You sell 3,572 units of Sturdy wood to break even.

Pristine wood's breakeven point in units is less than half of the Sturdy wood's (1,500 units versus 3,571 units).

A contribution margin of $20 (Pristine wood) beats a contribution margin of $7 (Sturdy wood) any day of the week. The difference in fixed costs is $5,000 — not a big difference. Pristine has a much larger contribution margin to cover fixed costs. That's why Pristine wood's breakeven point is so much lower.

Applying target net income to two products

After you compute the breakeven points on two products, you can decide on target net income for the period. Assume again that you sell Pristine and Sturdy wood, and your target net income for both types of wood is $10,000. You target a $5,000 profit for each product type.

Pristine wood's calculation is

$5,000 = sales – variable costs – fixed costs

$5,000 = (units × $50) – (units × $30) – $30,000

$5,000 = units × $20 – $30,000

Finish the calculation, and you see that it takes 1,750 units of Pristine wood to reach target net income of $5,000.

For Sturdy wood, plug in the variables. You need to sell 4,286 units to reach target net income.

The total profit for both products is $10,000 ($5,000 + $5,000).

Adjusting product sales to reach target net income

If one product's sales are lower than planned, you can still reach your target net income. Higher sales in one product can make up for lower sales in another product.

For example, say the economy is bad, and customers aren't eager to buy Pristine wood, so you sell only 1,600 units. The profit calculation is

Profit = $50 × (1,600) − $30 × (1,600) − $30,000

Profit = $80,000 − $48,000 − $30,000

Profit = $2,000

Your target net income for Pristine wood is $5,000, so you're $3,000 short of your goal. To reach your total target net income, maybe you can shift that $3,000 profit "burden" to Sturdy wood.

To determine how much more you need to sell, just change the Sturdy wood profit to $8,000, and compute the new number of units sold:

$8,000 = (units × $25) − (units × $18) − $25,000

$8,000 = units × $7 − $25,000

Finish the calculation. The number of units to reach your profit goal is $33,000 divided by $7. Therefore, if you sell 4,715 units of Sturdy wood, you generate $8,000. Your total target net income of $10,000 is based on $2,000 from Pristine wood and $8,000 from Sturdy wood.

The Tax Man Cometh, the Profits Goeth

Do you consider taxes when you make a spending decision? Does a bear live in the woods? The answer is "yes" to both questions. If you're considering a major purchase, think about the income you need to earn and the tax bite. There's going to be an impact on your profit. CVP analysis can help you figure everything out.

Understanding pre-tax dollars

Assume the business needs a car. The cost is $5,000. You have to earn more than $5,000, pay tax on that amount (say 30 percent), and then pay for the car. How much do you have to earn? Here's a formula to compute how much you need to earn, which I refer to as *pre-tax dollars:*

Pre-tax dollars needed for purchase = cost of item ÷ (1 - tax rate)

Pre-tax dollars needed for purchase = $5,000 ÷ (1 - 0.30)

Pre-tax dollars needed for purchase = $5,000 ÷ 0.70

Pre-tax dollars needed for purchase = $7,142.86

The cost of the car in pre-tax dollars is $7,142.86.

When you allow for taxes, it takes $1.43 to buy $1.00 worth of car. $7,142.86 ÷ $5,000 equals 143% (with rounding). To purchase the car, you need 143% of $5,000, or $7,142.86. The taxes paid in this example are $2,142.86, the difference between $7,142.68 and $5,000.

Adjusting target net income for income taxes

It's a smart move to assess the impact of taxes on target net income. Assume your business, Pizza Gone Wild, earns a $100,000 profit. That profit doesn't account for income taxes. It assumes that as the owner, you keep $100,000 in your pocket with no taxes paid. Assume a 30 percent tax rate. You can calculate the pre-tax dollars needed to earn $100,000 after taxes:

Pre-tax dollars = cost of item ÷ (1 - tax rate)

Pre-tax dollars = $100,000 ÷ (1 - 0.30)

Pre-tax dollars = $100,000 ÷ 0.70)

Pre-tax dollars = $142,857.14

The taxes paid are $42,857.14. And you're probably saying, "Oh, I get it. To earn $100,000 *after tax,* I need to increase my sales to cover the taxes." And you're right. Ideally, sales prices and volume are sufficient to cover the burden of taxes.

Consider an example, using pizza gone wild. The plan for profitability was to sell 10,000 units at $20 each, but that won't pay the taxes. Calculate the number of units you need to sell to cover profits and taxes ($142,857.14):

$142,857.14 = (units × $20) − (units × $8) − $20,000

$142,857.14 = units × ($20 − $8) − $20,000

$142,857.14 = units × $12 − $20,000

To finish the calculation, add $20,000 to both sides of the equation. Then divide both sides by $12.

You need to sell 13,571 units to handle the $142,857.14. That's 10,000 units for your profit and 3,571 units to handle the taxes. You gotta sell a lotta dough to make a little dough.

Chapter 4

Estimating Costs with Job Costing

*J*ob costing is a costing methodology you use when your customers incur unique amounts of costs. Job costing assesses costs by the job and allows you to provide detailed price estimates based on the product constructed or service provided.

By contrast, *process costing* (the topic of Chapter 16) assumes that individual product costs are nearly the same for every customer. For example, if you manufacture office chairs, each chair of a particular model has the same costs. You use the same amount of metal and material, and assemble the chair using the same amount of labor. If you calculate the cost for one chair, you know the cost for every chair of that model. In other words, the customer does not have the option to create his or her own unique product with unique costs.

Roofs (for example) aren't like chairs. If your business puts roofs on houses, each client's costs will be different. The amount of material depends on the type of roof and the square footage. Labor time varies, depending on the roof's size, pitch, and unique angles. This is an example of *job costing*.

When you're deciding on which costing method to use, keep in mind how specific or unique your product or service is. Do the costs differ a great deal from one customer to another? If they do, your business should probably use job costing. Otherwise, use process costing.

In this chapter, you see when job costing is the appropriate costing method to use. You also see how to apply both direct and indirect costs. (If you're not sure about the definitions of direct and indirect costs, they're covered later in this chapter.)

Understanding How Job Costing Works

For some businesses, nearly every customer job has different costs, and that's where job costing asserts its value. You need a job costing estimate in order to get the customer's business, and you need to track costs accurately so you generate a reasonable profit.

The different costs for different jobs will often be self-evident. Material costs, labor hours, mileage cost, and type of equipment used are likely to vary. For example, a tree trimming company would incur more costs to remove a 30-foot tree than to remove a small stump. The big tree takes more labor and different equipment.

Some factors could lower costs and make a business more competitive in price (or improve its bottom line). For example, every few months I receive a flyer in the mail or a knock on my front door from a tree trimming company working on a job in my neighborhood. They offer me a free estimate while they are in my neighborhood. It's a smart business move. If you've incurred the cost to locate your employees and equipment in a certain area, why not perform as much work as possible while you're there? You can spread some costs (mileage, for example) over several jobs. As a result, your cost per job in that neighborhood is lower, and you increase your profit.

The business lesson is that a little bit of flyer can go a long way.

Proper use of job costing

Here are a few examples of job costing. Look at three business sectors.

Service-sector businesses provide a service to clients.

Job costing: Law firm, accounting practice, consulting businesses

Merchandising-sector businesses sell products as a retailer. (Think of a department store.)

Job costing: Shipping expensive goods, customized product sales

Manufacturing-sector businesses make things.

Job costing: Home builder or remodeler, swimming pool contractor

Cost objects: The sponges that absorb money

A *cost object* is anything that causes you to incur costs. Think about a cost object as a sponge that absorbs your money. The object can be a customer, job, a product line, or a company division. Carefully identifying cost objects will help you cost your product or service accurately.

Assume you manage a group of plumbers. You're reviewing the month's mileage expense (the equivalent of gasoline) for your staff and notice a 20 percent increase from the prior month. Why? You start asking questions. As it turns out, the customer demand for plumbing work required your staff to drive more miles. The average customer lived farther away.

You grumble, "That driving ran up a lot of costs!" Yes, it did, and you do the driving to meet the needs of your customers. In this example, the cost object was the group of customers for the month. Without any customers, you wouldn't have paid for all of the gas. (Well, you wouldn't have had any income either, but never mind that.) No cost object means no costs incurred.

Direct costs are *traced* to the cost object, and indirect costs are *allocated* to the cost object.

Indirect costs can be fixed or variable. Insurance costs on vehicles would be a fixed indirect cost. The premiums are fixed, and the cost is indirect to the job because you can't trace the vehicle insurance cost directly to a specific job. Utility costs for the office (such as heating and cooling) are variable indirect costs. Costs vary with the weather, but as with the insurance premiums, you can't trace them directly to any one job.

This list explains how fixed and variable costs are assigned to cost objects:

- ✔ Direct costs

  Variable direct costs, such as denim material, where denim jeans is a cost object

  Fixed direct costs, such as a supervisor salary at an auto plant, where an automobile produced is the cost object

- ✔ Indirect costs

  Variable indirect costs, such as utility costs for a television plant, where a television produced is the cost object

  Fixed indirect costs, such as insurance for a plumbing vehicle, where a plumbing job is a cost object

Charging customers for direct and indirect costs

To bill a customer and calculate a profit, you must add up all the costs for that customer, whether they are direct or indirect costs.

If, for example, you manufacture kitchen countertops, you would want to include all direct and indirect costs of a custom countertop installation in order to bill the customer. A direct cost might be marble (for material). To find the total cost of material for the job, you'd compute direct material cost as (marble) × (quantity used).

Indirect costs are different. If your kitchen countertop business makes lease payments on an office building, the cost is indirect. You can't know the exact amount of indirect costs for the client. You also can't trace the cost directly to a specific customer, but you can allocate it using a cost allocation base.

For job costs to be accurate, you need to collect information before you bill the client. You also need to consider the difference between your cost estimate and the final bill. Your client needs to understand how costs higher than the estimate will be handled. Should the customer expect to pay it, or will you absorb the cost (and lower your profit)? If this isn't handled correctly, the customer may be upset. Unforeseen things happen, of course, and you should explain when you hand the customer the estimate that the final bill may be different. A customer would likely accept additional labor costs. That's because the exact cost of labor is probably hard for you to predict.

Think about allocating indirect costs this way: There's a dollar amount of cost to allocate (say, $100). You spread that cost over a group of customers, a level of production, or some other activity level. In this section, you see how that might work.

A carpenter owns trucks that require repair and maintenance expense. That cost can't be traced to specific customers; instead, these indirect costs are allocated to a cost object. You find a "best" method to assign repair and maintenance expense to clients, perhaps labor hours worked for the customer.

The logic is that if you worked more hours for a specific customer, you probably used your truck more. If you used the truck more, that customer should absorb more of your truck's repair and maintenance cost.

It's virtually impossible to trace the repair and maintenance cost of the truck back to a specific customer. So you make your best educated guess to distribute the cost.

Cost allocation is the process of connecting an indirect cost to a cost object (see Chapter 2 for more). A *cost pool* is a grouping of similar costs. You can think of a cost pool as a bunch of similar cost objects thrown together. In this case, the cost object is a specific customer job.

A *cost driver* is an item that changes the total costs.. If you drive the trucks more, they require more repair and maintenance. An activity (driving to see customers) drives up your costs (repair and maintenance).

Just to clarify: The cost object is the "sponge" that absorbs the cost. The cost driver adds to the size of the sponge. A bigger sponge absorbs more cost.

Assume the total repair and maintenance expense for three carpentry trucks is $3,000. During the month, your workers provide service to 300 clients. Each customer is allocated $10 of repair and maintenance expense ($3,000 ÷ 300 clients).

If the cost driver increased to 400 clients per month, the plumbers would drive more miles. As a result, the trucks would require more maintenance and possibly repairs. Your monthly repair and maintenance expense would be higher.

At 400 customers for the month, assume total repair and maintenance expense for three carpentry trucks is $3,600. Now each customer is allocated repair expense of $9 ($3,600 ÷ 400 clients). The cost driver increase (number of customers) changed your total cost to $3,600. Because you also have an increase in total customers (400), the $3,600 is spread over a larger group. The total cost increased, but the cost allocated per customer declined.

You can see how the cost allocation process can get complicated.

It's often beneficial to group similar costs together into the same cost pool when the cost driver is the same. Consider a cost pool for the indirect costs for the plumbing trucks. In addition to repair and maintenance expense, the company pays for insurance and depreciation on the three trucks. None of these costs can be traced to a specific customer; instead, you need to allocate these costs. A good cost pool would include depreciation, insurance, and repair costs on the trucks. This cost pool can be allocated just like the repair and maintenance in the previous example.

Implementing job costing in manufacturing: An example

To implement job costing in a manufacturing company, first think about dividing your costs into two piles: direct costs and indirect costs. In a manufacturing setting, you have direct materials and direct labor you can trace directly to the job. So far, so good. Next, think about what's driving indirect costs. You spread those indirect costs to the work you perform.

As an example, Reliable Fencing manufactures and installs wooden fences for the residential market. Reliable has a manufacturing component and a service component.

Reliable provides the customer a cost estimate. The estimate is based on the type of fence, fence height and length, and labor hours needed for installation. Because nearly every job has a different set of costs, Reliable Fencing uses job costing. This system allows Reliable to compute costs accurately. And from that, Reliable can calculate a selling price that generates a reasonable profit.

Imagine that you're the manager of Reliable Fencing. The Johnsons have requested an estimate for a fence in their backyard. To provide the estimate, you discuss the fence models and types with them. You measure the length needed for the fence and the height requested. Finally, you consider any extra labor costs you might incur. For example, the Johnsons would like the fence to jog around several trees so the fence doesn't damage the tree trunks.

The Johnsons' fence is the cost object. Reliable will incur costs if the client orders a fence and work starts on the project. But before getting an order, you have to provide a cost estimate.

Computing direct costs

Reliable combines the cost of wood, paint, and a waterproofing treatment for the wood. That combined cost represents direct materials. As the manager, you compute direct material costs:

Direct materials = quantity of materials × unit price paid for material

You buy material measured in square feet. The unit cost is the price per square foot (see Chapter 2). Here's the amount of material needed and the cost:

Direct materials = 600 square feet of material needed × $5 per square foot

Direct materials = $3,000

Your other direct cost is direct labor. Your staff must cut the wood, paint it, waterproof it, and build the fence. Thinking through it further, your staff must measure and dig postholes. They then fill the area around the posts and nail the fence boards onto the posts, all while keeping everything level. Not easy! It takes real skill and planning. As a result, the owners of Reliable Fencing know it's best to hire skilled people and pay them a reasonable hourly rate.

Your experience as Reliable's manager allows you to estimate the labor time needed, based on several factors. You consider the square footage of material needed; the length and height of the fence; and any extra work, such as going around those tree trunks. Here's your formula for direct labor costs:

Direct labor = hours of labor × rate paid for labor

Note a difference in terms: *Price* is used for materials, and *rate* is the term used for labor. That distinction comes up in the world of cost variances.

You estimate that 2 people working 20 hours can complete the job. Using these numbers, you determine the labor cost:

Direct labor = hours of labor × hourly rate paid for labor

Direct labor = 2 workers × 20 hours × $20

Direct labor = $800

Consider one more direct cost. You saw a discussion of mileage expense earlier in chapter. Let's dust off that formula and use it here:

Cost per mile = cost per gallon of gas ÷ miles per gallon for the vehicle

Mileage costs = miles needed for client × cost per mile

You calculate 15 miles (round trip) from your office to the job site. However, the work will be completed over several days. You estimate 45 total miles.

Your trucks get 20 miles to the gallon, and your fuel cost is $4 per gallon. It's not much, but here is the direct cost for mileage:

Cost per mile = $4 gallon of gas / 20 miles per gallon

Cost per mile = 20 cents per mile

Mileage costs = 45 miles needed for client × 20 cents per mile

Mileage costs = $9.00

So you have three direct costs: materials, labor, and mileage. They are direct costs because they can be traced to the cost object: the Johnsons' fence.

Calculating indirect costs

To allocate indirect costs, you decide on two cost pools. One pool is your vehicle and equipment costs, and includes depreciation, maintenance, repair, and insurance costs. The other pool is office cost, which includes salary, benefits, accounting costs, and legal costs for your company. The cost object for allocating these indirect costs is the customer base:

Vehicle and equipment costs	$4,000
Office cost	$7,000
Customers serviced	200

After you resolve how to allocate costs, try to keep it simple. You combine the indirect costs into one amount ($4,000 + $7,000 = $11,000). You then divide the indirect cost total by the number of clients for the month:

Indirect cost allocation rate = $11,000 ÷ 200 customers = $55 per customer

Indirect cost allocation rate = $55 per customer

Your office assistant asks a question: "Is that really fair? What if one client has a $3,000 job, and another's project is only $500? Should we be charging the same amount of costs to both?" You think about the issue over lunch.

After lunch, you stop by your office assistant's desk and say: "You know, a client should expect that if we show up for a job of any size we're going to incur some office and vehicle costs. I don't think a client will be surprised by those fees."

The assistant thinks for a minute. "Yeah, that's fair. If they showed up at my house for a job, those indirect costs seem okay. I guess I'd expect to pay for it somehow. As long as the cost charged to a small job is not huge, I think charging a rate per customer is reasonable."

The discussion with your office assistant may convince you that your indirect cost allocation should be more specific. If you could show the client how their specific job generated indirect costs, he or she would be more inclined to agree with your billing.

You need to weigh the cost and time needed to allocate costs with the benefit of knowing more specific information. If customers generally accept the $55 allocation rate as reasonable, great. Probably no reason to dig further into your indirect costs.

If the majority of your customers have a problem with the rate, you should consider more detailed analysis and present a more detailed indirect cost billing. If not, you may lose the opportunity to do more work with the same group of clients.

Presenting total job costs

Table 4-1 shows the total costs for the Johnsons' fence job.

Table 4-1	Job Cost Sheet — Johnson Fence Job		
Type of Cost	*Amount or Quantity*	*Price or Rate*	*Total*
Direct material	600 square feet	$5 per square foot	$3,000.00
Direct labor	40 hours	$20 per hour	$800.00
Mileage	45 miles	$.20 per mile	$9.00
Indirect costs	1 customer	$55 allocation	$55.00
		Total job costs	$3,864.00

Taking a Closer Look at Indirect Costs using Normal Costing

In this section, you apply indirect costs to your product or service. You also plan direct and indirect costs using a normal costing system. Actual costs represent what comes out of your checkbook. You determine actual costs after the work is completed. *Normal costing* instead uses budgeted data, which is generated before the work is completed. Normal costing uses a budgeted price or rate and multiplies that rate by the actual quantity used.

It's difficult to plan your work without some budgeted rates of cost. That's the purpose of normal costing. The process creates budgeted rates that you can use to plan your work. You don't have to wait until the end of the job and determine your actual costs. You can find more on budgeting in Chapter 6.

Let's say you operate a landscaping company. Changes in costs can make planning difficult, and the changes may be higher or lower. Maybe the costs you pay for materials, labor, and other costs change as the year goes on. The cost of grass seed may go up, increasing your material costs. Or your labor costs decline because the economy slows. More people with the needed skills are looking for landscaping work, so you can offer a lower pay rate.

If you use actual costs, which change over time, it's difficult to price your product to generate a reasonable profit. For example, if you had a 15 percent profit above costs, a cost increase will eat away at your profit. Maybe higher costs lower your profit to 10 percent.

It's also harder to plan your cash needs. If you need to buy $10,000 of grass seed in the next 30 days, what if the price goes up? Maybe a shortage increases your grass seed cost to $12,000. That means that the check you need to write will be $12,000, not $10,000. Now you need to have $2,000 more cash available.

Budgeting and cash management is similar to planning a vacation. First, you determine the costs (airline, car rental, hotel, gas). Next, you plan your cash flow to pay for the vacation cost. If the prices are constantly changing, planning is difficult. Many people try to book a vacation trip well in advance, so prices are fixed for the trip!

Budgeting for indirect costs

When you budget for indirect costs, you spread those costs to cost objects, based on a cost driver (refer to the section "Cost objects: The sponges that absorb money"). Before you spread the indirect cost, you come up with a rate to allocate the costs to the product or service. The indirect cost rate allows you to price your product to produce a reasonable profit.

As the manager for the landscaping company, you decide on a cost pool for indirect costs. Your only indirect cost is for vehicles and equipment (depreciation, insurance, and repair costs). Your company is new, with virtually no office costs to consider yet.

Many companies have planning meetings around the end of their fiscal (business) year. In the meetings, they make assumptions about many issues, including next year's costs. This is when a company plans *predetermined or budgeted indirect cost rate.* The predetermined overhead rate depends on total indirect costs and the cost driver you select.

During a planning session, you consider the prices and rates you paid last year. You think about how prices and rates have changed, and consider your estimates of miles driven each month. Based on that analysis, here is your budgeted indirect cost rate:

Predetermined or budgeted indirect cost rate = $7,500 ÷ 1,400 miles

Predetermined or budgeted indirect cost rate = $5.36 per mile

It isn't until the end of the year that the company knows what the actual total indirect costs will be and the actual miles driven. Here is the actual indirect cost rate for the vehicles and equipment (using miles driven for the month as the cost object). The formula is explained in the section "Computing direct costs and indirect costs":

Indirect cost allocation rate = $8,000 ÷ 1,300 miles

Indirect cost allocation rate = $6.15 per mile

Predetermined or *budgeted* means planned in advance. Your budgeted monthly rate has a lower monthly cost level ($7,500 versus $8,000) but more monthly miles (1,400 versus 1,300). As a result, the budgeted overhead rate is lower. You use this rate to apply indirect costs to every job during the year.

At the end of the year, you realize that you didn't allocate enough costs to your jobs. As a result, your actual profit will be lower than what you budgeted. Because actual costs aren't known until the end of the year, you almost always have a difference between budgeted and actual results.

Following a normal job costing system

Put together your budgeting process for indirect costs with a plan for direct costs. Think of the combined process as *normal costing.* I'll keep hammering away at this point, but it's important: You trace direct costs and allocate indirect costs.

Normal costing combines indirect cost rate with actual production. The process gets you closer to actual total costs for your product.

Computing direct costs and indirect costs

Here are the two steps to implement normal costing:

- ✔ **Direct costs:** Traced to the cost object by multiplying (actual prices/rates) × (actual quantity for a specific job object)

- ✔ **Indirect costs:** Allocated to the cost object multiplying (predetermined or budgeted indirect cost rate) × (actual quantity for a specific job object)

Note that both direct and indirect costs use actual quantity in the formula. While you come up with an indirect cost rate in planning, the rate is multiplied by actual quantities. In this case, the quantity is jobs for the month.

Introducing the job cost sheet

A *job cost sheet* lists every cost you've incurred for a particular job. That includes direct material, direct labor, and all indirect costs. The job cost sheet is your basis for computing your sale price and your profit. You use this document to prepare a cost estimate for a client. Table 4-2 shows a job cost sheet using normal costing for a landscaping job.

Table 4-2	Normal Job Cost Sheet — Landscaping Job		
Type of Cost	**Amount or Quantity**	**Price or Rate**	**Total Cost (Rounded)**
Direct material	100 square feet of grass seed	$12 per square foot	$1,200
Direct labor	15 hours of labor	$15 per hour	$225
Mileage	30 miles driven	$0.18 per mile	$5
Indirect costs	30 miles driven	$5.36 per mile	$161
		Total job costs	

The indirect cost calculation (vehicle and equipment costs) uses the actual quantity (miles driven) and the estimated rate per mile. The other direct costs on the job sheet use actual quantities and actual prices/rates.

Following the Flow of Costs through a Manufacturing System

Costs flow through a manufacturing system, from buying materials for a product all the way to the customer sale. When you envision the flow of costs, you find it easier to collect all the product costs you need to price a product. When you know all the steps, you remember all of the costs related to those steps!

Control starts with control accounts

Control accounts are temporary holding places for costs. Managing costs has to start somewhere, and in accounting, that process most often starts out with control accounts.

Labor, materials, and indirect costs start off in control accounts. It may sound strange, but these accounts and their balances don't appear in the financial statements. That's because the balances are eventually moved to other accounts. All the checks you write for manufacturing costs are posted first to control accounts.

For many manufacturers and retailers, inventory is the biggest investment; more cash is spent on inventory than any other asset. Because of that, a big part of operating a profitable business is to control the costs of inventory.

Inventory is an asset you eventually sell to someone. (That's a little different, of course, from buildings and equipment.) For manufacturers, inventory has three components: *raw materials, work-in-process,* and *finished goods,* whereas retailers just have finished goods. Raw materials inventory is, broadly, products not yet started; work-in-progress inventory is partially completed products; and finished goods inventory is completed products.

The three kinds of inventory are assets, because you eventually sell the goods to a customer. When you do, the inventory asset becomes an expense — cost of goods sold. Managing inventory starts in a control account.

Table 4-3 lists control account titles for each component of inventory.

Table 4-3	Control Accounts for Inventory
Type of Costs	*Control Account*
Materials	Materials control
Labor	Wages payable control
Indirect costs	Overhead control

✔ **Materials:** You buy materials (such as wood for making kitchen cabinets) in advance of making your products. *Materials control* is the term for the control account for material costs.

✔ **Labor:** Consider labor costs. Employees report the hours they work on *time cards* each week. Those cards list hours worked on various projects. For custom cabinets, the time cards list customer jobs that employees completed, and the hours worked. *Wages payable control* is the term for the control account for labor.

✔ **Indirect costs:** A business (such as the kitchen cabinet business) has indirect costs (for example, machine repair and maintenance). Your firm has some method to allocate those costs to clients (see "Budgeting for indirect costs"). However, you may not get to the allocation until after you write checks for the cost. *Overhead control* is the term for the control account for indirect costs.

Control accounts (materials, labor and overhead), work-in-process, and finished goods) are inventory accounts, which are assets. Cost of goods sold (COGS) is an expense account. When you make a sale to a customer, you "use up" the asset. The asset becomes an expense.

Explaining the debit and credit process

You increase and decrease account balances using *debits* and *credits*. Business owners need to know these terms because they can't understand your accounting process without them.

Don't be frustrated if you need to read this section a few times. I've taught the concept for years, and it requires some review before you fully understand it. Here are rules that never change:

✔ **Debits:** Always posted on the *left side* of an account

✔ **Credits:** Always posted on the *right side* of an account

All accounts are formatted like this:

Material Control

Debit   Credit

In accounting, *debit* and *credit* don't mean the same things they do in common talk. Debit can refer to an increase or a decrease. It depends on what type of account you're working with. The same is true of a credit. Here are the rules for the purposes of this book:

Asset accounts:

> **Debits:** Always *increase* the account balance. A big debit in the Cash account (an asset) is a good thing
>
> **Credits:** Always *decrease* the account balance

Control accounts, work-in-process, and finished goods are all inventory accounts, making them asset accounts. Cost of goods sold is an expense account. Debiting increases all of these accounts. The balance for any of these accounts is equal to debit balance less credit balance.

Liability accounts:

> **Debits:** Always *decrease* the account balance
>
> **Credits:** Always *increase* the account balance

Income accounts:

> **Debits:** Always *decrease* the account balance
>
> **Credits:** Always *increase* the account balance

Expense accounts:

> **Debits:** Always *increase* the account balance.
>
> **Credits:** Always *decrease* the account balance

There's an accounting mantra: "What's the impact of this transaction on the general ledger?" Always ask. There are several answers, depending on what you're doing, but in time you will know them all. And it's not as though if something goes up something else goes down. For example, when you sell something, cash (an asset) gets a debit and goes up. On the other side of the transaction, income gets a credit and goes up.

Walking through a manufacturing cost example

Say you're the manager of Karl's Kustom Kitchen Kabinets. You order $20,000 in lumber. You then take $5,000 of the lumber and start making cabinets for a customer.

When you bought the lumber, cash (an asset) went down, but the material control account (as asset) went up. The material control account was increased (debited) when you bought the lumber.

The material control account balance decreases (credit) when you take $5,000 in lumber to start using the material for a customer. Now how would your material control account look?

Material control account

Debit	*Credit*
$20,000	
	$5,000

If the month ends with no other activity, the ending material control balance is $15,000 (20,000 – $5,000).

But the $5,000 didn't just vanish. When you put materials into production, you reduce (credit) the material control account and increase (debit) the work-in-process control account.

Work-in-process control account

Debit	*Credit*
$5,000	

You reduce one asset (material control account) and increase another asset (work-in-process control account).

Now assume that the people on the shop floor finish some cabinets and move $2,000 of the $5,000 work-in-process to moved to finished goods.

Work-in-process control account

Debit	*Credit*
$5,000	
	$2,000

You reduce one asset (work-in-process control account) and increase another asset (finished good control account). If the month ends with no other activity, the ending balance is $3,000 ($5,000 – $2,000).

Again, there's no disappearing money. The "other side" of the transaction hits the finished goods control account.

Finished goods control account

Debit	Credit
$2,000	

So one more time, you reduce one asset (work-in-process control account) and increase another asset (finished goods control account).

At some point, you sell what you made. You've got $2,000 in finished goods. Because you make custom cabinets, there's one customer. The finished goods control account shows this:

Finished Goods

Debit	Credit
$2,000	
	$2,000

You are almost home. When goods are sold, you reduce (credit) the finished goods account and increase (debit) cost of goods sold. And *that's* an expense account. At last!

Cost of Goods Sold

Debit	Credit
$2,000	

The difference between your sale price and the cost of goods sold is your profit.

Why do you go with the flow? The reason you do this exercise is to fully track where your inventory money is. For custom cabinets, it can be a big deal, if you're building for, say, 20 customers at once. For off-the-shelf cabinets, it can be a very big deal. You might be delivering 2,000 cabinets per month.

The flow not only lets you see where the inventory money is, but also spot production logjams. Too much in the material control account suggest that you're overbuying or not producing. Too much in the work-in-process control account suggests that you're not producing. Too much in the finished goods control account suggests that you're not selling and you have "dead inventory."

Applying the methodology to other control accounts

Use the same flow process for labor and indirect costs. Labor costs accumulate in the control account until they're traced to a customer or product line. At that point, the cost moves to work-in-process. When the goods are completed, the costs move to finished goods. When goods are sold, the cost moves to cost of goods sold. The labor cost process mirrors the system for material costs listed above.

I define cost allocation in the "Budgeting for indirect costs" section. For example, you're recognizing depreciation expense and repair costs on vehicles. Those costs are in an overhead account. You plan a budgeted rate to apply indirect costs to products. As those costs are incurred, the overhead control account is increased (debited).

When you allocate indirect costs to a customer or product line, you reduce (credit) the overhead account and increase (debit) work-in-process control account. After that, the process is the same as with the other control accounts. Costs move from work-in-process to finished goods to cost of sales.

Chapter 5

More Activity, More Cost: Activity-Based Costing

As a business owner or manager, you can always use more useful information — information that helps you make informed decisions.

Chapter 4 introduces two widely used costing methods: job costing and process costing. Now dig deeper for better information on costs. Pull apart your product or service, and find out more about the activities that create cost. The result is an activity-based costing system.

Activity-based costing (ABC) is a methodology that focuses on activities. When compared to other costing methodologies, it assigns indirect costs (overhead) more accurately. Because ABC uses more detail, your cost estimates become more precise. As a result, you price your products more effectively.

Avoiding the Slippery Peanut Butter Costing Slope

Activity-based costing is an effective costing system that focuses on activities. You incur costs when production and sales happen. When you take an order over the phone, manufacture a product, or place a box on a delivery truck, the activities generate costs. The *activity* becomes the focus to assign costs. Because you're connecting cost to the activity that creates the cost, your cost per product will be more accurate, and so will your pricing.

Despite the benefits of ABC costing, many business managers use *cost smoothing,* or *peanut butter costing,* instead, which spreads costs over a broad range of cost objects. When you spread peanut butter, you smooth it over the entire slice of bread. You don't pay much attention to how much cost is assigned to any particular part of the bread. Likewise, cost smoothing spreads the cost without paying too much attention to how much cost is assigned to any particular cost object. The trouble is, costs won't be assigned as accurately as they should be.

Cost allocation is the process of allocating indirect costs to products and services. The cost allocation base is the level of activity you use to assign costs. Maybe you use 1,000 machine hours or 200 labor hours. Also, keep in mind that direct costs are *traced* to products and services, not *allocated.* Stroll over to Chapter 4 for more.

To help you understand the benefits of ABC, you need to see the slippery slope of peanut butter costing. Here's the setup: Say you're a food distributor. You have five restaurant clients that order meat, fish, and poultry every day. You take orders, package them, and deliver the food to these businesses every day. Your restaurant clients have high expectations; they expect high-quality, fresh food to be delivered quickly so they can prepare their meals.

Your order manager handles the details of order processing. Her salary, benefits, and other costs total $5,000 per month, and it's an indirect cost. The cost needs to be charged to the restaurant clients. You can't *trace* the cost of the order manager to your service. Instead, you need to *allocate* it.

The following sections explain how to allocate indirect costs using one type of activity. You'll see that using single indirect cost allocation can lead to errors in assigning costs.

Recognizing a single indirect cost allocation

A *single indirect cost allocation* uses one cost pool. (Chapter 4 defines cost pools.) The food distribution setup uses one pool of costs — order manager costs. With ABC, you end up dividing the costs of order management into more cost pools, and you're better off for it.

Everybody pretty much starts by creating a predetermined or budgeted overhead rate (described in Chapter 4). When you plan at the beginning of the year, using a single indirect cost pool, you come up with an overhead rate for the order manager's cost, such as the following:

Annual budgeted indirect cost rate = cost ÷ orders

Annual budgeted indirect cost rate = $60,000 ÷ 1,250

Annual budgeted indirect cost rate = $48 per order

The order manager's cost of $5,000 per month amounts to $60,000 per year. The five restaurants order nearly every business day of the year. You figure that total orders will be 1,250 — 250 orders per year from five customers. (Isn't it great that in samples all customers order exactly the same number of times?)

The single indirect cost allocation spreads the cost (order manager) uniformly over the cost object (orders). That's $48 dollars per order. This is an example of peanut butter costing, where all services receive the same or similar amounts of cost.

A fly in the peanut butter: Dealing with different levels of client activity

If some customers or activities eat up more costs than others, peanut butter costing isn't a true reflection of the costs. A customer or activity that demands more effort should get a larger cost allocation. So companies that use peanut butter costing miss the chance to allocate costs more precisely.

You no doubt know from experience that some customer orders are always smooth as glass. Other orders, from problem customers, always require your staff to jump through extra hoops.

For example, say you notice that your order manager is spending a lot of time with two customers in particular. The Steak Place and Riverside Fishery are making big demands.

It's typical for them to change their orders at the last minute at least once a week. When this happens, the order manager has to cancel the original invoice (the bill), make a new one, and email it. Then she also has to change the shipping instructions document; you don't want the wrong goods put on the truck and sent to the restaurant. So the order manager cancels the original shipping instructions and makes new instructions.

"It's really frustrating," the manager says. "Sometimes they call so late that I have to call the driver and tell him not to leave the dock. We unload the truck and start over." Well, no doubt you'd like to be known for your high level of customer service, but this is getting ridiculous.

There's another issue. When the invoice and shipping order change, the goods coming out of inventory also change. Your pickers are taking products off the shelf, putting them back, and then taking different products. These constant changes eventually lead to mistakes in inventory. A picker might move a product in or out and not record it in the accounting records.

And here's another point to consider: Your business supplies meat, fish, and poultry, items that aren't known for having a long shelf life. The excesses of The Steak Place and Riverside Fishery may leave you with bunches of spoiled products.

You decide to take another run at allocating the office-manager cost. "Why don't we track the time spent on each client? Let's try that for three months and see how your time shakes out. It sounds like we should assign more costs to the two customers you mentioned." You change the cost allocation from orders placed to time spent per customer.

After three months, you review the time spent per customer. Fortunately, you've been tracking time carefully, and you're using an excellent spreadsheet program.

The office manager works 24 days per month, 8 hours per day. Her total monthly hours are 192 hours (24 days × 8 hours). Table 5-1 shows the breakdown.

Table 5-1	Order Manager — Monthly Hours Per Customer	
Restaurant Customer	*Hours for Month*	*Percent of Total*
Apple Core Diner	30	15.6
Blue Lantern	30	15.6
Meadowbrook Grill	30	15.6
Riverside Fishery	56	29.2
The Steak Place	46	24.0
Total hours	**192**	**100.0**

Aha! The situation is just as the order manager told you, but now you have some metrics. Half the costing battle is measuring reality to confirm your instincts.

To summarize, with peanut butter costing, you spread the cost evenly. You assigned 20 percent of order-manager costs to each customer. Now you see that two customers account for more than 50 percent (!!!) of the order manager's effort. It's time to reallocate the cost.

Missing the mark: Undercosting and overcosting

If you use cost smoothing, it's likely that you will incur product undercosting or product overcosting.

- ✔ *Product undercosting* occurs when a product or service uses more resources (costs) than you assign.
- ✔ *Product overcosting* is the opposite. The product or service uses fewer resources (costs) than you assign.

If either of these costing errors occurs, the cost of the product won't be accurate, and your profit calculation will be incorrect.

Discussing product-cost cross-subsidization

Undercosting or overcosting creates *product-cost cross-subsidization*. Is that a mouthful, or what? Product-cost cross-subsidization means that if you undercost one product, you will overcost another. It's common sense and simple math. There's a fixed amount of cost to assign. If you're "over" in one product, you'll be "short" in the other. That situation throws off your cost and profit calculations.

Say you have two products, A and B. (Obviously, your marketing department needs to come up with better product names.) The total cost to be allocated is $100. You allocate $50 of costs to product A and $50 to product B. If you've overcosted product A by $10, you've allocated $10 too much. That means you've undercosted product B by $10. In other words, the actual costs should have been $40 for product A and $60 for product B.

You started with $100 in your "bucket" of costs. When you allocated too much for product A, there was too little to allocate to product B.

Undercosting or overcosting direct costs is relatively easy to figure out and fix. How do you catch mistakes? You *trace* direct costs, so you can determine the exact cost of material used in production. Undercosting or overcosting of indirect costs is harder. *Allocating* indirect costs is less precise than *tracing* direct costs.

For example, it's a bit difficult to allocate utility costs in a factory. You can't do it easily, but you can do it. The cost accounting "secret" is to invest time investigating the activities that result in utility costs. For example, if one of the manufacturing machines runs twice as long as another, that activity is probably consuming twice as much electricity. The higher machine activity should result in twice as much utility expense.

Table 5-1 shows that investigation pays off. Two customers were chewing up over 50 percent of the order manager's effort by requiring more hours of her time. The investigation of the activity produced metrics, which form the basis of a better cost allocation plan.

For the tools and techniques, see the section "Designing an Activity-Based Costing System."

Underallocating or overallocating messes up pricing

Underallocating or overallocating costs impact your product price and your profit. If your product costs aren't accurate, you can't price your product correctly.

Say you overallocate costs for retailing a men's dress shirt. You think total shirt cost is $31 in direct and indirect costs, and you'd like a $10 profit per shirt. You therefore price your shirts at $41.

But that may not be correct! If the true cost of the shirt is only $30, $1 is over-allocated. As a result, your profit is $11 ($41 – $30).

Well, what's wrong with that? You'd rather make $11 a shirt instead of $10. Consider this: By pricing your product at a higher price, you may lose some sales. Most people have a *price point,* a maximum price that they're willing to pay based on the value they perceive. There's trouble ahead, because the apparel industry is highly price-driven.

If a lot of customers say to themselves, "The most I would pay for that shirt is $40," you may lose sales at a $41 price. Although you make another dollar per shirt at $41, your sales may decline to the point where you make less total profit.

A bigger pricing problem may be when a product's cost is underallocated. Assume that you underallocate another men's dress shirt by $5. You think the total cost is $50. To make a $10 profit per shirt, you set the sales price at $60, so everything's fine, right? Wrong! If costs are allocated correctly, the real profit is $5 ($60 – $55). Underallocation has resulted in a sales price that's too low, and that reduces profit.

There's no way you can make up this deficiency through volume sales. Usually, shirts selling for $60 don't go flying off the display table.

Designing an Activity-Based Costing System

If your ABC system is well designed, you allocate costs more precisely. This section helps you carefully separate costs between direct costs and indirect costs. You also consider the specific activities that drive the indirect costs higher. Finally, the indirect costs are allocated to the activities that cause those costs to be incurred.

Refining your approach

ABC is a *refined costing system,* or a more specific way to assign costs to cost objects. The system avoids using big, generic categories, such as splitting a cost evenly between divisions. Instead, it allocates indirect costs to the activities that generate those costs. The result is likely to be more accurate costing and product pricing.

There are three tasks for the refined costing system:

- ✔ **Direct cost tracing:** Review your direct costs and categorize more costs as direct costs, if possible.
- ✔ **Cost pools:** Review cost pools and create more pools, if necessary.
- ✔ **Cost-allocation bases:** Decide on cost-allocation bases using cause-and-effect criteria.

Direct costs are traced to cost objects. As a result, the amount of cost is fairly easy to determine. For example, it's easy to determine the amount of leather used to make the leather handbags.

Cost pools should be *homogeneous.* Those are cost pools in which each of the costs has the same cost allocation base. The costs have a similar cause-and-effect relationship. Therefore, if you have more than one allocation base, you should have more than one cost pool.

A good example is a cost pool combining vehicle depreciation, repair and maintenance, and fuel costs. The costs all increase when your vehicles drive more miles. The cost allocation base should be mileage, and you simply allocate a dollar amount of indirect cost per mile driven.

Grouping costs using a cost hierarchy

A *cost hierarchy* groups costs into cost pools based on cost drivers or cost allocation bases. A cost hierarchy has levels, which explain how broadly you look at costs and activities.

Here are levels you might use in a cost hierarchy:

- ✔ **Unit-level costs** are cost activities performed on an individual unit, whether a product or service. If you make blue jeans, your unit is one pair of jeans. An individual tax return is a unit, if you prepare tax returns for clients.

- ✔ **Batch-level costs** are cost activities that generate costs at the batch level. For example, when an automobile plant changes from one car model to another, it's changing batches and incurring setup costs. The plant is "retooling," and that might include moving machinery, and certainly includes changing out the dies and reprogramming the welding robots.

- ✔ **Customer-level costs** are cost activities generated for one customer. If you're remodeling a kitchen, your labor costs, materials used, and overhead costs incurred for a specific customer are all customer-level costs. Customer-level costs may include multiple orders from the same client.

- ✔ **Product-sustaining costs** are cost activities that support a particular product or service line, regardless of the number of units produced. A product-sustaining cost extends the life of a product, and technology products are good examples. To stay relevant with customers, software companies come out with endless new versions of software. Extending a product's life is supposed to keep customers buying it. Design costs can be product-sustaining costs. To keep the technology product current, you change the design. You can allocate product-sustaining costs to a product or to an entire product line (sometime called a "product family" in high tech).

- ✔ **Facility-sustaining costs** are cost activities that support the overall company, such as legal and accounting activities. The rent, insurance, and maintenance on the company's building are facility-sustaining costs, because the building is essential to keeping the entire company running. The costs should be allocated over the entire company. Companies with multiple buildings sometimes cost allocate for each building to see if a building is too expensive to occupy.

If you use a fine-enough granularity, you can get really precise costing. On the other hand, too much granularity will make you crazy. The financial benefit of precise costing should be greater than the time and expense to track the cost information. The financial benefit is more accurate product costs and more exact profit calculations.

Testing your ABC design

The following example begins by separating direct and indirect costs. You also see descriptions of the activities that generate indirect costs. This example allocates indirect costs and calculates the full cost of the product.

For this example, assume you manage a company that makes and installs automobile windshields. You have a forward-looking product called a smart windshield, and it uses lasers, infrared sensors, and a camera to help drivers with vision problems drive well. You sell two products: sedan windshields and van windshields.

The company wants to implement activity-based costing for indirect costs. Ready, set, go!

Dealing with direct costs

You begin by sitting down with the production manager to get a handle on direct costs. You produce 1,500 windshields each year (750 for sedans and 750 for vans). You trace $300 of direct materials per windshield and $500 in direct labor per unit. Table 5-2 shows direct costs.

Table 5-2	Windshield Direct Costs	
Type of Cost	*Units × Cost*	*Total*
Direct material	1,500 units × $300	$450,000 ($225,000 per type)
Direct labor	1,500 units × $500	$750,000 ($375,000 per type)

Diving into the cost pools

Next, you and the production manager list the indirect cost activities to manufacture and install windshields. Your goal is to pull apart the cost pools. In other words, you make sure that each cost pool is based on a specific activity. The more specific the cost pool, the more likely you're allocating costs to products correctly. Table 5-3 shows the indirect costs for producing and installing windshields.

Table 5-3	Indirect Cost Activities — Windshield Production and Installation
Activity	*Description*
Molding setup	Install mold in machine to create a windshield
Machine operation	Run machine to convert material in mold to a windshield
Quality inspection	Review product for defects
Packaging and delivery	Pack windshield, load into truck for delivery to client
Installation	Install windshield at client location

You review to see if any of these costs are direct costs. That would be good, because it gets you out of the cost allocation business. It's better to have a direct cost *traced* to a product than an indirect cost *allocated* to a product.

Applying indirect costs using a cost allocation base

The next step is to link the indirect costs to the cost pools (the activities) using a cost allocation base. At the start, you agree that labor hours should be used to allocate indirect costs for each activity, except for machine operation. The machine cost will be allocated based on machine hours. Table 5-4 allocates each cost pool (activity) based on the total hours it takes to complete each activity. You perform this analysis for all products.

Table 5-4	Cost Allocation Rates			
Activity	*Allocation Base*	*Total Cost*	*Total Hours*	*Allocation Rate/Hour*
Molding setup	Labor hours	$20,000	150	$133/hour
Machine operation	Machine hours	$500,000	5,700	$88/hour
Quality inspection	Labor hours	$100,000	1,050	$95/hour
Packaging and delivery	Labor hours	$50,000	525	$95/hour
Installation	Labor hours	$30,000	900	$33/hour

Allocate and celebrate: Assigning the cost allocation rates to the products

You have the allocation rate per hour (either machine hours or labor hours). Now decide how many hours to use to apply the rate. The goal is to tie the cost allocation to the activity as closely as possible.

Each product has a different mold. Your company changes the windshield being produced by changing the mold. Because of the sedan windshield's curve, it takes more labor hours to set up the sedan's mold.

It takes more machine hours to produce the van windshield, simply because the van windshield is bigger. The van's larger windshield also requires more time to inspect, package, and deliver.

Installation costs are the same for both products. Table 5-5 lists the cost allocation for each product and the percentage of the total hours for each activity.

Table 5-5	Cost Allocation As a Percentage of Total Hours		
Activity	**Allocation Rate/Hour**	**Sedan Cost and (Percent Hours)**	**Van Cost and (Percent Hours)**
Molding setup	$133	$13,333 (67)	$6,667 (33)
Machine operation	$88	$236,842 (47)	$263,158 (53)
Quality inspection	$95	$42,857 (43)	$57,143 (57)
Packaging and delivery	$95	$21,429 (43)	$28,571 (57)
Installation	$33	$15,000 (50)	$15,000 (50)

At long last, you review the total product costs for sedan and van windshields (see Table 5-6).

Table 5-6	Total Costs By Type — Sedan and Van Windshields		
Type of Costs	**Sedan (750 Units)**	**Van (750 Units)**	**Total (1,500 Units)**
Direct material	$225,000	$225,000	$450,000
Direct labor	$375,000	$375,000	$750,000
Molding setup	$13,333	$6,667	$20,000
Machine operation	$236,842	$263,158	$500,000
Quality inspection	$42,857	$57,143	$100,000
Packaging and delivery	$21,429	$28,571	$50,000
Installation	$15,000	$15,000	$30,000
Total costs	$929,461	$970,539	$1,900,000
Cost per windshield	$1,239.28	$1,294.05	

The cost per van windshield ($1,294.05) is slightly higher than the cost per sedan windshield. The higher cost for vans makes sense. You can use the total costs in Table 5-4 and the percentages in Table 5-5 to assign costs. You get the same cost allocation that's calculated by using the rates per hour in Table 5-5. You need the cost allocation rates to easily assign costs to all of your production. That's why the rates per hour are important.

Take a look at indirect costs. Installation costs are evenly split, so disregard that cost pool. Consider the other indirect costs. Other than molding setup, all of the remaining indirect cost pools have a larger allocation to the van. That's reasonable, because the van windshield is bigger than the sedan windshield. It costs more to run it through a machine, to inspect it, and to package it.

Using Activity-Based Costing to Compute Total Cost, Profit, and Sale Price

The only constant is change. Demand for your product is probably always changing. Material costs may increase (seems like they rarely go down). Increased competition may force you to lower your prices to prevent sales from slipping. Luckily for you, activity-based costing is a tool to manage indirect cost allocations effectively as conditions change.

Take a look at the following example, which shows how cost allocation is used to compute total cost, profit, and a sale price.

Say you operate a lawn care business that provides two services: flower bed planting and care, and lawn planting and care.

You plan and price your work based on a 25-square-foot area. One unit for your business is 25 square feet, whether it's a lawn or flower bed. You refer to one unit as one customer yard. Table 5-7 shows a summary of the cost objects for the business.

In planning, you determine that your business will service 500 units in the upcoming year. Assume that the sales will be evenly split between the two services (250 yards each).

Table 5-7	Flower Bed and Lawn Care Costs	
Type of Costs	**Flower Bed**	**Lawn Care**
Direct materials	Mulch and fertilizer	Sod, grass seed, and fertilizer
Direct labor	Clear area, plant, or install material	Clear area, plant, or install material
Estimator cost (indirect cost)	Flower bed inspection and analysis	Same as Flower Bed column
Transportation cost (indirect cost)	Depreciation, insurance for vehicles, and mileage	Same as Flower Bed column
Office cost (indirect cost)	Costs for dispatcher/accountant	Same as Flower Bed column

Allocating indirect costs evenly by product

Initially, you allocate indirect costs by splitting the indirect costs between the product types. Table 5-8 shows an even allocation of indirect costs. The direct costs are traced to each service you provide, either flower bed work or lawn care.

Table 5-8	Costs and Profit by Product — Flower Bed and Lawn Care		
Cost (250 Units of Each Product)	**Flower Bed**	**Lawn Care**	**Total**
Direct material	$25,000	$30,000	$55,000
Direct labor	$37,500	$25,000	$62,500
Estimator cost (indirect cost)	$15,000	$15,000	$30,000
Transportation cost (indirect cost)	$7,500	$7,500	$15,000
Office cost (indirect cost)	$12,500	$12,500	$25,000
Total costs	$97,500	$90,000	$187,500
Add: Profit (10 percent of cost)	$9,750	$9,000	$18,750
Total sales	$107,250	$99,000	$206,250
Cost per unit (yard)	$390	$360	
Sale price per unit	$429	$396	

Estimator cost, transportation cost, and office cost are evenly split.

Now think about profit as a percentage of total costs. In Table 5-8, the flower bed profit calculation is $9,750, or 10 percent of costs ($97,500 × 0.10). To compute your sale price for flower beds, add the total cost to profit. That's $107,250. Finally, divide both the total cost and total sales by 250 yards. That provides cost per unit of $390 and sale price per unit of $429 for flower beds.

Analyzing and reallocating cost activities

A key point of activity-based costing is basing each cost pool on a specific activity. This puts you on the road to more accurate costing of your product. To learn more, you ask your staff in detail about their activities.

The estimator's job is to discuss each project with the client. She assesses the current condition of the yard, and the labor and materials needed for the project. Finally, she supervises the work until completion. You ask your estimator to track the amount of time she spends on each type of product. It's simple: She will post her time to a flower bed column or a lawn column on a spreadsheet.

After a few months, you find that the estimator spends 70 percent of her time on flower bed projects. "Flower beds take more time to discuss with the client," she says. "Most of time, there are already some flowers and other plants in the flower bed. The customer decides what to keep and what to throw out. Lawns are easier. There's not much to discuss, other than the current condition of the grass." From this, it's clear that you should assign 70 percent of the estimator's cost to the flower bed product.

At the same time, the estimator tracks mileage on the trucks and vehicles. "If you look at this map, you'll see that most of our flower bed work is in the wealthier area of town. That's farther from our office than most of the lawn work." She looks through her mileage log. "I calculated that 60 percent of our drive time and mileage is spent on flower bed work." Okay, more progress! It looks like you should allocate 60 percent of the transportation costs (vehicle depreciation, insurance, and fuel) to the flower bed product.

Your last stop is your office assistant's desk. "You know we get a lot of cancellations and rescheduled work for lawn care." He pauses for a minute. "I think because the work isn't complicated, and there are a lot of competitors, people don't take it as seriously. They change and cancel without much thought."

Well, a cancellation or rescheduling fee would reduce the problem, but that's a cost story for another day. For now, just consider the activities that generate office costs. The office assistant's cost (salary, office supplies, and computer) can be allocated based on his time. When a customer cancels or reschedules, the office assistant spends time on the phone with customers, the estimator, and employees. In addition, the paperwork for the project has to be changed. After more analysis, the two of you decide that 60 percent of the office assistant cost should be allocated to lawn work.

Changing allocations to cost pools

You investigated indirect costs and made some changes. Table 5-9 shows the cost allocation changes to the three indirect cost pools. The direct costs didn't change, because they are *traced* directly, not *allocated.* Total costs are still $187,500. That makes sense, because activity-based costing changes cost allocations, not cost totals. Costs change by product but not in total for the company. Sales are still $206,250.

Because the per unit sale prices stay the same, the profit calculations changes. Profit for flower beds is now $4,750 ($107,250 – $102,500). Profit for lawn care is now $14,000 ($99,000 – $85,000).

Table 5-9	Activity-Based Costing by Product — Flower Bed and Lawn Care		
Cost (250 Units of Each Product)	*Flower Bed*	*Lawn Care*	*Total*
Direct material	$25,000	$30,000	$55,000
Direct labor	$37,500	$25,000	$62,500
Estimator cost (indirect cost)	$21,000	$9,000	$30,000
Transportation cost (indirect cost)	$9,000	$6,000	$15,000
Office cost (indirect cost)	$10,000	$15,000	$25,000
Total costs	$102,500	$85,000	$187,500
Profit (total sales less total costs)	$4,750	$14,000	$18,750
Total sales	$107,250	$99,000	$206,250
Cost per unit (yard)	$410	$340	
Sale price per unit	$429	$396	

In Table 5-9, the flower bed total cost increased by $5,000 (from $97,500 to $102,500). As a result, profit for flower beds declined by $5,000 (from $9,750 to $4,750). ABC had the opposite effect on the lawn care business. Lawn care costs went down by $5,000 (from $90,000 to $85,000). Profit increased by $5,000 (from $9,000 to $14,000).

Changing prices after ABC

You overcosted lawn care and undercosted flower beds. When you reallocate that from lawn care to flower beds, the change throws off your profit calculation!

You wanted a profit of 10 percent for each product, but flower beds are producing only a 4.6 percent profit ($4,750 profit ÷ $102,500 in sales). The lawn care profit produces a 16.5 percent profit ($14,000 ÷ $85,000). The profit and sales numbers are explained above.

Here's the problem: 4.6 percent may be too small a profit margin. You're spinning your wheels for a bunch of petunias.

Calculate the new sale price for flower beds, based on the ABC and a 10 percent profit. This is shown in Table 5-10.

Table 5-10	Calculating a New Sale Price for Flower Beds
Cost (250 Units of Each Product)	*Flower Beds*
Total costs in Table 5-9	$102,500
Profit (10 percent of total cost)	$10,250
Total sales	$112,750
Cost per unit (yard)	$410
Sale price per unit	$451

The original price per unit for flower beds was $429. The new flower bed unit price is now $451, $22 higher than before ($451 to $429). To make a 10 percent profit, change the flower bed sale price to $451 per unit.

At the old price, you weren't making your desired profit. Now you will. And *that's* the value of using ABC.

You could make up for the lower profit on flower beds by earning more on lawn care. But really, you should assess each product on its own and price each one to produce the correct profit.

Part II
Planning and Control

The 5th Wave   By Rich Tennant

"Have someone in accounting do a cost-volume-profit analysis, run a variance analysis, and finish this Sudoku puzzle for me."

In this part . . .

Accountants love to plan, so plan on this part covering methods for creating a budget and getting budgets to fit together. I also lead you through a pleasant discussion on overhead costs and why they're often misused or ignored in cost analysis. You say you want to learn about inventory and how that may generate your largest costs? Well, you're in the right place . . . er, part.

Chapter 6

What's the Plan, Stan? Budgeting for a Better Bottom Line

. . . .

In This Chapter

▶ Seeing the master budget and its component parts

▶ Appreciating the importance of budgeting

▶ Planning production, sales, and cash

▶ Working costs into the budget process

▶ Assigning responsibility, using a budget as a guide

. . . .

You need accurate information to make smart decisions about your business. A well-planned budget may be most important piece of information you use.

Budgeting is a proactive process. It's the thinking person's accounting. You anticipate future outcomes and can maximize them. You anticipate problems and may be able to minimize or eliminate them. That's a lot better than operating in ignorance and reacting to events as they come up.

In this chapter, you look at budgets, consider how to anticipate costs, and work through some essential budget documents.

Brushing Up on Budgeting Basics

As you know, a *budget* is a financial plan that includes both financial and non-financial information. Its most obvious features are a projection of revenue (how much you anticipate selling) and expenses (how much you anticipate spending). The budget can also contain non-financial information, such as how many employees you think you need.

A budget is a forecasting document, but businesses use it as a financial control tool, as well. A *financial control* is a tool to monitor activities in your business. One control is to review spending and ensure that you don't exceed your budgeted spending. Often, a company (or a division or department within it) isn't allowed to spend more than has been budgeted.

Budgets cover a specific period of time, most commonly a year. And a budget looks into the future. Although you use historical information to put together your budget, the activities you plan happen in the future.

When you budget, you're in good company. Businesses and governments, both large and small, create budgets. So do millions of people.

Seeing the master budget and its component parts

A *master budget* is a summary of your financial plan and your operating plan. The master budget gives you a "big picture" and sets your course of action for an upcoming period. It's critically important.

- ✔ The *financial plan* (financial statements, really) is what you share with outside parties who need your budgeted information. The bank where you have a loan may want to see your financial budget. In some cases, a government regulatory agency may want to review your budget. If you manufacture food, the Food and Drug Administration (FDA) is the federal agency that regulates food. The FDA might want to review your budget. Financial information comes from three financial statements: budgeted balance sheet, budgeted income statement, and budgeted statement of cash flows.

- ✔ The *operating plan* (also known as the *operating budget)* is used internally. Imagine sitting in a meeting with your managers. Your managers need to understand how much they can spend this year and how they are allowed to spend it. Managers also need to understand how much money the company is forecasting as a profit. The projected profit affects the manager's sales plans. These details are contained in the operating plan. You hand out the operating plan to each manager, and the managers implement the plan.

The master budget is a comprehensive picture of your plans for the future and how the plans will be accomplished.

Operating plans can contain non-financial information. Decisions about production, hiring, and selling effort are components of operating plans.

Why budgeting is important

To put it simply, when you put together a budget, you determine how you plan to use your resources. *Assets* are resources; cash is the most famous asset. Other property, like vehicles, for example, are assets, too. The reason you spend cash for materials and labor is to earn money for your business. The reason you buy a truck for use in your business? Same thing: to earn money for your business.

In theory, you could sell all your assets. Of course, then you wouldn't have a business, but that's what happens when you dissolve a business — the assets are used to pay off the company's liabilities. A *liability* represents a "claim" on your assets. A claim means that someone has a potential right to your assets if you don't pay him or what you owe. A bank loan is a company liability. So are your utility bill and other bills you need to pay. If you don't pay your bills, the companies you owe could file lawsuits. A court might force you to pay. That's what is meant by a claim on assets.

A budget helps you forecast how much of your assets you use and how much revenue (sales) the asset generate. If you use your assets (resources) wisely, you increase your profit.

Assets such as trucks *depreciate.* They're worth a little less every day as you use them up. The more you drive your company trucks, the more costs you recognize. Note that you can budget for operating costs and depreciation, such as what you'll see with a truck.

Take landscapers as an example. Landscapers are a smart bunch. They drive the wheels off their trucks until maintenance costs become too great. They milk all the revenue they can out of an asset before disposing of it. It's simple: A load of steer manure doesn't care whether it's being driven to the jobsite in a brand-new dually with crew cab or a 15-year-old junker. You have choices about using resources. If you choose to use resources to make product A (and generate revenue), you're giving up the opportunity to use those same resources to produce product B (which would have generated revenue, too). This is called *opportunity cost.* You make the decision to produce either product A or B in your budget.

Opportunity cost is the decision to go one way instead or the other. It's mainly about deciding how to allocate resources. Opportunity cost confronts you when you look at your product line (what you plan to sell), your expenses, your vehicles, and so forth. It even operates when you choose which restaurant to go to on Saturday night. Maybe the pricey place is close by and the cheaper place is a long way away, so what do you do? Either option gives you something and costs something.

Your budget also helps you figure out product mix. How much of each product or service will you sell? Take a look at Chapter 3 to see how to use sales mix to reach a target level of income.

Cash flow is the cash inflows and outflows your business generates. When you produce a product or perform a service, you spend cash (cash outflow). When you're paid for a sale, you get cash (cash inflow). You plan sales in your budget. As a result, you plan cash inflow and outflows, too. The key cash flow question is this: Does my budget include enough cash inflows to pay the outflows?

If an accountant recognizes revenue based on cash inflows, he or she is using the using *cash basis* accounting. Cash basis accounting recognizes expenses when you have a cash outflow. Most companies use the accrual method of accounting, which is different. Both of these methods are defined in the "Budgeting with Cash Accounting or Accrual Accounting" section, later in this chapter.

Planning strategically

Businesses generally plan for the long term. Occasionally, you get existential and ask, "What's it all about?" Your strategic plan has the answer.

A *strategic plan* is your business's road map to the future. The plan reminds you, your employees, and third parties what you do, how you do it, the customers you do it for, and maybe even how you will do it in a superior way. "It" means making jet fighter aircraft, selling chocolates in a mall, or whatever the business does.

The plan summarizes where the business is, where it wants to go, and how it's going to get there. In theory, everything you do day to day contributes to advancing the goals in the strategic plan. Everything you do can affect costs, profits, and company growth.

Your budget, of course, is an important part of strategic planning. The budgeting process forces you to think, make decisions, and come up with reasonable forecasts. You can't sidestep potential negatives, either. That would be like a farmer pretending that a drought doesn't exist.

In the world of startup businesses and bank loans, you generally hear the question "Do you have a business plan?" A *business plan* is very much the same thing as a strategic plan. You probably won't get venture capital (VC) money or a loan without a plan that assures the investor or lender of your credit-worthiness.

VC firms buy equity (ownership) in companies that are just starting out. The companies that VC firms invest in typically don't have a track record of sales and profits. VC firms take large risks, because the investment in a startup firm may be lost if the company fails. If the new business succeeds, the VC firm can earn a large rate of return on the investment. You may have heard the term "Go big or go home." That describes what a VC firm does.

Strategic planning begins in a practical way but quickly requires you to be a visionary. A good example is the late Steve Jobs, considered to be a great business visionary of the 20th and 21st centuries. Jobs was able to imagine the types of technology products customers wanted long before other people could. Apple created lots of innovative products based on Jobs's vision.

Strategic planning methods exist in abundance and seem to be a thriving cottage industry. They contain more letters than ten cans of alphabet soup, and include SWOT, PEST, STEER, EPISTEL, ATM, and RCA. Be cautious, and use common sense before embracing a planning methodology. *Strategic Planning For Dummies,* by Erica Olsen (published by John Wiley & Sons) is a great resource for this topic.

Planning How to Plan: Factors That Impact Your Budgeting Process

Planning is time consuming, but it pays off. There's no single difficult part, so the biggest challenges are to bring the right information to the game and use your head. Good information comes from your experience, what you know about timing, the facts and figures your staff gives, and what you judge about sales projections.

Experience counts

Business owners without much experience in an industry often plan poorly, in part because they don't have much personal history to go on. Also, some people have trouble accepting the reality of their business prospects. For example, they really want the business to grow 30 percent but can't accept the fact that 10 percent is more realistic.

I worked with three brothers who were opening a pizza-parlor franchise. The franchise was successful in other parts of the county. The brothers were opening a store in a new area of town. All good. None of the brothers had any restaurant industry experience. Two of the brothers sold business envelopes, and the third was a professional golfer. Not so good.

The four of us did an analysis and determined that the profit margin was only 5 percent. That profit margin was so small that a seemingly insignificant change from the budget (budget versus actual) could result in a loss.

The brothers went forward with the business in spite of the small profit margin. They wanted to start their own business very badly, so they were willing to take the risk that it wouldn't succeed financially. After a few years, the brothers closed the business. The pizza parlor never generated enough profit to pay the owners a reasonable salary.

The pizza-restaurant owners planned poorly. They didn't have any industry experience. If they had, they might have realized that the profit level they were projecting was not realistic. If they had agreed that the projected profit was too low, they might have passed on opening the restaurant.

Timing is everything

Different business decisions have different timelines. Those timelines depend, in part, on the dollar amount of the decision you're making. Understanding your timeline will help you make intelligent decisions about spending.

For example, if you decide to use a different supplier for your materials, you could start buying materials from that company immediately. No problem. On the other hand, completing a move into a newly constructed building might take a year or more. You need to consider timelines for your more expensive business decisions. If you're building a new office, determine how long the construction will take. Based on the timeline, you can plan your payments for the building and how you'll generate cash to make the payments.

Explain your timeline in your business plan. If you're providing financial statements (discussed later in this chapter) for one year, you may need to explain payments for a building (asset) that isn't yet completed. It's perfectly reasonable to expect a business to pay for major assets over a long period. Just make sure that it's explained to your investors or lenders. You may have a one-year *operating* budget, along with a *capital expenditure budget* for three to five years. The capital expenditure budget is the big-things-I'll-buy-and-pay-for-long-term budget. This budget helps you and others visualize your long-term plans and spending.

People get you headed in the right direction

The budgeting process isn't just about numbers; it also involves people. Part of planning your business involves talking to people — lots of people! A budget is something that a group of people typically reviews and eventually comes to an agreement on. Involve people and get their opinions, or there won't be agreement on the budgeted results. If the company's managers don't generally agree on where you're headed in your budget, you may need to revise.

Talk to your staff. If you're concerned about wasting material in the manufacturing process, talk to people on the factory floor. Maybe you'll find out that poor quality is the reason some material is wasted during production. Maybe some denim you use to make jeans tears too easily and has to be thrown out. The problem isn't the employees; it's poor-quality material from a supplier. You may never find that out unless you spend some time on the factory floor.

Talk with the sales staff to plan sales for the year. Good salespeople know their clients. They may know about a client's purchasing plans for next year. They may even know a client's budget to buy your product! Also, a good salesperson might know the financial condition of the customer. If the customer's business is growing, he or she might buy more from you. If the business is in financial trouble, that might mean decreased sales.

Have a conversation with the accountant during planning. She knows how cash flow turned out last year. You can look at the data on how quickly you collected cash for sales. Also, your attorney will remind you of any legal issues that might generate expenses during the year. There may be costs for legal services or costs to settle litigation. Those costs require cash, and you need to include them in your plan.

When your budget is in good shape, you can present it to your staff and explain where the company is headed. They'll feel more confident knowing the company's direction and prospects.

Sales projections pay off

Sales projections help answer the question of how you earn a reasonable level of profit. Of course, the answer is complicated if there are competitors selling the same product or service, because it suggests you might have to lower prices to stay competitive. If you want to cut prices to attract business, you need to plan your costs so your profit level remains reasonable. Another possibility is to improve the design of your products and not change prices. If you do that, you add the cost of design to product costs. But increased sales without cutting prices may offset the cost of design.

Company goals, employee compensation

Ideally, your employees can connect your budget goals to their proposed salary increases and bonuses. I once sat in a sales meeting with a company president and his sales staff. The salespeople were paid a bonus based on their individual sales, regardless of overall company results. The president was paid a bonus based on company profits. It was early November, and the president was trying to determine if enough sales would come in before year end so the company could reach its profit goal (which would be good for the president).

Keep in mind that the additional business would need to meet an accountant's defini-

tion of a legitimate sale. If you'd like to know more, check out the book *Financial Accounting For Dummies,* by Maire Loughran (published by John Wiley & Sons).

I knew that none of the salespeople were close to meeting the sales level for bonuses. They had no motivation to bring in sales before the end of the year (which would be bad for them). They wanted to close sales and get credit in the following year, when they counted toward their next year's bonus. Needless to say, the salespeople stayed quiet. The president didn't connect the company's profit goals with the salespeople's compensation.

Good planning is useful, and poor planning leads to projections (of profit, sales, and company growth) that aren't useful. If you use unrealistic plans, you use assets in ways that won't maximize your profits. Simply put, you end up spending time and money on the wrong activities.

Say you're a homebuilder with a 50 percent growth in sales last year. This year's budget assumes a 30 percent sales growth. You don't take a lot of time to analyze that assumption; you just figure that because last year was great, and expected orders for the beginning of this year look promising, why not 30 percent? That's no method of projecting sales growth.

Part of the answer is market research. It's a marketing concept but may be useful here. Assume that you're selling running shoes in the United States. The first step is to determine the size of the market, and you find that 10 million people buy running shoes each year. On average, they spend $80 for a pair. Fortunately, you've priced your shoes at $78, so you're right around the average.

Next, you estimate that your firm can capture 10 percent of the U.S. running-shoe market. That means a total sales volume of 10 percent of a 10 million-unit market, or 1 million units sold in a year. At $78 a pair, you project your sales to be $78 million. Finally, you consider whether the market is growing or shrinking. If the running-shoe market is growing at 10 percent per year, you could reasonably increase your sales projection by 10 percent each year, also. Of course, market growth is impacted by the economy overall and the specific industry (sporting goods, in this case). Competitors may also impact your growth. All of these issues would need to be projected before coming up with a reasonable sales forecast.

The sales growth rate drives decisions about spending, employee hiring, and cash planning. If you're selling 30 percent more, you can plan to increase your spending and hire employees to manufacture 30 percent more of your product. You also probably can expect a 30 percent increase in cash inflow as a result of growth, too.

But wait! If a more careful review indicates 10 percent growth, your 30 percent projection creates some problems for you. You increased your spending and hiring assuming the 30 percent level, but the sales and cash inflows will only come in at 10 percent. Put simply, you're planning on spending 20 percent too much. Whether you're building homes or selling running shoes, the numbers still apply.

The Nuts and Bolts (and Washers) of Budgeting

Budgeting takes time. In fact, a well-designed budget can take a lot of time to create. The good news is that the process gets easier over time.

Begin by deciding what company entities require a budget. Also decide how detailed your budgeted data should be. The budget can be for the whole company, or maybe each of five company divisions should have its own budget. Maybe you want to produce budgets for each of three departments within each of the five divisions. The process takes time and involves people, so the benefit of having the budget must outweigh the cost of putting it together.

In budgeting, you begin with some assumptions. The assumptions are called *standard costs* and are the specific planned levels of cost and activity. For example, you might assume a standard labor rate (cost) of $20 per hour for a sewing-machine operator. You might assume a standard material rate of $75 per square foot for marble for kitchen countertops.

When you create your budget (based on reasonable assumptions) and start the year's business, you have actual costs and levels of activity to review. A difference between an actual cost and standard cost is a *variance* (see Chapter 7). A variance is a scorecard that tells you how close your budget assumptions were to actual results. Fortunately, you can make modifications to your budget to deal with variances.

Understanding the budgeting financials

Your budget becomes a set of *pro forma* financial statements. Pro formas are what-if statements, filled with budgeted, planned, and forecasted items. Unless you have a crystal ball, your budget is always a collection of educated best guesses about the future.

To keep things simple, there are three basic financial statements for budgeting: the balance sheet, the income statement, and the statement of cash flow (mentioned earlier in this chapter). Another aspect is an explanation of your source of funds.

Source of funds

Your budget determines if you have enough funds to run your business. Hopefully, you get all the money you need from selling products or services, but that's not always the case.

The *financial plan* (also loosely called the *business plan)* explains the source of funds to run the business. You can raise money by borrowing cash (debt) or by offering investors ownership in the business (equity) in exchange for cash.

If you borrow, you repay a creditor the original amount borrowed (principal) and interest on the loan, usually on a written schedule. The interest cost and principal repayment must be included in the budget.

You can also raise funds by selling ownership in your business, offering investors equity. Equity investors are rewarded in two ways: *stock appreciation* and *dividends.*

The most common way to sell ownership is to sell common stock. Investors expect you to explain (through your budget) how you plan to generate a profit for the year. If the company is profitable, the value of their ownership in your business increases. They could eventually sell their ownership interest to someone else for a profit.

You also need to think about whether or not to pay dividends. Dividends are a share of the profits earned by the company paid to equity investors. Of course, without any company earnings, you can't pay dividends.

Using the balance sheet

The *balance sheet* lists the company's *assets, liabilities, and equity* (essentially the difference between assets and liabilities) as of a certain date. Think of the actual balance sheet as a snapshot in time; think of the budgeted balance sheet as a pretty good estimate of the actual financial statement.

Liabilities are claims on your assets. A *liability* means that you owe someone money. Liabilities include items such as unpaid utility bills and payroll costs you have not yet paid. Future interest and principal payments on a loan are also liabilities. When you pay a liability, you use an asset (cash, in most cases) to make payments.

This gets you to the basic formula for the balance sheet:

Assets – Liabilities = Equity

I describe it this way: Assume you own a little shop. You sell all your assets — your inventory, furniture, and your building. You use the cash you receive to pay off all your liabilities — utility bills, payroll, and bank loan. Whatever cash is left after you pay off your liabilities is your equity. Equity is the true value of your business. Equity is the residual — after you use your assets to pay off all liabilities. So now you can see the logic behind the balance sheet formula: Assets less liabilities equals equity.

Working with the income statement

The *income statement* shows revenue, expenses, and net income (profit). For most business owners, the income statement is the most important report. The income statement shows if a business was profitable over a period of time (such as a month, quarter, or year), whereas the balance sheet shows assets, liabilities, and equity as of a specific date. The nice thing about modern accounting software is that it's pretty easy to instantly display and print an income statement. Think of the budgeted income statement as a pretty good projection of your company's sales, expenses, and profit.

The income statement formula is incredibly simple:

Revenue – Expenses = Net Income

Analyzing the statement of cash flows

The *statement of cash flows* analyzes your sources of cash (cash inflows) and your uses of cash (cash outflows) over a period of time. Cash flows are grouped into three categories: operating, financing, and investing activities. When an accountant puts together a cash flow statement, she reviews every transaction that affected cash. A very simple model is what's in your checkbook. If inflows are good, you probably have enough cash to operate. If the checkbook shows that you're overdrawn, outflows have exceeded inflows, and you've got trouble.

The goal is to assign every cash transaction to one of three categories, although most of your cash activity is in the operating activities section. I always suggest that people find financing and investing activities first because there are usually fewer transactions. The remaining transactions are operating activities.

The three cash flow categories are

- ✔ **Operating activities** occur when you run your business each day. You buy material, pay for labor, ship goods, pay interest on loans, and collect cash from customers.

✔ **Financing activities** occur when you raise money for your business, and when you pay lenders or investors. You receive cash when you sell equity, and you receive cash when you borrow. You pay cash when you pay dividends, and you pay cash when you pay down a loan (pay back some of the principal).

✔ **Investing activities** occur when you buy or sell assets. If you write a check for a new vehicle or receive cash when you sell equipment, those are investing activities.

The statement of cash flows lists the beginning cash balance; all the cash activity for the period, grouped into three categories; and the ending cash balance:

Ending cash balance = (net cash flow of operating activities) + (net cash flow of financing activities) + (net cash flow of investing activities)

A simpler formula is

Ending cash balance = (beginning cash balance) + (cash inflows for the period) – (cash outflows for the period)

The ending cash balance in the statement of cash flows equals the cash balance in the balance sheet (well, it's supposed to, anyway). For example, if the statement of cash flows is for March, the ending cash balance should equal the balance sheet cash balance for the last day of March.

When you create your budget, it should include all three financial statements (balance sheet, income statement, and statement of cash flows).

Reviewing revenue and production budgets

Revenue and production budgets, put simply, forecast how many units you plan to produce and how many units you plan to sell. For more info, check out the flow of manufacturing costs in Chapter 4.

Say you're budgeting to manufacture garage doors. You need to forecast how many sales you expect. Then you consider how many garage doors you already have in inventory and plan how many you need to manufacture to meet the sales forecast. Ta da! When you know the number of doors you need to make, you can budget for material and labor costs.

Direct costs are pretty straightforward, and you can use an activity level to assign indirect costs. See Chapter 5 for more on assigning indirect costs. Revenue, production, inventory, direct materials, direct labor, indirect costs (overhead), and cost of goods sold all are budgeted items.

Applying the revenue formula

Say you forecast selling 200 garage doors in March. Consider how many garage doors you need to manufacture. Assuming a sales price of $300 per door, here's your revenue budget:

Revenue budget = 200 units × $300

Revenue budget = $60,000

Using the inventory formula

And now for the famous inventory formula:

Ending inventory = beginning inventory + production - sales

Your production will change based on how many garage doors you already have in inventory. So if you already have 75 completed garage doors in beginning inventory, it's clear that you won't need to manufacture all of the 200 units you plan to sell.

But wait! Do you want any garage doors in ending inventory? If you think you'll have orders during the first few days of the next month, you probably do. So maybe you decide on an ending inventory of 50 garage doors.

Take the inventory formula and calculate the garage door production you need. Assume x is production in units, and solve for x:

Ending inventory = beginning inventory + production - sales

$50 = 75 + x - 200$

$x = 175$

This simple algebra problem shows that production should be 175 units. Table 6-1 shows a production budget.

Table 6-1	Garage Door Production Budget		
Cost	**Quantity**	**Price**	**Total**
Direct material (wood)	80 square feet	$1 per square foot	$80
Direct labor (labor)	2 hours	$25 per hour	$50
Indirect costs allocated	1 hour	$15 per hour	$15
Cost per unit			**$145**
	Units	**Unit cost**	**Total cost**
Production cost	175	$145 (above)	**$25,375**

The production budget includes direct materials, direct labor, and indirect costs (overhead). In this example, the indirect cost is allocated based on machine hours. Add the costs to get a unit cost. Then multiply units to be produced by the cost per unit. That amount is the total cost of production of $25,375.

Assessing cost of goods sold

The goods you produce for customers end up in one of two places: You either sell them (cost of goods sold), or they're still on the shelf (finished goods inventory). Beginning inventory and production don't matter. For more info on cost of goods sold, see Chapter 4.

What costs should be attached to the goods you sell? How much did they cost to produce? (If you're a retailer, how much did they cost to get?) To continue with the garage door manufacturing example, assume that the first goods you sell are from beginning inventory. Because all 75 units of beginning inventory are sold, use a formula to determine how many units of the March production are sold:

March production sold = total sales - beginning inventory

March production sold = 200 - 75

March production sold = 125

Assume also that the cost per unit of beginning inventory is $143. That cost is different from the March production cost of $145. (Why the change? Because it seems like the costs of materials and labor to make a garage door go up all the time.) Table 6-2 displays the cost of goods sold budget.

Table 6-2	Garage Door Cost of Goods Sold Budget		
	Units	*Cost Per Unit*	*Total Cost*
Beginning inventory	75	$143	$10,725
March production sold	125	$145	$18,125
Total	200		$28,850

The total cost of goods sold is higher ($28,850) than total production cost in Table 6-1 ($25,375). That makes sense, because Table 6-1 deals only with producing 175 units. You sold 200 units, but 75 units were from inventory. Because of adjustments for beginning and desired ending inventory, you don't always need to produce in a month the number of units you sell in a month.

One more calculation. (There's always one more calculation.) Now calculate your ending inventory budget:

Ending inventory budget = units × per unit cost

Ending inventory budget = 50 × $145

Ending inventory budget = $7,250

You've planned revenue, production, and inventory. Great! Now you need to figure out how to pay for it all. If you don't have a budget for an adequate cash amount to operate, you can't do business.

Budgeting with Cash Accounting or Accrual Accounting

Accounting was easier in the days of the cave dwellers. Og said to Gog, "I give you three spear points. You give me that deer." After that, accounting got more complex, and every civilization has kept business records in one form or another.

The credit for modern accounting goes to Italian mathematician Luca Pacioli, a Franciscan friar who hung out with Leonardo da Vinci. Pacioli developed double-entry accounting, which every business (except street merchants, and maybe some of those, too) uses.

There's a choice for small business: You can use cash basis accounting or accrual basis accounting. Both methods can be used for budgeting, but accrual is better and is used by all large organizations.

Cash basis accounting: Using your checkbook to budget

Cash basis accounting posts revenue and expenses to the financial statements based solely on cash transactions. Nothing happens until you take cash in or send it out. It's a simple way of doing things — no accounts receivable and no accounts payable.

By contrast, *accrual basis accounting* states that expenses are matched with revenue, regardless of when cash moves in or out of the checkbook. The accrual basis is a better method to account for cash, because revenue and expenses are matched more precisely. See the section "I accrue, you accrue, we all accrue with accrual accounting."

On a very basic level, your cash budget is a reflection of your checkbook. It's the sum of the deposits you make (revenue) and the checks you write (costs). The budgeting result of cash basis accounting is a *cash budget.*

Such a budget assumes that all your customers pay for sales in cash during the month of sale, and it assumes that you pay all costs during the month that the goods are sold. This is very unlikely for most businesses.

It's more likely that you write a check in February for materials for a product you sell in April. Similarly, you might pay an employee in December for work to make a product that's sold in January.

Assume you own a gift shop that sells greeting cards, flowers, and gifts. Your beginning cash balance for the month is $100,000. Table 6-3 displays a cash budget for a gift shop.

Table 6-3	Gift Shop Cash Budget — Month of March
	Amount
Beginning cash balance	$100,000
Add customer payments for sales	$50,000
Less:	
Inventory purchases	$20,000
Payroll costs	$10,000
Utilities costs	$1,000
Lease cost	$3,000
Ending cash balance	$116,000

This cash budget has a $16,000 increase in cash during the month ($116,000 - $100,000). You had $50,000 in sales. If you hadn't collected any cash from customers during March, your cash balance would decrease by $34,000, the total of all the cash outflows. If that happened, you'd start the next month with $34,000 less cash. You need to consider if your April cash budget (next month) would work with a lower beginning balance in cash. You don't want to start in the red.

If you don't think you'll have enough cash for a period, you can consider how to get it.

The cash budget is similar to the statement of cash flows. Table 6-4 shows an example statement of cash flows for the gift shop.

Table 6-4	Gift Shop Budgeted Statement of Cash Flows
	Amount
Beginning cash balance	$100,000
Cash flow from operations	$16,000
Cash flow from financing	$0
Cash flow from investing	$0
Ending cash balance	$116,000

Note that the beginning and ending cash balances in Table 6-4 agree with the cash budget ($100,000 at the beginning and $116,000 and the end). The cash flow calculation from operations is

Net cash inflow from operations = customer payments - cash outflows

Net cash inflow from operations = $50,000 - $34,000

Net cash inflow from operations = $16,000

All the cash flows for the gift shop are related to day-to-day operations. None of the cash activity is related to financing or investing.

I accrue, you accrue, we all accrue with accrual accounting

An effective budget applies the *matching principle*. The principle says you should match the timing of the expenses of creating and delivering your product or service with the timing of getting revenue from the sale. This is *accrual basis accounting* (as opposed to *cash basis accounting*).

Accrual accounting ensures that revenue is better matched with the expenses incurred to generate revenue. In simple terms, with accrual accounting you realize or recognize expenses when you incur them, not when you pay them. You realize revenue when you generate it, not when the customer pays.

When you create an invoice, the accounts receivable (A/R) system generates a *receivable,* even though the customer may not pay for, say, 30 days. When the payment comes in, the receivable *goes flat,* meaning it's been satisfied by the payment. Accrual accounting is considered to provide a more accurate reflection of business activity than cash accounting. By the way, the system still allows for straight cash sales — where you sell *now* and the customer pays *now.*

The same is true of purchases you make. When you buy now and pay later, you create a *payable*. When the bill comes and you pay it, the payable goes flat. Of course, the system allows you to make straight cash purchases — where you buy and pay your vendor *now*.

Say you manage a catering business. The food, preparation cost, and delivery expenses related to the Jones family reunion should be matched with the revenue from Jones family. Ideally, you want the expense and the revenue to be posted in the same time period. You wouldn't want the Jones expenses posted in March and the Jones revenue posted when they paid (say, in April). That's not the best reflection of your business activity.

The downside of accrual accounting is that your income statement revenue and expenses rarely match your cash inflows and outflows. You can be rich in receivables and darned poor in cash. All companies still prepare a cash flow statement even if they are using accrual accounting.

Budgeting to Produce the Income Statement and Balance Sheet

A final step is to create a budgeted balance sheet and budgeted income statement. Your balance sheet and income statement, whether budgeted or actual, are the two great financials. They are the bottom line, showing how you're doing.

The well-balanced balance sheet

Your balance sheet is a fine indicator of business health. Table 6-5 shows a pretty darned healthy balance sheet.

Table 6-5	Budgeted Balance Sheet
	Amount
Assets	$100,000
Less liabilities	$50,000
Equals equity	$50,000

As you review your balance sheet budget, keep in mind the goal is to maintain enough assets to run your business, which includes production (if you make things), buying inventory (if you're a retailer), or employing people (for manufacturing, retailing, or service businesses).

The balance sheet should include assets needed for selling and distributing your products. Managing your business generates liabilities, too (accounts payable, long-term debt, and so forth). That's okay, as long as you have a plan to pay them.

If revenue doesn't supply you enough of the best asset — cash — you need a plan to raise capital. Capital represents an investment in your business. If a business owner invests $20,000 into his business, the $20,000 is considered capital for the business. That means you likely are either issuing debt or selling equity.

The incredible income statement

Most business owners are most interested in the income statement. The owner will typically plan this budget document first.

Table 6-6 shows a nice income statement.

Table 6-6	Budgeted Income Statement
	Amount
Revenue	$50,000
Less expenses	$25,000
Equals net income	$25,000

Here's the thought process: You figure out how much revenue the company can generate. Then you subtract likely expenses from the revenue, and the result is your net income. After that, think about how cash will "move" (the cash flow statement) and where your company will get sufficient assets to operate (the balance sheet).

As you move forward in managing your business, don't be surprised if cash flow becomes the most important budget item for you. Without enough cash flow, not much can happen.

Chapter 7

Constant Change: Variance Analysis

∙ ∙

In This Chapter

▶ Comparing static and flexible budgets

▶ Recognizing variances and why they're important

▶ Using variance analysis to improve financial performance

▶ Analyzing price variances to make decisions about spending

▶ Reviewing efficiency variances to improve productivity

∙ ∙

*I*n Chapter 6, you review how to set standard (budgeted) prices and rates in the planning process. You budget at the beginning of the year and then review your actual results at year-end. Don't be surprised when your actual results are different from your standards. That difference is called a *variance*.

When you budget, you necessarily make assumptions about total costs and levels of activity (also known as standard costs). *Standard costs* are based on projected prices and your planned levels of usage. If you manufacture blue jeans, you'll determine the hourly rate you need to pay workers. You'll also estimate the total number of hours they will work during the year. No one (not even giant corporations) has a crystal ball, so reality (actual cost) is guaranteed to vary from assumptions (standard cost).

Variance analysis amounts to a series of techniques used to spot changes that can happen on both the revenue side and the expense side. These changes can occur for practically any reason. For example, if a disaster affects sales, revenue goes down. If the cost of materials spikes unexpectedly, expenses go up.

Business is risky. You often see unfavorable variances, results that are poorer than you wanted. But sometimes results are better than expected, and you see favorable variances.

In this chapter, I introduce several types of variances methods. I go over the concept of management by exception. This concept raises red flags that call attention to business problems, including variances. I identify variances using a flexible budget. When a variance is found, I show how to determine if the variance is favorable or unfavorable.

When you can identify a variance and understand why it occurred, you can make changes in your business to improve your productivity and your profit. The end result for you is a new, better set of assumptions, which operate until you do another variance analysis.

Variance Analysis and Budgeting

A *flexible (flex) budget* adjusts for changes in activity. A *static budget* assumes that the sale price, volume of sales, and all costs are fixed. The static budget does not change with any level of activity (like production or sales). In most situations a flexible budget is more useful than a static budget. That's because your actual production and sales levels will likely be different from your budget.

Using management by exception to recognize large variances

Management by exception is a variance analysis method that identifies the largest variances between actual results and standard plans. The largest variances need fixing; they are a priority for you.

Say your company makes leather coats that use a plastic zipper. As you review your actual and standard costs for the month, you notice that the actual price you paid for zippers is 20 percent higher than your planned price. None of your other variances for cost or revenue is greater than 1 to 2 percent. Something's going on! The variance doesn't tell you what happened, but it prompts you to investigate.

Management by exception is the red-flag method of variance analysis, and that 20 percent variance in the zipper price is a big red flag. It's a large difference that you need to investigate. It's not only statistically significant, but also, if your product is tightly costed (a small margin in the price for profit), the price increase is eating into your margins.

The increase may have happened because of a product shortage, meaning that your usual supplier couldn't meet your needs, and you had to go to another supplier and pay a lot more. Find out why the exception happened so you can make changes to prevent such a variance in the future.

Possible changes might be

- Find a different zipper that won't be subject to a product shortage.
- Find a different supplier who has a bigger inventory of the zipper you need.
- Find a cheaper zipper.
- Consider whether your business strategy is effective or not. Assume your leather coat's budgeted cost is $75. If your actual cost is getting higher, maybe the $75 cost per coat isn't a realistic budget amount.

Seeing the problem in using a static budget

A *static budget* (also referred to as a *master budget)* is a summary of operating and financial plans. After the budget is created, it doesn't change with the level of activity (sales, production) in your business.

A static budget is the starting point for determining a reasonable profit for your business. But a static budget assumes one level of output that never changes. This can create problems that are fixed by using flexible budgeting.

Table 7-1 shows a static budget for a toy manufacturer.

Table 7-1	Toy Manufacturer — Static Budget	
	Per Unit	**Total**
Units sold		120 units
Revenue	$45	$5,400
Variable costs		
Direct material	$12	$1,440
Direct labor	$8	$960
Indirect (overhead) costs	$6	$720
Contribution margin	**$19**	**$2,280**
Fixed costs		$1,200
Operating income		$1,080

Your static budget assumes only one level of production: 120 units. But direct material, labor, and indirect (overhead) costs are variable costs. They change as production changes. (Actually, you should keep in mind that indirect costs can be fixed or variable.) If you produce more or less than 120 units, you will have a variance that is caused just by volume (production). In fact, there are three major types of variances you might come across:

- ✔ **Volume variance:** You produce more or less than planned. That may mean that you use more or less material than budgeted. You may also use more or less labor than planned.

- ✔ **Price or rate variance:** The price you pay for materials, or that rate you pay for labor costs, is different than what you budgeted.

- ✔ **Sales variance:** You sell more or less than planned.

Note an important difference: Volume variances are all about *usage*. Price or rate variances relate to the *price* you pay — regardless of how much you use.

Operating with operating income

Operating income is your profit from the day-to-day activities of running the business. A growing operating income is a measurement of a successful business. In Table 7-1, you subtract fixed costs from contribution margin to get operating income.

If you make toys, your operating income is derived from just toy production and sales. Other types of income are not considered operating income. If your company happened to sell a building for gain, that gain wouldn't be part of operating income. The gain on sale of the building is a line in the non-operating income section of the income statement.

Table 7-2 lists the actual results for toy manufacturing.

Table 7-2	Toy Manufacturer — Actual Results	
	Per Unit	**Total**
Units sold		100 units
Revenue	$50	$5,000
Variable costs		
Direct material	$10	$1,000
Direct labor	$8	$800
Indirect (overhead) costs	$5	$500
Contribution margin	**$27**	**$2,700**
Fixed costs		$1,000
Operating income		$1,700

There are some differences between Tables 7-1 and 7-2. The actual units sold were less than budgeted (100 versus 120 units). The actual sale price per unit was higher than planned ($50 versus $45). There were also some differences in costs per unit that generated a higher actual operating income ($1,700 versus $1,080 budgeted).

You can breathe a little easier. It appears that your new Malibu Margi Beach House and Fun Set is selling pretty well and costs a little less than you expected to produce.

Table 7-3 is a static budget variance breakdown for the toy company. It shows what happens when real-life results differ from planned results.

Table 7-3	Toy Manufacturer — Static Budget Variance		
	Actual Results	**Variance**	**Static Budget**
Units sold	100 units	(20 units)	120 units
Revenue	$5,000	($400)	$5,400
Variable costs			
Direct material	$1,000	($440)	$1,440
Direct labor	$800	($160)	$960
Indirect (over-head) costs	$500	($220)	$720
Contribution margin	$2,700	$420	$2,280
Fixed costs	$1,000	($200)	$1,200
Operating income	$1,700	$620	$1,080

Talk about management by exception! There's a giant variance in actual versus budgeted operating income. That's a nice surprise, but be careful. Surprises can go both ways.

Understanding favorable and unfavorable variances

Variances can be *favorable* or *unfavorable*. If you understand the differences, you can take action and improve your business.

Keep in mind that Table 7-3 displays *static variances*. These are variances between actual results and the static budget, and they suggest that a static budget has some limitations.

A *favorable variance* increases your operating income over the planned amount. A favorable variance occurs when actual spending is less than budgeted. That's a good thing. Also, a favorable variance occurs when you sell more units than planned (budgeted). That's a good thing, too.

The flip side is an *unfavorable variance* decreases your operating income over the planned amount. When actual spending is higher than budgeted, the variance is unfavorable. Also, when actual sales are less than budgeted, the variance is unfavorable.

You always put the actual results on the left. To compute a variance, subtract the actual results (left) from the budgeted amounts (right). For example, here's how you compute the Table 7-3 revenue variance:

Revenue variance = actual revenue – static budget revenue

Revenue variance = $5,000 – $5,400

Revenue variance = -$400

Because this is a revenue variance, a negative number is unfavorable. You sold less than budgeted. If actual revenue were higher than budgeted, you'd get a positive number (more revenue than planned). For revenue or sales variances, a positive number is a favorable variance.

Yes, but now you're asking, "What about a cost variance?" It's the same process. Take the actual costs (on the left) and subtract the budgeted cost (right):

Direct material cost variance = actual material – budgeted material

Direct material cost variance = $1,000 – $1,440

Direct material cost variance = -$440

Because this is a cost variance, a negative number is good; you spent less than planned. A negative variance is a favorable variance that increases your operating income over the plan.

You treat contribution margin and operating income in the same way as revenue: More actual activity is better (favorable). The positive variances for contribution margin and operating income in Table 7-3 are favorable.

Opting for a flexible budget

A flexible budget adjusts or changes for different levels of activity (sales, production volume, and so forth). To me, this is more realistic.

It's very unlikely that your budgeted sales volume will match the actual results exactly. Whereas you create a static budget at the beginning of a period, you put together a flexible budget at the end of the period, when actual sales volume results are known.

Put another way, the flexible budget is what your static budget would look like if you had a crystal ball and knew the actual level of sales in advance. So now, to create your flexible budget, you take all the budgeted per-unit amounts from the static budget in Table 7-3 and multiply them by actual sales volume (100 units) rather than static budget sales volume (120 units).

Handling fixed cost in a flexible budget

Fixed costs hold true within a range of production. If you go above that range, you need to revise fixed costs as you need more capacity, and that's likely to cost more. Understanding *relevant range* is critical if you want to plan investments in assets.

For example, if you use a machine that produces up to 15,000 units of product a month, the fixed costs for that machine are constant — as long as you don't need to produce more than 15,000 units. If your production goes higher, you need to buy another machine.

Working a machine to capacity is a little like redlining the engine when you're driving your car. Your car can run at 7,000 rpm for only so long. In time, it will break down because it's not designed for that sustained level of use. The same is true for machines, tools, and equipment you use in your business.

You're probably familiar with the relevant ranges for the equipment your company uses. And you very likely know that overworked machine tools wear out, and welding rigs must be "rested" to prevent failure. Computer printers specify monthly duty cycles in their sales literature.

For a flexible budget, use the static budget amount of fixed costs. If you go above your relevant range, you'll need to rethink the fixed cost amount. Consider if you need to invest in more fixed costs to maintain your higher level of production.

In Table 7-3, that is $1,200. To justify using the static budget amount, consider that actual production (100 units) was obviously within the relevant range for the static budget (120 units).

Reviewing the components of a flexible budget

The next two tables show two variances that you use for flexible budget analysis. Table 7-4 shows flexible budget revenue and costs.

Table 7-4	Toy Manufacturer — Revenue and Cost Variance		
	Actual Results	*Variance*	*Flexible Budget*
Units sold	100 units	None	100 units
Revenue	$5,000	$500	$4,500
Variable costs			
Direct material	$1,000	($200)	$1,200
Direct labor	$800	none	$800
Indirect (over-head) costs	$500	($100)	$600
Contribution margin	$2,700	$800	$1,900
Fixed costs	$1,000	($200)	$1,200
Operating income	$1,700	$1,000	$700

The actual results column is the same as Table 7-3. The flexible budget column uses all of the per-unit revenue and cost amounts from Table 7-1 and multiplies each item by 100 units, the actual sales in units.

The variance column in the middle of Table 7-4 provides the *flexible budget variances*. For example, the flexible budget variance for revenue is $500. Because that's a positive number for revenue, it's a favorable variance. Contribution margin and operating income are also favorable variances because their variance amounts are positive.

The direct material variance is ($200). Because the number is negative for a cost variance, it's favorable. The actual cost of $1,000 was less than the flexible budget cost of $1,200. The overhead cost and fixed cost variances are favorable variances. The variance for operating income is $1,000 favorable.

Now compare the differences between the flexible budget and your original static budget. This is called the *sales volume variance*. Remember that all of the per-unit revenue and cost amounts were the same between static and flexible budget. The only difference causing the variance is sales volume.

Table 7-5 shows a sales volume variance.

Table 7-5   Toy Manufacturer — Sales Volume Variance

	Flexible Budget	Variance	Static Budget
Units sold	100 units	(20 units)	120 units
Revenue	$4,500	($900)	$5,400
Variable costs			
Direct material	$1,200	($240)	$1,440
Direct labor	$800	($160)	$960
Overhead costs	$600	($120)	$720
Contribution margin	**$1,900**	**($380)**	**$2,280**
Fixed costs	$1,200	none	$1,200
Operating income	$700	($380)	$1,080

If actual sales volume is less than planned, you have an unfavorable variance. Also note that revenue, contribution margin, and operating income amounts are all less than planned. As a result, each of these items has an unfavorable variance also. The sales volume variance in total, the variance for operating income, is $380 unfavorable. You see the impact of selling less than you planned.

The formula for static budget variance is

Static budget variance = flexible budget variance + sales volume variance

Static budget variance = $1,000 + ($380)

Static budget variance = $620

Keep in mind that the numbers are taken from the operating income variance at the bottom of each table. A $620 static budget variance is a favorable variance because it relates to income.

Investigating budget variances

Just like it says on the first page of this chapter, when you understand why you have a variance, you can make changes in your business to improve your productivity and your profit.

There are some likely reasons for variances, so after finding variances, you need to put on your thinking cap and figure out the causes.

Seeing the cause of a flexible budget variance

To understand why you have a flexible budget variance, keep in mind that both actual and flexible budgets use actual units sold. This means that the variance can't be due to a difference in units sold; the variance must be due to something else. There are two likely causes:

- ✔ **Price per unit:** The $50 actual price per unit is higher than the $45 flexible budget price per unit. The static budget prices and costs are used for the flexible budget. So what happened? Maybe you decided to raise your actual price, based on customer demand or competitor pricing. You were able to sell the same number of units (100 units) at a higher sales price! As a result, the revenue variance is a $500 favorable variance.

- ✔ **Costs per unit:** Note the $10 actual direct material cost per unit is lower than the static budget material cost of $12. The actual overhead is also lower than budgeted overhead cost ($5 versus $6). The material variance ($200) and overhead variance ($100) are both negative. For cost variances, a negative number is a favorable variance.

Considering reasons for a sales volume variance

Analyzing sales volume variances is easier than analyzing flexible budget variances because the differences in the flexible budget and static budget are due only to the difference in sales. You use this analysis to see the impact of sales on other areas of your business.

In the toy manufacturing examples, the flexible budget was prepared with 100 units sold (actual sales). The static budget assumed 120 units sold.

The per-unit revenue and costs are the same for both actual and flexible budgets. Here are the primary reasons why actual sales may be lower than the static budget:

- ✔ **Product demand:** Overall product demand has declined. All sellers of the product (including you) see their sales go down.

- ✔ **Competition:** Increased competition has reduced your sales volume. Some customers now feel that your price is too high when compared with your competitors'.

- ✔ **Quality:** Clients are buying less because of a concern about product quality.

- ✔ **Unrealistic budget:** The per-unit budget numbers from the static budget don't reflect actual costs and accurate product prices.

The same previously listed factors can explain *higher* actual sales as well. For example, less competition, higher demand, or reduced competition can increase your sales.

Demand and competition are broader concerns. They relate to the outside world, such as events that are happening outside of your company. As a result, you have less control over demand and competition.

Quality and budgeting are areas that you can change more easily. You can improve the quality of your product or service. You can also do more research and improve the accuracy of your budgeting process.

Analyzing in Material Price and Efficiency Variances

This section separates material variance analysis from labor variances analysis. You find that your material variances are caused by differences in price (how much you pay) and by differences in usage (how much you use in production).

There is a similar pattern with labor variances. A labor price (rate) variance occurs when your actual price paid per labor hour is different from your plan. A labor efficiency variance occurs when you use more or fewer labor hours than planned.

If your analysis is more specific, you make better decisions. Those decisions help you reduce your costs or even eliminate them.

A *price variance* is the difference between actual and budgeted price for something you purchase. Here's the formula for price variance:

Price variance = (Actual price – budgeted price) × (actual quantity)

An *efficiency variance* is the difference between actual and budgeted quantities you purchased for a specific price. Here's the formula for efficiency variance:

Efficiency variance = (Actual quantity – budgeted quantity) × (standard price or rate)

A standard is a planned amount per unit. Note that there are two terms in the efficiency formula: standard price and rate. This is a distinction you need to remember for cost accounting. *Standard price* refers to material variances. You pay a certain price for materials. *Standard rate* refers to labor variances. When you pay an hourly rate, you're working with labor variances.

To summarize the distinction between the two variances, you either *paid* more or less than planned (price variance) or *used* more or less than planned (efficiency variance).

Applying price variances to direct materials

An obvious way to reduce your costs is to analyze the prices you pay for materials. Say you operate a bicycle factory, and you use aluminum to manufacture bike frames. During planning, you come up with a standard or budgeted price of $5 per pound for aluminum. When you review your actual costs, you find that the real price paid was $5.75 per pound. Assume you purchased 10,000 pounds of aluminum. Table 7-6 shows your material price variance for the year.

Table 7-6	Material Price Variance — Aluminum for Bikes
Actual Quantity × Actual Price	*Actual Quantity × Budgeted Price*
10,000 lbs.	10,000 lbs.
Multiply by $5.75	Multiply by $5.00
Equals $57,500 (A)	Equals $50,000 (B)
Material price variance (A) – (B) $7,500	

The material price variance is $7,500 unfavorable because your actual costs ($57,500) were more than the actual quantity at budgeted price ($50,000). The only difference in this variance is the price paid for aluminum.

Applying efficiency variances to direct materials

Another way to improve your business performance is to be more efficient — "to work smart," as the business cliché goes.

Looking at budgeted input quantity

During planning, you also determined a *budgeted input quantity allowed for actual output* of 12,000 pounds of aluminum for bike production. (Wow! That's the longest title for a concept in this whole book.) This term multiplies the number of units you plan to produce by some amount of material per unit. This is the calculation for amount of aluminum for the bikes:

Budgeted input quantity= budgeted units produced × lbs. used in a unit

Budgeted input quantity= $2,000 \times 6$

Budgeted input quantity= 12,000

To produce 2,000 bikes, you plan to use 6 pounds of aluminum per bike, or a total of 12,000 pounds. Assume that for the same 2,000 bikes produced, you used only 5 pounds of aluminum per bike (because you were so efficient, of course). This means that you only used 10,000 pounds of aluminum. Your material cost would be lower, which would increase your operating profit.

Table 7-7 shows your material efficiency variance for the year.

Table 7-7   Material Efficiency Variance — Aluminum for Bikes

Actual Quantity × *Budgeted Price*	*Budgeted Quantity* × *Budgeted Price*
10,000 lbs.	12,000 lbs.
Multiply by $5.00	Multiply by $5.00
Equals $50,000 (A)	Equals $60,000 (B)
Material efficiency variance (A) – (B) ($10,000)	

A negative variance for a cost is favorable, so the material efficiency variance is favorable.

Look back at the price and efficiency variances in the last two tables. Here's the flexible budget variance calculation for direct materials:

Flexible budget variance = price variance + efficiency variance

Flexible budget variance = $7,500 + -$10,000

Flexible budget variance = -$2,500

You have a $7,500 unfavorable price variance and a $10,000 favorable efficiency variance. Because this is a cost variance, a negative number indicates less actual spending than planned, and that's a good thing.

Laying out reasons for price and efficiency variances

The real reason you go through all of this analysis is to identify areas where you can improve. By "improve," you want to reduce costs, increase demand, or raise prices to generate a higher profit.

Here are some reasons you might find a material price or efficiency variance:

- ✔ **Material purchasing decisions:** You're able to negotiate a lower price per unit. You may find a new supplier with a larger supply of material. To reduce their inventory, that supplier may be willing to sell at a lower price. These decisions may create a favorable material variance. On the other hand, a shortage of the material in the marketplace may mean that you pay more for materials. The additional spending may create an unfavorable variance.

- ✔ **Personnel and hiring decisions:** Due to a slow economy, you're able to hire workers with the skill set you need, but for a lower hourly rate. Also, you may have a staff that's so productive they get work completed faster than you planned. Finally, you're able to plan production so that workers don't wait during setup time. Less setup time means more hours producing the product. Of course, higher wages, less productivity, and poor decisions may create an unfavorable variance.

Implementing price variances for direct labor

Use your price variance knowledge to improve operations. You manage a lamp manufacturer (you're done with leather coats, toys, and bicycles). You hire employees to run machinery and also perform more delicate tasks by hand.

During planning, you come up with a standard rate (the hourly pay rate) of $25 per hour. Your actual labor rate is $22 an hour. During the year, you use 20,000 hours of labor to produce lamps. Table 7-8 shows your labor price variance for the year.

Table 7-8	Labor Price Variance — Labor Hours for Lamps
Actual Quantity × Actual Price	**Actual Quantity × Budgeted Price**
20,000 hours	20,000 hours
Multiply by $22	Multiply by $25
Equals $440,000 (A)	Equals $500,000 (B)
Labor price variance (A) – (B) ($60,000)	

A negative variance for a cost is favorable, so the labor price variance is favorable. The actual labor price (hourly rate) was $22, versus $25 budgeted. The actual quantity of hours is the same in both calculations.

Sizing up efficiency variances for direct labor

You can easily get a sense of whether your staff is efficient. Calculate budgeted input quantity allowed for actual output. Assume that you plan to use 7 hours of labor per lamp, and you actually produce 3,000 lamps. This is the labor hours needed to produce lamps:

Budgeted input quantity = budgeted units × hours per unit

Budgeted input quantity = 3,000 × 7

Budgeted input quantity = 21,000

To produce 3,000 lamps using 7 hours of labor per lamp, you expend 21,000 hours of labor (see Table 7-9).

Table 7-9   Labor Efficiency Variance — Labor Hours for Lamps

Actual Quantity × Budgeted Price	*Budgeted Quantity × Budgeted Price*
20,000 hours	21,000 hours
Multiply by $25	Multiply by $25
Equals $500,000 (A)	Equals $525,000 (B)
Labor efficiency variance (A) – (B) ($25,000)	

You end up with a favorable flexible budget variance of $25,000 for direct labor (hours):

Flexible budget variance = price variance + efficiency variance

Flexible budget variance = -$60,000 + -$25,000

Flexible budget variance = -$85,000

The ($60,000) price variance comes from Table 7-8, and the ($25,000) efficiency variance) comes from Table 7-9. Together, they yield a ($85,000) favorable flexible budget variance. Because this is a cost variance, a negative number indicates less actual spending than planned.

Using Your Findings to Make Decisions

The reason you analyze variances is to take action and reduce your costs. This section goes over the process of decision-making as it relates to variances. You decide when a variance is large enough to be considered important. The term accountants use for important is relevant.

In addition to lowering costs, you'll use variances to improve your entire production process. For instance, identifying a variance may help you reduce the number of defective products you produce. Successful companies make improvements continuously.

Your variance decisions lower your costs, improve your production process, and increase your profits.

Following up on variances

If you think investigating a variance is tough, try ignoring one sometime. Yes, following up takes time and may involve phone calls, discussions with your staff, or additional research into supplier relationships. But if the variance is relevant, you gotta do it.

Researching the relevant

In accounting, you see the term *relevance* used frequently. Relevance refers to something that's worth noticing. You need to decide what variances are important to you.

Here's some simple advice: If a variance amounts to a big percentage difference between actual results and plan, or if it amounts to a big out-of-pocket cash difference, you should investigate.

No waffling on the impact of defective products

If you produce defective products, you're spending production costs on goods that cannot be sold to customers. As you find later in the book, you may be able to repair the product and sell it, but that will require more costs, too. So defective products result in unfavorable cost variances. You spend more than you planned.

You also may see a decline in sales, as unhappy customers stop buying your product. The sales decline means an unfavorable sales variance. You sell less than you planned.

A defective product will kill you ten ways to Sunday. Any defect in any product qualifies. The impact won't be good. The first thing you don't need is diminished sales, and the last thing you need is dozens of bad comments on a consumer website.

This isn't just a matter of a cost accounting variance. A defective product is the core of ruined image, publicly aired complaints, and a general undermining of confidence in your entire product line.

Simple advice is for you to look at the defect, find the cause, correct the cause, and make things right with your customer base. And for that matter, take what steps are necessary to reduce the chances of producing defective products in the future. The time investment is worth the effort.

You don't have to spend a lot of time on the Internet to find stories about companies that were seriously damaged by making defective products and failed to handle the problem.

Picking a minimum dollar amount or percentage

For variances other than serious product defects, pick a dollar amount or percentage as a big red flare. That is, choose a guideline for investigating variances.

Say you're making watches. It doesn't matter whether you put out costly Rolex watches at $15,325 or inexpensive Casio watches at $6.95. Each line suggests a guideline for concern.

You might decide that a variance of 10 percent or more from your standard amount is an issue. If your standard direct materials cost (cost × quantity) is $50,000, a variance, either favorable or unfavorable, of $5,000 or more ($50,000 × 10%) should be reviewed. The same is true if your standard direct material cost is $5,000,000. It's still 10 percent or more.

My personal opinion is that big-ticket items can absorb a variance better than small-ticket items. An affluent customer base is likely to accept price increases, which overcomes variances. The economic law is that consumers buy more of a good when its price is lower and less when its price is higher; however, that law doesn't seem to apply to luxury items.

Keep in mind that the standards you create in planning (costs, quantities, and so forth) are *only* an estimate. You can expect some difference between standard and actual amounts. You don't have a crystal ball to get the standards exactly right. Finally, your company should include the guidelines for variance investigation in your written accounting procedures. That way, everyone in your organization knows the ground rules for variances.

Moving on to continuous improvement and benchmarking

Continuous improvement is the process of continually improving your efficiency and thereby reducing costs over time. By reducing costs a small amount each year, you increase your profit over time. You can find areas to reduce costs by investigating variances.

Over time, it may be more difficult to find cost reductions. As with many things in life, you try to do the easy fixes first; you make those changes that are obvious. As time goes on, the changes make your production more efficient. Finding new changes gets harder, but great companies stay at it. They make the effort to find more ways to reduce costs without sacrificing product quality.

If you want to compete, it's a good idea to compare your performance to other companies in your industry. *Benchmarking* is the process of comparing your company's performance to that of similar companies. That performance could mean many things: how quickly you deliver a service or how well you produce a product that minimizes defects. If you do competitive benchmarking, you're in good company. Some of the largest corporations in the world have such programs.

The purpose of benchmarking is to suggest areas where you can make improvements. If, for example, you can produce and deliver a product faster or reduce costs without affecting product quality, your company can be more profitable.

What you measure relates to what you do. If you're in a service industry, you might benchmark how quickly you do things: how long a customer waits in line at your store or how quickly can you make a home delivery.

If you manufacture products, you might benchmark product quality. *Quality* might mean tracking the number of product defects or the percentage of sales that are returned by customers.

Judging the effectiveness of your employees

Variance analysis is one criterion you can use to evaluate employees (but of course it shouldn't be the only one).

As mentioned earlier, all of your managers should participate in the budget process. After your planning is complete, each manager should receive a budget for his or her department. A good manager communicates the budget expectations to each employee. So everyone should be in the loop on the budget plans.

If the budget expectations are communicated effectively, you can use variance analysis to assess the performance of your employees. That's the purpose of this section.

Evaluating the purchasing manager

Good decisions by your purchasing manager can create favorable material price variances. If she purchases well, you may pay a lower material price, which can create favorable price variances.

The good purchasing manager not only makes good choices, but also tries to avoid bad choices. There are several key factors in making sound purchases:

✔ A low price is a low price if there aren't any strings attached.

✔ Quantity pricing can be a good thing in the short run. However, when you buy more, you're out of pocket more cash. And in the long run, there are other concerns. For example, the manager may have paid a lower price by buying more material than was needed. Eventually, you need to move that excess material into production. In the meantime, you have to store it somewhere.

✔ A reliable supplier is important. A good supplier should offer a quality product, in the quantities you need, delivered in a timely manner, at a reasonable price. The grass is not always greener on the other side on the fence. If you change suppliers to get a lower price, you may not get the same level of quality. You also might not get the same supplier response time when you need to resolve a problem.

✔ The quality of the material is vital. You often pay a price for buying cheap stuff, and you may ultimately spend more money than you save. Just think blemished leather, poorly produced denim, contaminated chemicals, and impure metal. Poor quality can result in waste, costly redos, or (worst case) defective products. Maybe most important, you may lose a client who is upset about the defective product or poor service.

If you're evaluating an employee, make sure it's based on the long-term result of their decisions, not a short-term gain to create a favorable variance. Short-term decisions to create favorable variances may create more cost and less profit in the long term. (Note that new CEOs at big corporations do this all the time, sometimes to the detriment of their companies.)

Here's another issue: Managers may set standards (budgeted amounts) artificially low. After all, they're being evaluated on outperforming a variance. If variance outcomes are only part of the evaluation, your staff won't be tempted to create unrealistic standards.

You may need to apply variance in evaluating your market research, design, and marketing departments. Customer tastes change, and your products may not be attractive to a retailer. The retailer may decide to buy less of a product (or not buy the product at all) because customers aren't interested. You might have a sales volume variance because actual sales to retailers are less than plan. (Technology products are great examples. That industry requires manufacturers to constantly change product design to meet customer demands.)

Tying supply chain concepts to variance analysis

A *supply chain* is the flow of goods, services, information — and, most important, costs — through a company. It's the entire process, from buying direct materials to delivering a completed good or service to the customer. Here is a simple supply chain:

Supplier to manufacturer to retailer to customer

You can envision how costs move through this chain.

Just in time manufacturing (JIT) is obsessed with shortening the supply chain. There are many benefits to JIT, and the methodology certainly reduces carrying costs for in-process inventory. Carrying costs represent the cost to store inventory. Not only do you need storage space for inventory, but you also need to insure it against damage or theft. However, it's a highly orchestrated ballet that might give you ulcers.

Attaching ABC costing concepts to variance analysis

You can allocate costs at different levels: unit level, batch level, and so forth. A batch is a group of units, just like a batch of cookies you bake in the oven. You can analyze how you produce batches (for example, batches of a simple, high-volume product compared to batches of a complex, low-volume product) and possibly reduce your costs. That's better than spreading costs uniformly, which can result in distortions.

Say you make glass bottles. You're in a great environment for cost allocation by batch. A machine shapes the glass into bottles and imprints your logo. Your static budget assumes that the cost of loading and unloading bottles is allocated based on a batch of 50 bottles. Table 7-10 shows an analysis of your loading costs.

Table 7-10   Glass Bottles — Labor Cost Allocation by Batch

	Actual	*Static*
Bottles produced (A)	10,000	12,000
Batch size (B)	50	48
Batches produced (A × B)	200	250
Labor hours per batch	3	2.5

	Actual	*Static*
Total labor hours (C)	600	625
Cost per labor hour (D)	$22	$21
Total labor costs (C × D)	$13,200	$13,125

You have just traced labor costs at a different level in cost hierarchy. Instead of tracing costs to a unit, you've traced costs to a batch.

Applying a flexible budget

It's not hard to apply flexible budget techniques to a batch. When you know how to apply the per-unit static budget amount to actual production, it's a short step to applying the per-batch static budget amount to actual production.

Table 7-11 calculates flexible budget cost.

Table 7-11	Glass Bottles — Flexible Budget Calculation
Actual units	10,000
Divide by static batch size	48
Equals number of batches	208
Multiply by static labor hours per batch	2.5
Equals flexible budget labor hours	521
Multiply by static labor rate per hour	$21
Equals flexible budget labor cost	$10,938

Putting price and efficiency variances together

The best way to reduce costs is to analyze multiple variances (in fact, analyze as much data as you can). You see labor price and efficiency variances in tables earlier in the chapter. Now apply the concepts at the batch level. Table 7-12 is a labor price variance calculation; Table 7-13 is a labor efficiency variance.

Table 7-12 **Glass Bottles — Labor Price Variance**

Actual Quantity × Actual Price	Actual Quantity × Budgeted Price
600 hours	600 hours
Multiply by $22/hour	Multiply by $21/hour
Equals $13,200 (A)	Equals $12,600 (B)
Labor price variance (A – B) $600	

Because the price variance relates to cost, the negative variance of $625 is favorable. You spent less than planned in the static budget.

Table 7-13 **Glass Bottles — Labor Efficiency Variance**

Actual Quantity × Budgeted Price	Budgeted Quantity × Budgeted Price
600 hours	625 hours
Multiply by $21/hour	Multiply by $21/hour
Equals $12,600 (A)	Equals $13,125 (B)
Labor efficiency variance (A – B) -$525 Favorable	

The negative labor cost variance is favorable. You spent less than planned. Now calculate the flexible budget variance:

Flexible budget variance = price variance + efficiency variance

Flexible budget variance = $600 + -$525

Flexible budget variance = $75

Chapter 8

Focusing on Overhead Costs

. . . .

. . . .

*I*ndirect costs, also referred to as *overhead,* can be fixed or variable. For example, the salary of a foreman who manages the factory floor is a fixed overhead cost because the total cost does not change. Trucking costs to ship products to customers is a variable overhead cost. That's because shipping costs do change, depending on your production and sales. Both types of costs, however, relate to production. That's why both costs are considered overhead that is allocated to the cost of your product.

This chapter looks at how fixed and variable overhead costs are calculated and how you can use variance analysis (see Chapter 7) to reduce your costs and increase your profit.

Using Cost Allocation to Minimize Overhead

Most company managers don't spend enough time or thought correctly analyzing overhead costs; they have to think carefully about the activities that cause them to incur these costs. Because this process is time consuming, managers tend to rush the process of allocating costs. As a result, the costs aren't assigned to products properly. If the cost allocation isn't correct, there could be a problem in interpreting the true cost and profit margin of a product.

The best way to manage an overhead cost is to analyze it frequently. That way, you can start removing (or reducing) the cost sooner. Also, think carefully about new overhead costs, such as factory utility costs or an equipment lease, before you start incurring them!

A phrase to keep in mind for overhead costs is "Do only what you need to do to produce your product or deliver your service." Accountants also use the phrase *essential costs,* or costs that add value. Recall that overhead costs are *allocated,* not *traced,* like direct costs (see Chapter 2 for more). Because you allocate costs, it's difficult to get at how much overhead you really need in your business.

When you incur an overhead cost, it can be difficult to stop paying it! For example, if a fixed overhead cost is an employee, ending that cost by terminating the employee can be complicated. There are legal issues and human resources issues. And there are your own emotions to consider. A decision to let someone go is challenging.

If your variable overhead cost to repair machines is based on a contract, removing that cost is another legal issue. You may need to consult an attorney to determine when and how to end the contract.

In Chapter 5, I define a cost allocation base. To put it simply, the *cost allocation base* defines how you determine the amount of cost you assign; it's your yardstick (or your tape measure) for costs.

The most common cost allocation base is to use labor hours or machine hours worked during the period. Assume you calculate a cost allocation rate of $5 per machine hour for repair overhead. You then multiply the allocation rate of $5 per hour by the number machine hours worked to make a product. That amount is your total repair overhead cost allocated to the product.

The following sections show you how to connect the cost allocation process to other overhead costs.

Paying for the Security Guard: Fixed Overhead Costs

Fixed overhead costs are costs that stay the same even as the level of activity changes. Your goal is to reduce fixed overhead costs and generate more profit.

Planning fixed overhead costs

T' ame for overhead is to look at the activities that cause you
t le if those activities are necessary for production. This
echniques that can prevent and remove unneces-

e that you'll pay more because
ufacturer schedules
e it's better to maintain
wn. Follow a program of
e maintenance) to keep
unning production around the
me waiting for a machine to be

osts and stick to your spending plan.
aintain a reasonable profit level. When
ending money without fully considering

pending when you plan your spending.
nd if possible, buy office supplies and simi-

using process. For example, perform a monthly
rev. s. Based on that review, make a month-end purchase o . e monthly purchase will reduce the likelihood of
frequent, unp. se buys of items you don't really need.

I'm not much of a shopper. When I need to go to the mall, I find what I want
online, call the store to see if they've got it, go buy it, and leave. My process
eliminates the temptation to impulse-buy. I don't walk by something and buy it
without any plan to do so.

Considering capacity needs

Any asset that you own (equipment, machinery, vehicles, and so forth) has a
limit on its use. For example, a car can operate well for only so long. At some
point, repairs become excessive. A machine can produce a product only for
a certain number of hours per day. That's the *capacity* or *duty cycle*. If you try
to operate beyond that level, similar to the car, the machine — or *asset* —
eventually breaks down.

Relevant range defines the maximum amount that you can produce using the asset. Jump to Chapter 2 for more info. Obviously, when you plan fixed overhead costs, you need to consider the relevant range of your assets.

Capacity planning is the process of figuring the production capacity you need to meet changing demand for your products. You must have the necessary assets in place to meet production requirements. Assume you need to produce 20,000 shirts for the month. If your machinery can produce only 15,000 shirts, you've got trouble. But you have choices, each one with consequences.

You could buy or lease another machine (which costs some money), or you could turn away some business (which means less revenue). Maybe you find another manufacturer who can help fill the orders (which means more costs to you). As is often attributed to economist Milton Friedman, "There ain't no such thing as a free lunch." The better you anticipate production requirements, the better the decisions you make.

Allocating fixed overhead costs

The more accurately you allocate fixed overhead costs, the more accurately your product's total costs are reflected. If total cost is accurate, you can add a profit and calculate an accurate sale price. To more accurately allocate fixed overhead you use cost pools and cost allocations to compute a cost allocation rate (see Chapter 5).

Computing a cost allocation rate

Say you make car tires. Your cost pool for fixed overhead includes machine depreciation, utility costs, and salary costs for your security guard. The annual budgeted costs total $120,000, and you have 20,000 total machine hours budgeted. Use these formulas and these numbers to compute your cost allocation rate:

Budgeted cost allocation rate = $120,000 cost ÷ 20,000 machine hours

Budgeted cost allocation rate = $6 per machine hour

You determine that a budgeted quantity per unit (per tire) is 30 minutes. Here is your budgeted fixed manufacturing overhead cost per unit:

Fixed overhead cost per unit = .5 hours per tire × $6 cost allocation rate per machine hour

Fixed overhead cost per unit = $3

Each tire has direct costs (steel belts, tread) and $3 in fixed overhead built into it.

Applying actual costs and the static budget

Take the total cost pool of $120,000 and simply divide it over 12 months. Your monthly static budget is $120,000 ÷ 12 months. That's $10,000 per month.

Calculating flexible budget variances

You can now calculate a *fixed overhead flexible-budget variance* (sometimes referred to as a *spending variance*). A flexible budget changes as activity levels (sales, production) change. Because fixed costs do not change within a relevant range, there is no adjustment of budgeted fixed costs from a static to a flexible budget. This holds true as long as actual costs are within the relevant range.

Bad news. The static budget simply took the annual cost pool amount of $120,000 and divided by 12 months. But say total actual costs for April are $11,000. You have a variance, and it is not favorable. Here's the formula:

Fixed overhead flexible budget variance = actual cost − static budget

Fixed overhead flexible-budget variance = $11,000 - $10,000

Fixed overhead flexible-budget variance = $1,000 unfavorable variance

A fixed overhead flexible budget variance is also called a *spending variance.*

The variance is unfavorable because your actual spending ($11,000) was more than the static budget ($10,000). If you're dealing with a spending variance, a positive number is an unfavorable variance. You spent more than planned. See Chapter 7 for more on variances.

Using production volume variances

An efficiency variance means that you used either more or less of the input (material, labor) than you planned. The variance reflects how efficiently you used your inputs to create a product or service.

For fixed overhead, there isn't an efficiency variance. The fixed cost is what it is. You incur the same amount of fixed costs regardless of how efficiently you produce your goods. If your actual production is higher or lower than planned, it doesn't change your flexible budget total for fixed overhead variance.

Whatcha gonna do? Instead of efficiency variance, fixed overhead variance uses something called a *production-volume variance*. Because fixed costs are fixed, the production volume variance measures how much output you got for the fixed costs you put in. The focus is on the output, not the amount of costs you put in (the input). This variance reveals how efficient you were at producing goods using a fixed level of budgeted costs.

This variance compares budgeted fixed overhead and allocated fixed overhead, based on actual output. (That's a mouthful.) Here's another way of saying it: You take the budgeted fixed overhead and apply it to actual output.

For fixed overhead analysis only, budgeted fixed overhead, flexible budget, and static budget all mean the same thing. This is because fixed costs don't changes as the level of volume changes. That relationship is true when you operate within the relevant range.

Assume actual tire production for April is 3,500. Table 8-1 shows budgeted fixed overhead applied to actual output.

Table 8-1 Budgeted Fixed Overhead — Applied to Actual Output

Budgeted cost allocation rate (A)	$6 per unit
Budgeted machine hours per tire (B)	0.5 (30 minutes)
Actual tires produced (C)	5,000
Budgeted overhead applied (A × B × C)	$15,000

Production volume variance = budgeted fixed overhead - budgeted fixed overhead applied

Production volume variance = $10,000 - $15,000

Production volume variance = ($5,000) favorable variance

The negative variance is favorable because this is a *cost* variance. Spending less is what you want to do.

What this variance tells you is that even though you planned to spend only $10,000 in fixed costs, you were able to produce more tires for the same budgeted amount of money. In theory, producing 5,000 tires should have cost you $15,000 in budgeted fixed costs. However, you made them within the $10,000 budget. This saved you $5,000, because you were more efficient at producing your goods than you planned.

What you saw for fixed overhead analysis were two variances: the flexible budget variance and the production volume variance.

Assessing potential causes of fixed overhead variances

Fixed overhead variances determine if you measured the amount of required fixed costs accurately. You probably didn't, or you wouldn't have a variance. During the budgeting process, you made a judgment on the amount. Either you judged wrong, or something changed.

When you find an unfavorable cost variance, it means that you've spent more than you planned or that you were less efficient than you had hoped. Your estimate of fixed overhead costs was too low. A favorable cost variance means that you spent less or were more efficient than planned; your estimate of fixed overhead costs was too high. You completed production while spending less than you expected.

Those Vexing Variable Manufacturing Costs

Now shift your thinking from fixed costs to variable costs. *Variable manufacturing costs* (or *variable overhead)* increase as your activity levels (that is, production) increase. You may find variable manufacturing costs easier to visualize than fixed costs. Examples of variable manufacturing costs are

- ✔ Utility costs may vary with individual machines, how many machines are in use, and how long they run. Some costs are strictly proportional. Costs vary according to power consumption and amount of use.

- ✔ Repair and maintenance costs may vary according to the amount of time a machine uses. More use suggests more frequent maintenance.

- ✔ Design-engineer labor, sometimes referred to as *expert costs,* can vary from product to product, depending on the level of effort required to develop the products.

When you analyze variable manufacturing costs, chances are good that you find ways to reduce costs and increase your profit.

Working with variable overhead costs

You plan variable overhead costs using a process similar to planning fixed overhead. Your goal is to plan overhead costs, compare your plan (budgeted) amounts to actual spending (real life), and review any variances. When you understand the variances, you may be able to make changes to reduce costs.

Considering variable overhead in planning

Think (try always to think, think, think) about variable overhead costs in the planning stage before you start writing checks. The idea is to avoid a knee-jerk decision that may result in false allocation of costs, causing you to spend more than necessary. You saw this in the fixed overhead section of the chapter: Any time you fail to plan or schedule, you may end up reacting to a situation when you should have implemented a plan. You run the risk of over-spending; then you have to work twice as hard just to put out the fire. Trust me: Poor allocation of overhead costs gives you gray hairs, and constant hassles shorten your life span.

There's good news with variable overhead: It's easier to spot and fix variable overhead overspending than fixed overhead overspending. By definition, variable overhead changes (being variable) with the level of activity, so if you think you're overspending on variable overhead, you may be able to slow — or stop — the production process and investigate.

You're less concerned with your required capacity when you plan variable overhead. You can start and stop production, which means that you can start and stop variable overhead spending. If for some reason you need to increase production by 10,000 units, you can add variable overhead as needed.

Figuring budgeted costs and activity levels

Say you manage a business that produces tires for cars. You need to compute a cost allocation rate for your tire production. This rate explains how much variable overhead you've budgeted, based on some measurement of activity (see the "Computing a cost allocation rate" section, earlier in this chapter). In planning, you determine that the cost pool for variable manufacturing overhead is repair and maintenance costs for the machinery. The annual budgeted cost is $36,000. Your cost allocation base is machine hours, the same basis as for fixed overhead. The total budgeted machine hours are 20,000.

Compute a cost allocation rate:

Budgeted cost allocation rate = cost ÷ machine hours

Budgeted cost allocation rate = $36,000 ÷ 20,000

Budgeted cost allocation rate = $1.80 per machine hour

The $1.80 per machine hour is also the *flexible budget variable manufacturing overhead per machine hour*. This says that you are planning to spend $1.80 on repair and maintenance for every hour the machine runs. A flexible budget applies actual production to budgeted costs and activity levels.

Keep in mind that the allocation base for fixed and variable overhead isn't always the same. In this case, using machine hours for both types of overhead makes sense. That activity is driving both fixed overhead (utility cost, for example) and the variable overhead (repair and maintenance costs). The more the machines run, the more utility and maintenance costs you are likely to have.

Say the actual tire output for the period was 5,000 units (tires). You can now compute *flexible budget machine hours per output*. This is a new term that was not used for fixed overhead.

Flexible budget machine hours per output = machine hours ÷ units (output)

Flexible budget machine hours per output = 20,000 hours ÷ 5,000 units

Flexible budget machine hours per output = 4 hours

Each tire (unit) produced requires 4 hours of machine time. You use budgeted machine hours (from the cost allocation rate) and actual units produced.

Now pause for just a minute and consider the two previous formulas:

- ✔ Budgeted cost allocation rate: Total cost divided by total machine hours
- ✔ Flexible budget machine hours per output: Total machine hours divided by units produced

A cost allocation rate is always a total cost divided by some level of activity. In this case, it's machine hours. Machine hours per output is calculated as a level of activity (machine hours) divided by units produced. Read the bullet points and this paragraph a second time, if you need to. It's a difficult concept but an important one.

Adding in actual costs and activity levels

You need data from actual costs and activity levels to perform your variance analysis. Your actual variable overhead costs totaled $38,000. You used 18,000 hours of actual machine time.

Actual machine hours per output explains how many machine hours you used per actual unit produced:

Actual machine hours per output = actual machine hours ÷ actual units (output)

Actual machine hours per output = 18,000 ÷ 5,000

Actual machine hours per output = 3.6 hours

In the "Figuring budgeted costs and activity levels" section, you note a flexible budget of 4 hours per unit. The actual hours, 3.6, are less than you planned. Using fewer hours will generate a favorable variance. You used less than you budgeted.

You can calculate the cost for each machine hour by applying *actual variable manufacturing overhead per machine hour:*

> Actual variable manufacturing overhead per machine hour = budgeted cost ÷ budgeted machine hours

> Actual variable manufacturing overhead per machine hour = $38,000 ÷ 18,000

> Actual variable manufacturing overhead per machine hour = $2.11 per machine hour

Implementing variance analysis

This section dives into variance analysis as it relates to variable overhead. I cover spending and efficiency variances, the two components of a variable overhead variance. A spending variance occurs when the rate or price you pay different from your budget. An efficiency variance is incurred when you use more or less than you plan.

You implement variance analysis to understand differences between planned and actual costs. You hope to learn from the analysis and reduce your costs moving forward.

Comparing the use of the term flexible budget variance

Flexible budget variance is used in the fixed overhead costs section earlier this chapter. However, flexible budget variance has a different meaning for variable overhead.

Refer to the section "Calculating flexible budget variances," earlier in the chapter. That's where you see that for *fixed overhead,* the spending variance is also the flexible budget variance. For *variable overhead,* the flexible budget variance is the sum of two variances.

Here's a variance formula for variable overhead:

> Flexible budget variance (also variable overhead variance) = spending variance + efficiency variance

To keep this straight in your head, flexible budget variance refers to *one* variance for fixed overhead. Flexible budget variance is the *sum of two* variances for variable overhead.

Computing spending variance and efficiency variance

Spending and efficiency variances relate to other concepts you see in this book. In Chapter 7, you see the formula for price variance:

Price variance = (actual price - budgeted price) × (actual units sold)

The price variance formula is similar to the *variable overhead spending variance*. You already calculated both an actual and a budgeted cost in earlier sections of this chapter. You also see (in an example) the actual production in units (tires). Instead of actual units sold, this variance uses actual units *produced*. That's because you're applying overhead to production. You use actual and budgeted costs instead of prices. All that being said, here's the formula:

Variable overhead spending variance = ($2.11 - $1.80) × (18,000)

Variable overhead spending variance = $5,580

It's an unfavorable variance, because you spent more than you planned. Once again, if you get a positive number for a cost variance, it's unfavorable.

Now consider the variable overhead *efficiency* variance. If you have an efficiency variance, you used more or less than you planned. You need two calculations for this variance; then you compute the difference between the two amounts.

Here's the first calculation:

Actual quantity × budgeted price = 18,000 units × $1.80

Actual quantity × budgeted price = $32,400

The second calculation is *budgeted variable overhead applied to actual output*. Way back in Table 8-1, there's similar calculation for fixed overhead, Table 8-2 displays a related calculation.

Table 8-2	Budgeted Variable Overhead — Applied to Actual Output
Flexible-budget machine hours per output (A)	4
Actual output (units) (B)	5,000
Flexible-budget overhead per machine hour (C)	$1.80
Budgeted variable overhead applied (A × B × C)	$36,000

Variable overhead efficiency variance = $32,400 - $36,000

Variable overhead efficiency variance = ($3,600).

Because this is a negative cost variance, it's favorable. Now, you had a hint that this variance might be favorable earlier in the chapter. Roll back to the "Adding in actual costs and activity levels" section. You see that the actual machine hours per unit is a rate of 3.6. That rate is less than the budgeted amount of 4 hours So, it makes sense that the efficiency variance would be favorable. You used less than you budgeted.

The variable overhead variance is the sum of the spending variance and the efficiency variance. Here's your variance calculation:

Variable overhead variance = $5,580 + ($3,600)

Variable overhead variance = $1,980

Because the positive cost variance is unfavorable, that means your costs for variable overhead were more than planned.

One point bears repeating: You have a variance because you spent more or less than planned (the price or rate you paid had a variance), or you used more or less than planned. You can apply that thought to just about any variance in cost accounting.

Finding the reasons for a variable overhead variance

You want to know why variances occur so you can make changes to your business. Those changes (have you heard me say this before?) can lower your costs and improve your profit.

The spending variance was the difference in per unit cost (actual versus budgeted), multiplied by actual units produced. So you should consider why actual variable overhead costs would differ from your flexible budgeted cost.

There's one factor to put out there right up front: The variance can't be due to a difference in units produced. Both the budgeted and actual calculations used 5,000 (actual) units produced. Think about the check you wrote for variable overhead. In this case, your budgeted variable overhead was $36,000, but your actual cost was $2,000 higher ($38,000):

Variable overhead spending variance = ($2.11 - $1.80) × (18,000)

Variable overhead spending variance = $5,580

You should also consider machine hours. Actual machine hours used were less than budgeted (18,000 versus 20,000). That means the higher actual cost was spread over fewer units ($38,000 ÷ 18,000 units). As a result, the actual overhead per machine hour was higher than budgeted ($2.11 versus $1.80). You have an unfavorable spending variance, because the $2.11 actual rate per machine hour is higher than the $1.80 budgeted.

You can consider several reasons for the difference. You had to pay a higher total amount than planned ($38,000). Maybe the hourly rate for machinery repair was higher than budgeted.

Finally, the favorable efficiency variance is due to using 2,000 fewer machine hours than you planned (18,000 versus 20,000). Think about it. You used fewer hours than budgeted, so you spent less than budgeted. Variable costs change as total machine hours change.

Chapter 9

What's on the Shelf? Inventory Costing

. . . .

In This Chapter

▶ Determining what costs are included in inventory

▶ Understanding the methods for recognizing cost of sales

▶ Comparing variable and absorption costing

▶ Deciding on a method to determine production capacity

▶ Reviewing common problems in inventory accounting

. . . .

*I*f you're starting a retail business, one of your largest investments is inventory. Say you start a gift shop. To attract customers and meet their needs, you need to stock the products they want; you need to spend money to fill your shelves. Decisions you make on accounting for inventory have a huge impact on pricing your products and ultimately on your profit.

This chapter presents the types of costs that are inventory-related. The idea is to assign a dollar amount as the total cost for each product. That sounds obvious (of course every item has a cost), but there are different methods for assigning costs. Your inventory value decision affects your cost of sales, and that (of course) affects other things, like your operating profit.

This chapter also looks at capacity. For this book, *capacity* is the maximum amount of production and sales that you can generate, using all of the assets you currently have. Those assets include equipment, factory space, your staff, and your salespeople. Consider how much business (in terms of sales and production) you can realistically handle. As a businessperson, you should consider activity levels that are reachable, not just "pie in the sky."

Working with Inventoriable Costs

Inventoriable costs are all of the costs of your inventory item and are not immediately expensed. They first become assets — inventory. In a nutshell, inventoriable costs should include all costs to prepare the goods for sale. You need to know which costs are attached to inventory so you can price your product based on the total product costs. If you know your total cost, you can better compute a sale price that includes a reasonable profit. Later in this chapter, you see that inventoriable costs can remain with the inventory item for months.

Using the matching principle to calculate profit on sale

Profit is defined as revenue less expenses. To measure profit accurately, you need to match revenue with related expense. When you sell an item (create revenue) you need to account for or match the expenses you incurred for that sale. Applying this *matching principle* allows you to calculate an accurate profit on your sale.

Some textbooks talk about the matching principle, and by that they mean that there's a cause-and-effect relationship. If you write a check for inventory, you should include that amount as an inventory cost (of course), but there are other costs, too that you should include in inventory. Hard to say, but easy to demonstrate.

Checking out inventoriable costs

Say you own a gift shop and sell greeting cards. You write checks for greeting cards, which you enter into inventory. You also pay shipping costs and an insurance premium to insure against damage during shipment. All of these costs are part of your inventory (greeting cards) and should be included in the inventory cost.

Inventory is an asset account. Asset accounts are defined as having a future benefit. With inventory, the future benefit is that you can sell the inventory item and generate revenue.

As already mentioned (but worth stating again), inventoriable costs should include all costs to prepare the goods for sale. You couldn't put goods on your shelf without paying shipping and insurance costs. Those costs, in addition to the product cost, moved the inventory from your supplier to your gift shop's shelves.

Each greeting card in the gift shop should include a portion of all three costs — merchandise, shipping, and insurance. That way, the revenue from the greeting cards sales is matched with the related expenses. The inventory cost process is discussed later in this chapter.

FOB stands for *free on board.* It goes back to the days when goods shipped "on board" a vessel. FOB specifies which party (buyer or seller) *pays* for shipping and loading costs. It also describes who has title (ownership) to the goods during shipping — and, therefore, who bears the *risk of loss* due to damage or destruction. If the truck blows up on the freeway, either you or the seller bear the risk. If you are the buyer, specify "FOB destination" in your purchase orders. Say a seller's in Chicago, and your store is in St. Louis. Most likely, you'll pay shipping, and the order will say "FOB destination" or "FOB St. Louis." This means that you are not liable for damage to the goods until you receive them — which is what you prefer.

Working with non-inventoriable costs

By contrast, utility cost (such as the cost of heating and cooling, your water bill, sewer bill, and so on) isn't an inventoriable cost because it isn't a direct cost that you can trace to a product. While utility cost is certainly a business expense, it doesn't directly relate to inventory.

It's also difficult to allocate utility costs as an indirect cost. The activity (such as heating and cooling) doesn't relate to inventory sales. (See Chapter 2 for direct and indirect cost info.) If you can't trace or allocate the cost, you expense it as you incur it. A utility cost paid in May is expensed in May. Recording the expense immediately reflects the *principle of conservatism.* More on this principle in the next section.

When it comes to the matching principle, your utility bill is handled differently. You just saw that utility costs are expensed as they are incurred. To calculate profit, your May sales are matched with the utility costs for May. Here's a summary:

- ✔ Inventoriable costs are traced to the inventory item. The costs are expensed when the item is sold. So the revenue from the sale is matched with the cost of the sale.

- ✔ Non-inventoriable costs (like utility costs) are expensed each month as they are incurred. The costs are not traced to the inventory item. The expense is matched with the revenue for the month.

Erring on the conservative side

Because inventory is often your biggest asset account, the decisions you make about inventory are critical. When you make decisions, you should keep in mind the principle of conservatism. Applying this principle helps you generate financial statements that are not overly optimistic. The principle of conservatism helps the statement reader understand the true condition of your business.

Accountants stick to several principles. One of them is the principle of conservatism. Many actions an accountant takes involve judgment. Conservatism directs you to err on the conservative side of a decision. Consider which decision would make your financial statements look less attractive:

- ✔ If you're making decision about expenses, recognize the expense sooner than later. As a result, your profit will be lower. If you have to make a judgment, err on the side that shows less profit.

- ✔ If you have to make a judgment call about revenue, delay posting the revenue until you know you've earned it. Less revenue means less profit.

That's the big picture of conservatism at this point.

Costing Methods for Inventory

You buy inventory over time, not all at once (except, of course, when you first stock a store). How much you buy depends on customer demand and the amount of inventory you already own. Over time, the price you pay for inventory changes, both up and down. You need to select a method that best recognizes the cost of your inventory.

There are four methods: *first-in, first-out; last-in, first-out; weighted average;* and *specific identification.* After you understand and apply a method, you can attach an accurate cost to each inventory item. After you select a method, you need to stick with it, which is called the *principle of consistency.*

When you apply a consistent inventory cost method, your financials will be consistent. Someone reading your financial statements will see an apples-to-apples comparison of inventory costs. If you change from one method to another, you risk distorting your financial statements. At the least, you have to explain the change of method in the financials; it's only fair to those reading the information, such as investors.

For this analysis, you should assume that prices increase over time. That's normally what happens in real life. *Inflation* is defined as the overall increase in retail prices over time. *Overall* means the prices of a representative list of goods that people buy all the time, such as food, energy, medical services, and so forth. Those basic items are used to measure inflation. You can see a typical Consumer Price Index at the U.S. Bureau of Labor Statistics website, http://www.bls.gov/news.release/cpi.nr0.htm.

The effect of prices increasing over time is that your older inventory costs less than your more recent purchases. You use this assumption for all three inventory methods.

Say you own a hardware store. Table 9-1 displays purchase and sale dates, number of units, and prices for a rubber mallet.

Table 9-1	Rubber Mallet — Inventory Purchases and Sales		
Date	**Units Purchased**	**Price Per Unit**	**Total**
10/1	100	$10	$1,000
10/15	150	$12	$1,800
10/17	75	$15	$1,125
Total Units	**325**	**Total Cost**	**$3,925**
Date	**Units Sold**		
10/25	50		
10/31	50		

You need the info in Table 9-1 for all three inventory methods.

Here are a few keys things to remember for inventory costing:

- ✔ The number of units purchased and sold is the same for all methods.
- ✔ The units don't change. Only the cost placed on the units changes.
- ✔ The goods put on the shelf and then sold are the same in all cases.

There's a total cost at the lower-right corner of Table 9-1 ($3,925). That total cost ends up in one of two places. You either sell the inventory (cost of sales), or it stays on the shelf (ending inventory).

The cost of sales and ending inventory adds up to $3,925. This is true, regardless of which inventory method you choose. If you remember to account for all the units — and all the dollars — you correctly account for inventory.

Using the first-in, first-out (FIFO) method

The *first-in, first-out (FIFO)* method assumes that you sell the oldest items first. You can safely assume that inventory prices increase over time. In Table 9-1, the unit prices increase during the month (from $10 to $12 and then to $15). That means your older inventory items are less expensive.

At the grocery store, the stockers usually put the oldest milk (the milk that's closest to expiration) at the front of the cold case. The new milk is in the back. The store wants you to buy the oldest milk before it expires. You don't have to go that far with your inventory, but that's how you should think about FIFO. It's *as if* the oldest items are sold first. If prices increase over time, the oldest items will also be the least expensive.

Your goal is to account for your inventory cost accurately, so you know your total costs. Table 9-2 shows your cost of sales for the FIFO method.

Table 9-2	FIFO Method — Cost of Sales		
Date	*Units Sold*	*Price Per Unit*	*Total*
10/25	50	$10	$500
10/31	50	$10	$500
Total Units	**100**	**Total Cost**	**$1,000**

Here's how your units moved using the FIFO method:

Units in ending inventory = total units – units sold

Units in ending inventory = 325 – 100

Units in ending inventory = 225

This calculation shows the movement of dollars:

Ending inventory = dollars to account for – dollars for units sold

Ending inventory = $3,925 – $1,000

Ending inventory = $2,925

With these calculations, you account for all the units and cost in Table 9-1.

Notice that the top of Table 9-1 starts with the oldest purchases (10/1). As you move down, you move later into the month. This layout helps you choose the correct units for figuring the cost of sales.

For FIFO, you sell the oldest units first. Start at the top of Table 9-2 and work your way down. On 10/25, you sold 50 units. You start with the oldest purchases. The units you sold on 10/25 were from the 10/1 purchases. You take 50 of those 100 units purchased on 10/1 and move them into cost of sales. On 10/31, you sold another 50 units. For FIFO, start looking at the top of the table. You use 50 of the remaining units purchased on 10/1 and move them to cost of sales.

Table 9-2 displays the two sales at the 10/1 $10 purchase price. If you had sold any more units, you'd take units from the 10/15 purchase at $12 per unit. That's because all 100 units of the 10/1 purchase have already been sold.

Accounting with the last-in, first-out (LIFO) method

The *last-in, first-out* method assumes that you sell the most recent inventory items first. Take another look at Table 9-1. Because prices increased during the month, the last items purchased are more expensive than the first items purchased.

For LIFO, you start at the bottom of Table 9-1 and work your way up. You sell the most recent purchases first. With LIFO, you sell the 75 units you bought on 10/17 at $15 first. When you sell all 75 of the 10/17 units, you're "movin' on up." The next units are the units you bought on 10/15 at $12.

Table 9-3 shows cost of sales using the LIFO method. The sales dates and number of units sold are the same as FIFO (Table 9-2).

Table 9-3	LIFO Method — Cost of Sales		
Date	*Units Sold*	*Price Per Unit*	*Total*
10/25	75	$15	$1,125
10/31	25	$12	$300
Total Units	**100**	**Total Cost**	**$1,425**

Start at the bottom of Table 9-1. On 10/25, you sell 50 units. These are units you bought for $15 on 10/17. On 10/31, you sell another 50 units. For the remaining 50 units sold, you first sell the remaining 25 units at $15 (the 10/17 purchases). Then you move up one spot in Table 9-1. You sell 25 of the units you bought for $12 on 10/15. To fill the entire sale order of 100 units, you pulled units from two different purchase dates.

You're not selling the *actual* physical units from a particular purchase date. They all look the same in the stockroom or on the shelf. You're just using a costing method, *assuming* that the units sell *as though* they were from a particular purchase date.

The number of units sold (100) was the same whether you're using FIFO or LIFO. The inventory method you choose has no impact on the movement of units; however, your cost of sales is different. FIFO cost of sales was $1,000 (Table 9-2). LIFO cost of sales totaled $1,425 (Table 9-3). That's a big difference, but it's to be expected. Because LIFO sells the more recent (and more expensive) units first, you'd expect the LIFO cost of sales to be higher.

Here is the movement of dollars for LIFO. Note that you need to account for the same total dollar amount of inventory that you did with FIFO. That is, the sold and unsold items still total $3,925:

Ending inventory = dollars to account for – dollars for units sold

Ending inventory = $3,925 – $1,425

Ending inventory = $2,500

Because LIFO's cost of sales is higher, the ending inventory is lower ($2,500 versus $2,925). What's left on the shelf is less valuable.

Weighing the merits of weighted-average cost

The *weighted-average* method for inventory takes total inventory costs and divides it by total units. That cost per unit is assigned to every unit sold. This method simplifies your bookkeeping for inventory. Here's an example, using the same total cost and total units in Table 9-1:

Weighted-average cost per unit = inventory cost ÷ units

Weighted-average cost per unit = $3,925 ÷ 325

Weighted-average cost per unit = $12.08

FIFO and LIFO are difficult, because you're required to keep track of each purchase — the number of units and the cost. You also have to monitor each sale and the purchase price of the items you used to fill that sale. With either FIFO or LIFO, sometimes you have to fill orders by selling units from two (or more) purchases at two (or more) different prices. That's a lot to track!

Think of the benefit-cost ratio (BCR). There are cost versus benefit discussions throughout the book, and here's another one. You need to decide if the extra work of using the FIFO or LIFO method (cost) is worth it (benefit). The FIFO or LIFO method lets you see the impact of selling cheaper or more expensive goods first. The "impact" is the effect on profit.

If you decide that the extra information isn't worth it, you can simply use weighted-average cost per unit.

Considering specific identification method

The *specific identification* method puts a very fine point on your inventory cost. With specific identification, you select an inventory item sold. You use the exact cost of the item for cost of sales. You track inventory and cost of sales *by item*.

For example, if you're in the luxury or custom item business (expensive clothing, jewelry, cars, and so forth), you may want to track each individual item in inventory. If an item in inventory is expensive, you want to know where that item is at all times. By contrast, FIFO and LIFO account for purchases and sales by groups of items — lots.

Analyzing profit using FIFO and LIFO

The FIFO and LIFO methods use different ways to determine the cost of inventory sold. Cost of sales is different for each method (see Tables 9-2 and 9-3) and generate different levels of profit.

Table 9-4 uses the cost of sales from Tables 9-2 and 9-3. In each case, you sold 100 units. Assume you sold each unit for $20. Here's the profit calculation for FIFO and LIFO.

Table 9-4	Profit on 100 Units Sold — FIFO and LIFO	
	FIFO	*LIFO*
Sales revenue ($20/unit)	$2,000	$2,000
Cost of sales	$1,000	$1,425
Profit	$1,000	$575

FIFO generates a higher profit because it sells the older, less expensive units first. Your cost of sales for FIFO is lower. So after 100 units sold, you show a bigger profit using the FIFO method.

You've heard several times by now that the total units and total cost are the same with any inventory method. To explain it, Table 9-5 assumes that you sell the entire ending inventory (check out Table 9-1). Here's your ending inventory in units:

Ending inventory in units = units purchased – units sold

Ending inventory in units = 325 – 100

Ending inventory in units = 225

Assume that the remaining 225 units then sell at the same $20 each. Your revenue is 225 units × $20 per unit, yielding $4,500. Table 9-5 shows the profit earned by selling the ending inventory. In other words, the ending inventory moved to cost of sales.

Table 9-5	Profit on 225 Units Sold — FIFO and LIFO	
	FIFO	*LIFO*
Sales revenue ($20/unit)	$4,500	$4,500
Cost of sales	$2,925	$2,500
Profit	$1,575	$2,000

The LIFO method sells the newer, more expensive goods first. The LIFO ending inventory is made up of less expensive goods. So it's not surprising that the cost of sales (ending inventory) for LIFO is less than FIFO ($2,500 versus $2,925).

It all comes out the same in the end (see Table 9-6).

Table 9-6	Total Profit- FIFO and LIFO	
	FIFO	*LIFO*
First 100 units	$1,000	$575
Next 225 units	$1,575	$2,000
Total profit	$2,575	$2,575

Because you purchased 325 units overall and sold them all for the same price ($20 per unit), the total profit is the same. Sure, FIFO generated more profit when you sold the first 100 units (see Table 9-4). But that evened out when you sold the rest of the inventory. Over time, you end up with the same total profit.

FIFO and LIFO inventory methods create the same level of profit and cost of sales. The only difference is the timing of recognizing profit and cost levels. Table 9-6 proves that point. For any group of items purchased, there is no difference in profit and costs once all of the units are sold. That assumes that the same selling price is used for each costing method.

In fact, the same is true of weighted-average costs. That calculation generates the same total profit as FIFO and LIFO.

What's important is to select an inventory method and stick with it. This is the principle of consistency. (See the "Costing Methods for Inventory" section, earlier in this chapter.) If you stick with the same method, the financial statement reader can see how profits and cost of sales are generated.

So why the different methods? Different industries use different inventory methods. It's critical that you understand the financial impact of using one method or another. FIFO method means you will recognize profit sooner; LIFO recognizes more profit in later periods.

To judge the true profitability of a business, you need to understand when each inventory method recognizes profit.

Using Variable and Absorption Costing to Allocate Fixed Manufacturing Costs

You see a theme throughout this book: Determine how much you spend on an activity (a job, an hour of machine time, and so forth); then *trace* or *allocate* the cost to a product so you can calculate a sale price and a profit on its sale. Next, consider why you spent those dollars.

Variable costing and absorption costing both relate to how fixed manufacturing costs are dealt with on the income statement. Each method treats the fixed costs differently. *Variable costing* expenses the fixed manufacturing costs as incurred. *Absorption costing* attaches the fixed manufacturing costs to inventory. The cost isn't expensed until the inventory item is sold. At that point, the inventory becomes cost of sales.

The two methods reflect two different views of fixed manufacturing costs. The absorption costing view is that the costs are inventoriable. On the other hand, the variable costing view is that fixed manufacturing costs are incurred every month. The costs should not be attached to inventory.

The method you select to address fixed manufacturing costs has an impact on your inventory's value. If you choose absorption costing, your fixed manufacturing costs are attached to inventory. As a result, your inventory value is higher — and your immediate expenses is lower.

You'll delay recognizing the fixed manufacturing costs as an expense until the inventory is sold. The method you choose can have a large impact on your inventory value and your recognition of profit.

Defining period costs and product costs

According to Generally Accepted Accounting Principles (GAAP), a *period cost* is to be expensed immediately as it's incurred. A *product cost* "stays with" the product and first becomes inventory until the product is sold. Imagine that the cost is attached to your product or service. It's expensed when you sell the product to your customer. At that point, all of the product costs are expensed. GAAP requires this treatment of period and product costs on all external financial statements of public companies.

Variable costing, which is used only for internal financial statements (used to make decisions), considers fixed manufacturing costs as period costs. Under variable costing, these costs are expensed as incurred. Absorption costing (required by GAAP) treats fixed manufacturing cost as a product cost. Those costs are part of inventory and later become cost of goods sold. On the income statement, cost of sales and net income results are different, depending on which costing method you use.

If you have ending inventory, you have a difference in total costs and profit (net income). Recall that absorption costing "attaches" fixed manufacturing costs to inventory, so some of the cost is sitting on the shelf until you sell the item. Variable costing expenses that cost immediately. If you sell your entire inventory, no problem. All the expense has gone out the door under either method. It's all cost of sales, and both methods result in the same amount of income.

The problem comes in when you have ending inventory sitting on the shelf. If you use absorption costing, that inventory has fixed manufacturing costs attached. So that cost isn't expensed until you take the product off the shelf and sell it.

In the short term, you have less immediate expense with absorption costing. Less expense results in a higher profit. When your entire inventory is sold, your total costs and profit are the same, regardless of which method you choose.

Applying variable and absorption costing

Because variable and absorption costing generate different levels of cost and net income, you need to understand the differences so you can select a costing method to use internally for decision-making.

Say your business manufactures handsaws. Table 9-7 shows a summary of production, sales, and costs in Year 1

Table 9-7	Year 1 Production — Sales and Costs
Production (units)	3,000
Sales (units)	2,500
Sales (at $25 per unit)	$62,500
Fixed manufacturing costs	$21,000
All other product costs	$33,000

Because you didn't sell all of your production, you created ending inventory:

Ending inventory = units produced – units sold

Ending inventory = 3,000 – 2,500

Ending inventory = 500

Your fixed manufacturing costs are $7 per unit produced ($21,000 ÷ 3,000 units). Absorption costing requires you to assign $3,500 of fixed manufacturing costs to ending inventory ($7 × 500 units). Table 9-8 outlines the profit in Year 1, comparing variable and absorption costing.

Table 9-8 Year 1 Profit — Variable Versus Absorption Costing		
	Variable Costing	*Absorption Costing*
Sales (at $25 per unit)	$62,500	$62,500
Fixed manufacturing costs	$21,000	$17,500
All other costs	$27,500	$27,500
Total costs	$48,500	$45,000
Profit	**$14,000**	**$17,500**

Absorption costing deferred $3,500 of fixed manufacturing costs. The fixed manufacturing costs are only $17,500. You see that absorption costing has a $3,500 higher profit ($17,500 versus $14,000).

In Year 2, assume that your sales and sales price are the same. You also sell all your production, plus the 500 units that were in ending inventory. Your sales (2,500 units) are 500 units more than your production (2,000 units). Because you produced less in Year 2, the all-other-cost number declines to $22,500. Less production means less cost. Check out Table 9-9.

Table 9-9	Year 2 Production — Sales and Costs
Production (units)	2,000
Sales (units)	2,500
Sales (at $25 per unit)	$62,500
Fixed manufacturing costs	$21,000
All other costs	$22,500

Variable and absorption costing are the same if you sell all of your production. You don't produce any ending inventory, so you don't defer any fixed manufacturing costs into inventory items. Table 9-10 displays the profit in Year 2.

Table 9-10 Year 2 Profit — Variable Versus Absorption Costing	Variable Costing	Absorption Costing
Sales (at $25 per unit)	$62,500	$62,500
Fixed manufacturing costs	$21,000	$24,500
All other costs	$27,500	$27,500
Total costs	$48,500	$52,000
Profit	**$14,000**	**$10,500**

Five hundred units from Year 1 ending inventory are sold in Year 2. In Table 9-9, production of 2,000 is 500 units less than sales of 2,500. You had 500 units available for sale at the beginning of Year 2.

Fixed manufacturing costs for Year 2 are the same for both methods ($21,000). However, absorption costing added the $3,500 fixed manufacturing cost that was deferred in Year 1. The fixed manufacturing cost is $24,500 ($21,000 + $3,500).

The variable costing profit in Year 2 is $3,500 higher than the absorption costing profit ($14,000 versus $10,500). In Year 1, variable costing profit was $3,500 lower than the absorption costing. When Year 1 ending inventory is sold in Year 2, absorption picks up the fixed manufacturing cost that was deferred.

Over two years, all the production is sold. The total profit over two years is the same for both costing methods.

So I'm sure you're wondering about which method to use. Your profit *eventually* is the same under either method. In the long run, there is no advantage to using one method over another.

You should select a method and stick with it. By doing so, you're applying the principle of consistency. For a financial statement reader to compare your results year by year, you need to use the same method. It's the old idea of an apples-to-apples comparison. This principle comes up throughout the book.

Relating Capacity Issues to Inventory

Capacity refers to how much you can do, based on the assets (equipment, machinery, vehicles, and so forth) you have. In business, determining your true capacity level is a balancing act. You want to avoid investing too much and then find that the capacity isn't needed. The money you invest in unused production capacity could be better spent elsewhere.

On the other hand, you want to invest enough to fill every possible customer order. Your realistic capacity is somewhere in the middle. You want the ability to fill orders without biting off more than you can chew.

This section discusses four types of capacity. The first two types focus on production: *theoretical capacity* and *practical capacity*. Consider how much you could produce if customer demand was unlimited. The second two types focus on customer demand. *Normal capacity utilization* and *master budget capacity utilization* are driven by customer orders. Select a capacity method that makes sense to you, and use that as a tool to plan production and spending.

Reviewing theoretical and practical capacity

Theoretical capacity assumes that nothing in your production ever goes wrong. Accountants describe this capacity as working at full efficiency all the time.

Consider what your pie-in-the-sky or perfect-world capacity would be. It's a world in which everything runs perfectly and no machines or equipment ever break down. It's utopia where no worker ever makes a mistake. That would be great, wouldn't it? That's theoretical capacity, and you can't reach it. It seems silly, but you need to see this level of capacity to understand the others.

Say you own a business that makes athletic running shorts and other clothing. At maximum capacity, you can make 200 pairs of shorts per shift. You run three 8-hour shifts per day, 365 days a year. Based on those numbers, here is your theoretical capacity:

Theoretical capacity = shorts × shifts × 365 days

Theoretical capacity = 200 × 3 × 365 days

Theoretical capacity = 219,000

Unfortunately, this level of capacity isn't attainable. You need to take into account the unavoidable. That gets you to practical capacity.

Practical capacity is the level of capacity that includes unavoidable operating interruptions. Another description is unavoidable losses of operating time. Consider maintenance on equipment, employee vacations, and holidays. You're willing to accept a good, rather than perfect, capacity level.

The people in your company can help you determine your practical capacity. Your production and engineering staff can answer questions about machine capacity and repair time. Your human resources staff can forecast employee availability, based on vacations and holidays.

You determine that 250 days is a more realistic number of production days, given unavoidable operating interruptions. Also, you decide that two shifts per day are realistic. Here's the practical capacity calculation:

Practical capacity = shorts × shifts × days

Practical capacity = 200 × 2 × 250

Practical capacity = 100,000

The practical capacity is 100,000 units (pairs of shorts) per year.

Using normal and master-budget capacity

Normal capacity utilization is the level of capacity needed to meet customer demand over several years. *Master-budget capacity utilization* is the expected level of capacity needed for your current budget. You use both measurements to control costs.

Add the term *utilization* to the discussion. In this case, utilization means the amount of capacity you need to meet customer demand. That level may be less than the capacity levels you just reviewed.

Any available production capacity beyond the customer demand level isn't needed. You don't have customers to buy the extra products produced.

Consider whether your business is seasonal. Certain seasons produce more demand for certain product; then, when the season's over, retailers clear out merchandise. This is the clearance-sale concept. My friends who are smart shoppers always buy at the end of a season. They buy winter coats in April and swim suits in September. Stores are cutting prices to clear inventory that is no longer in season.

A lot is riding on your understanding this issue. You need to crank up production before your busy time of year. That means you need machinery, materials, and labor to be available during that heavy production time. Consider your cash position. You produce more goods, sell more goods, and collect more cash during your busy season. When things slow down, you produce less, and you need to plan your cash use to get through the slow times.

A two- or three-year period includes the impact of the seasonality of your business each year. If you sell outdoor athletic equipment, you have a busy spring and summer, and maybe a slowdown in winter. If you manufacture outdoor athletic equipment, you have a busy autumn and winter making products for retailers. An analysis over several years may pick up changes in the overall economy. Think about normal capacity as on-average capacity.

A *cyclical stock* is a term used in the investment business. This type of investment is affected by changes in the overall economy. Cyclical stock prices do well in good times and poorly in bad times. Picture companies that make or sell goods that are discretionary purchases. When the economy goes down, consumers buy fewer luxury items. Sales of expensive clothing, jewelry, and cars generally decline.

Master-budget capacity utilization is the expected level of capacity needed for your current budget. (Check out Chapter 7 for more on master budgets.) In planning, you make assumptions about costs and sales, and then you use the data to come up with a capacity level of production.

A word of caution: This year's budget may not reflect the same level of capacity needed over two to three years. Your master-budget capacity may reflect a great current economy and a high level of sales. Normal capacity might reflect an average economy over two to three years. The economy is like a roller coaster; there can be big highs and lows, and the changes can happen quickly. Keep your time period in mind as you make capacity decisions.

Choosing a capacity level

Your capacity-level decisions affect a product's total cost, pricing decisions, and financial statements. The process for evaluating employee performance is also affected by capacity. Capacity decisions have a ripple effect through your business.

If your decisions result in excess capacity, you spend more than you need to. If your decisions result in too little on capacity, you won't be able to fill all customer orders.

Costing your product

The concept of cost allocation is everywhere in this book. Cost allocation may spread a fixed cost over a level of activity. Your capacity is a level of activity, and it might impact your cost allocation decisions. If your capacity level isn't realistic, your cost allocation will be incorrect and impact your product's cost.

The section "Reviewing theoretical and practical capacity" shows that theoretical capacity is unattainable. Assume you use machine hours to allocate a $50,000 fixed manufacturing cost. Theoretical capacity calls for 5,000 machine hours. First, do a fixed manufacturing cost allocation:

Fixed manufacturing cost allocation (theoretical capacity) = fixed cost ÷ machine hours

Fixed manufacturing cost allocation (theoretical capacity) = $50,000 ÷ 5,000

Fixed manufacturing cost allocation (theoretical capacity) = $10 per hour

Next, take into account downtime for machine repair, holidays, and vacation time for your machine operators. You determine a practical capacity for 4,500 hours. Here's your fixed manufacturing cost allocation for practical capacity:

Fixed manufacturing cost allocation (practical capacity) = fixed cost ÷ machine hours

Fixed manufacturing cost allocation (practical capacity) = $50,000 ÷ 4,500

Fixed manufacturing cost allocation (practical capacity) = $11.11 per hour

Theoretical capacity's cost allocation is lower than practical capacity ($10 versus $11.11). Using theoretical capacity allocates too little fixed manufacturing cost to the product because the theoretical capacity was based upon perfect-world machine usage of 5,000 hours. You determine that 4,500 machine hours is more realistic.

Pricing decisions and capacity

The *downward demand spiral* is a bad thing. Say your company isn't willing to meet lower prices offered by competitors. By not lowering prices, you lose business. As you lose business, you have to spread the same costs over fewer products. Your per-unit cost increases. To maintain a profit, you raise prices. As prices increase, you lose more business. The more business you lose, the higher you must raise prices, which makes the situation worse.

You may have seen this type of scenario in a movie. A character makes a bad decision, and to fix things, the character makes even worse decisions, digging himself into an even deeper hole.

Okay, that sounds scary. So here's how you can prevent it from happening to you. When you're asked to meet a competitor's price, take a long, hard look at your cost assumptions.

Look at your capacity level. The downward-demand spiral is based on an *increasing decline* (how do you like that phrase?) in demand. To avoid the problem, use the practical capacity level.

Practical capacity is a capacity level based on production you can supply. If you use a capacity level based on *demand,* and it's too high, you have a problem. You're allocating a fixed cost based on too much capacity. As demand falls, the fixed costs are allocated to fewer units.

Now you're stuck in a downward demand spiral. As demand falls, the fixed costs allocated to each unit increases. The higher fixed cost forces you to raise your prices to maintain a profit.

If you make a small quantity of a costly product, it's easier to take that long, hard look at cost assumptions. If, for example, you own a rapid-prototype machine shop, you're probably dealing with one client who has a very special need. And you may be able to offer a well-thought-out lower price.

If you produce 100,000 pairs of running shorts per year, you're in a very competitive industry, and you may already have squeezed out costs from the product. Not to name names, of course, but the world's largest retailer demands cuts in price from vendors year after year. Those demands can run your business into the ground.

Capacity levels and employee evaluation

Assume you're a manager getting your annual review. You're accountable for cost variances in your department. If actual costs are more than budgeted (an unfavorable variance), it may count against you. Your boss considers the unfavorable variance to be a sign of weak cost control.

The trouble is, this scenario isn't an apples-to-apples comparison. The capacity cost was forecasted over several years; your review is for one year. To be fair, your company should use an annual capacity cost measurement. The master-budget capacity utilization is for one year. The company should use that one.

Focusing on uncertainty

In business, as in life, no amount of planning can remove all uncertainty. (I like the phrase "embrace the unknown" to feel better about it, but uncertainty is still unnerving.) Any capacity level you choose may result in unused capacity. Your estimate of production may be too high; your forecast of demand may also be too high. The good news is that you can analyze and correct.

However, unused capacity may not be all bad. That extra capacity can help you meet a sudden or unexpected demand for a product. Extra business is a nice surprise — *if* you're able to fill the orders. Although the unused capacity has a cost, it may pay off over time.

Part III
Making Decisions

The 5th Wave   By Rich Tennant

"Gentlemen, we stand on the shoulders of accountants."

In this part . . .

Some people groan at the thought of making decisions of any kind, let alone making decisions using cost accounting. But in this part, you learn about cost drivers, activities that cause you to incur costs, and relevance. You also address pricing, compute the cost of your product correctly, and calculate the proper price for your product. It's a good thing you decided to read the chapters in this part, huh?

Chapter 10

Cost Drivers and Cost Estimation Methods

*I*f you can understand cost behavior, you can understand and forecast costs. A *cost driver* measures how much cost an activity generates. I've described a cost object in other chapters as a "sponge" that's full of costs. The cost driver adds to the size of the sponge or subtracts from its size.

Cost behavior links an activity (such as sales or production) to a cost. *Cost functions* relate a cost to an activity level using a mathematical formula. You use a cost function formula to build a better cost/activity relationship.

This chapter helps you understand cost drivers and the activities that create them. You can use that knowledge to reduce costs and increase your profit. (Ah, that marvelous bottom line — again!) It guides you through the steps to determine a cost driver. And if you get stuck, check out Chapter 4 for more on cost drivers.

Working with Cost Behavior

Costs can be fixed, variable, or mixed. As the terms imply, *fixed costs* don't change with the level of activity, *variable costs* increase or decrease with the level of activity, and *mixed costs* have a fixed cost and a variable cost component. I cover that ground in Chapter 2. Now put the cost behavior in the form of a formula. You can plug levels of activity into the formula and compute the cost. Technically, this is called *plug and chug*. The object is to understand costs and reduce them.

Understanding linear and nonlinear cost functions

As a preliminary, keep in mind that you relate only one cost to one activity at a time. Also, the relationship holds true only in a relevant range of activity. An activity level above the relevant range may not have the same cost function. (See Chapter 2 for details on relevant range.)

Cost functions may be *linear functions* or *nonlinear functions.* A linear function in cost accounting looks almost exactly like the linear function you may have learned in high school algebra: $f(x) = mx + b$. If the formula isn't ringing a bell with you, the explanation below should help.

A linear costing function has this form:

> Total cost = fixed cost + (variable cost × activity level)

Try the formula with the first cellphone billing plan (fixed cost):

> Total cost = $200 + ($0 × 0)
> Total cost = $200

At any level of cellphone use, the cost is $200.

Next, try the formula with the second billing plan. You used 500 minutes.

> Total cost = $0 + ($0.05 × 500)
> Total cost = $25.00

For variable costs, you multiply the total cellphone minutes used by 5 cents, and there's no fixed cost component.

Here's the formula applied to the third plan, the mixed cost plan:

> Total cost = $50 + ($0.02 × 500)
> Total cost = $50 +10.00
> Total cost = $60.00

If you didn't use any minutes for the month, your cost would be $50. If you used 500 minutes for the month, you would pay $60.

All three types of costs fit into the formula; they're all considered linear costs.

If you plot a linear cost function on graph paper, it appears as a straight line (just like in high school). Conversely, a nonlinear cost function is a function where the graph won't be a straight line. Think quantity discount or sliding scale. See the section "Exploring Nonlinear Cost Functions," later in this chapter.

Linear costs increase or decrease at a constant rate. In the variable cost cell phone plan, each minute has a $0.02 cost. As you use more minutes, the cost increase is a constant $0.02 per minute. You also see the constant cost increase in the variable component of the mixed cost plan.

Discovering how cost drivers determine total costs

You can't assign costs and compute a total product cost without knowing the cost driver. An activity relates to a cost if there's a cause-and-effect relationship. Each of the following situations is a cause-and-effect relationship:

✔ A direct cost (material or labor) can be traced to the product. If you increase your production of denim jeans, you incur more denim material cost. The cause (more jeans production) has the effect of increased spending on denim material.

✔ A contract requires that you incur the cost for a particular activity. Assume a customer contract requires you to add six brass buttons to each pair of jeans. That cause (a contract) has the effect of increasing your spending on brass buttons. You also incur machine and labor costs to attach the buttons to the jeans.

✔ Based on your industry or product knowledge, you can relate the activity to the cost. Say your outdoor action line of jeans has reinforced stitching. It prevents the jeans from tearing when campers and hikers give them rough use. Based on your product knowledge, you know that labor and machine costs are higher for the outdoor action line than your other lines of jeans. The cause (product line) has the effect of increasing spending on labor costs and machinery.

Almost all activities are related to a cost. A cost and an activity relate only if the cause-and-effect relationship is reasonable. That requires judgment and common sense on your part.

Consider this scenario: You notice that the vast majority of your machine repair costs occur on Fridays, so you decide to do some analysis to see if there's a relationship. On average, your machine use isn't any higher than other days of the week.

Your payroll records tell you that the same employees work each day of the week. There are no differences in staffing between Friday and other days.

Your production manager speculates that breakdowns happen on Fridays because the machines have been running all week. After four prior days of use, they get overheated and tend to break down on Fridays. You don't use the machines over the weekend. By Monday, the machines have cooled back down.

You run machine diagnostics on each Monday and Friday for several weeks and conclude that your manager is correct. The heavy machine use during the week (the cause) results in higher repair costs on Fridays (the effect).

Considering Cost Estimation Methods

Your goal is to select a method to estimate each cost function. You can choose among four good ones. No matter what method you select, you need to collect information, make some assumptions (such as deciding what data are more important and less important), and consider the cost of implementing your cost estimation method.

The goals are simple. You're going after a method you can implement for a reasonable cost and one that gives you useful information to estimate costs. You end up deciding whether the benefit of having the information is worth the cost and time involved to collect it.

Walking through the industrial engineering method

The *industrial engineering method* (also called the *work-measurement method*) relates inputs to outputs. You analyze inputs (material, labor, overhead) and attach them to some level of output. For example, you may determine that five hours of machine time is required to cut and treat 12 square yards of leather to make purses. The input is machine time; the output is the treated leather.

If this sounds time-consuming, it is! Someone (maybe an analyst you hire) has to monitor dozens of inputs to see what comes out on the other end — the outputs. Because of the time and effort involved, this method is no longer widely used. It's also not very effective when estimating overhead costs. As you've seen, overhead costs are hard to judge. They're allocated, not traced, to production.

Agreeing on the conference method

As the name implies, the *conference method* uses a consensus of opinion from people within the company. That consensus view becomes the cost estimate.

There are several benefits. You use the collective knowledge from everyone in the organization. Presumably, that adds experience, and it spreads out the time needed over many people. Because the decision is based on consensus, it may carry greater credibility. Certainly, the group providing input believes in the process and the outcome.

However, the conference method may not yield an accurate cost estimate because the method relies more on opinion and less on analysis. People can include their own biases when they give their opinions.

Reviewing the account analysis method

The *account analysis method* may be the easiest method to understand and implement. There are three steps to this process:

1. Identify the type of activity that is driving the cost.

2. Divide the total costs into fixed, variable and mixed costs. Essentially, you are creating three "buckets" of cost.

3. Plug in the fixed, variable, and mixed cost totals into the cost function formula.

Here's a simple example. Assume an activity relates to $100,000 in total cost. You analyze the activity and determine that $60,000 of the total cost is fixed, and $40,000 is a variable cost driven by machine hours. You determine that the variable cost per machine hour is $20 an hour.

Now you can plug the data into the cost function:

Total cost = fixed cost + (variable cost × activity level)

Total cost = $60,000 + ($20 × machine hours)

You can plug in any level of machine hours and come up with a total cost. Because you're able to plug the activity and costs into the cost function, it's a linear function.

If you created a dollar of cost for a mixed cost, you would post the fixed portion to the fixed part of the cost formula and the variable per unit amount to the variable part of the cost formula.

What you've created is a cost function estimate that uses analysis (not just opinion) and is easy to understand. Keep in mind, however, that it's tough to know with certainty which costs are fixed and which are variable. As with many areas of accounting, you use your best judgment.

Checking out the quantitative analysis method

The quantitative analysis method uses more math than you've seen so far. You review your historical data, look at activities and costs you've incurred, and then plot the data on a graph.

Say the x-axis is the activity level, which in this case is labor hours. The y-axis is the related cost. For each level of activity on the x-axis, you plot a point for cost on the y-axis. Finally, you use the points on the chart to create a cost function. Figure 10-1 shows a linear function.

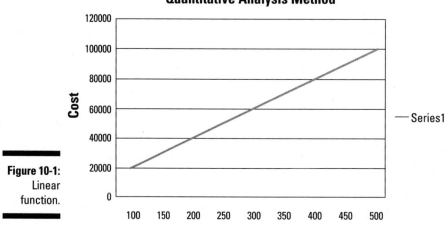

Quantitative Analysis Method

Figure 10-1:
Linear
function.

Bear in mind that the cost function is linear. Moving left to right on the graph, the cost function is a straight line.

Introducing the high-low method

The high-low method is the simplest form of the quantitative analysis method. It gives an idea of how quantitative analysis works for accounting analysis. You then know enough (for a beginner) to be dangerous. Going further requires more math and statistics than are discussed in this book.

Say that you're reviewing data for indirect machine cost. The cost driver is machine hours. You have two years of monthly data (24 months). You post each machine hour on the x-axis, find the cost on the y-axis, and plot the points. Figure 10-2 shows the data used. The top chart shows the cost per month. The bottom chart shows machine hours per month.

High Point: $100,000 cost, 1,600 machine hours
Low Point: $80,000 cost, 1,100 machine hours

No outliers

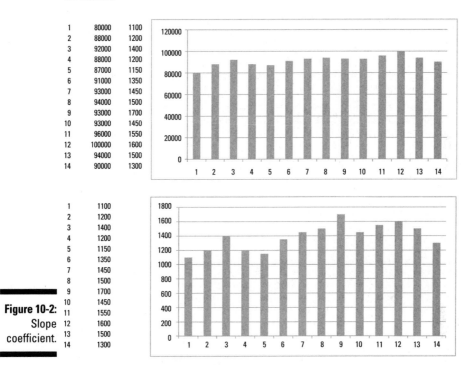

1	80000	1100
2	88000	1200
3	92000	1400
4	88000	1200
5	87000	1150
6	91000	1350
7	93000	1450
8	94000	1500
9	93000	1700
10	93000	1450
11	96000	1550
12	100000	1600
13	94000	1500
14	90000	1300

1	1100
2	1200
3	1400
4	1200
5	1150
6	1350
7	1450
8	1500
9	1700
10	1450
11	1550
12	1600
13	1500
14	1300

Figure 10-2:
Slope
coefficient.

Your first step is to find the highest and lowest activity (machine hour) points in that 24-month period. That's the bottom chart. Your next step is to find the cost points that align with the highest and lowest activity levels you selected. You use the top chart for that. Here are your high and low points:

High point: $100,000 cost; 1,600 machine hours

Low point: $80,000 cost; 1,100 machine hours

The graph at the bottom of Figure 10-2 displays the total hours for each month. The highest point on the chart is the ninth month. At the point, you see 1,600 machine hours. The lowest point on the same chart is in the 17th month. In that month, you incur 1,100 machine hours.

The high-low method requires you to select the highest and lowest activity *first*. You then use the activity to locate the related costs. The graph at the top of Figure 10-2 relates each month to the indirect machine cost. Sixteen hundred machine hours generate a $100,000 cost, and the 1,100 machine hours ties to an $80,000 cost.

Compute a *slope coefficient* and a *constant*. These two numbers provide the high-low estimate of your cost function. Those terms are defined next.

Computing the slope coefficient

The *slope coefficient* is the cost per machine hour. That's the accounting definition. This term has a math definition, too, but it's not critical to understand it for this cost estimation method.

The difference between highest and lowest cost is $20,000 ($100,000 to $80,000). The highest and lowest machine hour difference is 500 hours (1,600 hours to 1,100 hours). Here's the slope coefficient:

Slope coefficient = cost ÷ hours

Slope coefficient = $20,000 ÷ 500

Slope coefficient = $40 per hour

Finding the constant in the cost function

Now use the slope coefficient and the other data to compute the constant. You need all of this data for your estimate of the cost function. To find the constant, you can use either the highest cost and machine hours or the lowest. Here's the constant formula, using the highest data:

Constant (highest data) = highest cost − (slope coefficient × machine hours)

Constant (highest data) = $100,000 − ($40 × 1,600)

Constant (highest data) = $100,000 − ($64,000)

Constant (highest data) = $36,000

You can check your work by plugging the lowest cost and machine hours into the formula. You should get the same dollar amount constant. This formula computes the constant using the lowest cost and machine hours:

Constant (lowest data) = $80,000 − ($40 × 1,100)

Constant (lowest data) = $80,000 − ($44,000)

Constant (lowest data) = $36,000

Estimating the cost function

Finally, you use the slope coefficient and the constant to compute the high-low estimate of the cost function:

Total cost = fixed cost + (slope coefficient × activity level)

Total cost = 36,000 + ($40 × activity level)

To estimate your cost, you can plug in a number of machine hours and compute a cost estimate.

The high-low estimate of the cost function relies on just two data points. Those points might be unusual — far out of the ordinary. To avoid results that are misleading, consider using a *representative high and low*. Take a look at several of the high costs. If the highest cost is far different from the others (an *outlier*), don't use it in high-low analysis. Use another high cost that is closer to the other results. Do the same thing at the low end.

For example, the month with the highest cost and machine hours was due to unusually high customer demand. Maybe you were ending a product line that was very popular. Customers rushed in to get the product while it was still available, so you were working (and spending) at an unusually high rate.

You could also have a month at the other end of the spectrum. The month with the lowest cost and machine hours was quirky. Say you sell winter coats for hikers and campers. April is normally your slowest production month because the winter season is just about over. In May, you crank up production to meet fall and winter demand.

You have an unusually warm April, so customer demand is lower than expected. Production is low — maybe the lowest ever. If you use your April cost and machine hours for your cost function, your cost estimate would be distorted.

Choosing a cost estimation method

Now that you've seen several methods for estimating costs, consider some scenarios. You have to consider which cost estimation method to use.

Deciding between two cost drivers

Typically, the two most common cost drivers for indirect costs are machine hours and manufacturing labor hours. This concept has been addressed several times in the book.

Say that you're selecting a cost driver for machine repair costs. You're thinking about which activity drives the repair cost. Well, it could be machine hours. After all, the more you run the machines, the more likely they are to break down. On the other hand, the best cost driver could be manufacturing labor hours. The more employees you have running the machines, the more the machines break down.

You decide to use quantitative analysis to decide which cost driver is best. Specifically, you apply the high-low method. Compute a cost function for using each cost driver. You have a cost function for repair costs versus machine hours. You also have a cost function for repair costs versus labor hours. If you need to, refer to the section "Estimating the cost function."

You end up with two formulas. They both look like this:

Cost function estimate = constant + (slope coefficient × number of hours)

The constant is the fixed cost portion of the formula. The slope coefficient is the variable portion of the formula. The hours are either labor hours or machine hours. Next, plug values (hours) into the function, and see what your cost estimate is.

You decide on a cost driver by deciding which cost function results look the most reasonable. You're able to see which set of costs is the most plausible, producing outcomes that you'd expect.

You graph manufacturing labor hours cost function. You noticed that the relationship of costs to labor costs is haphazard. There's no pattern or trend that relates the cost to the labor hours.

Your graph of the machine hours, on the other hand, shows a definite trend. As machine hours increase, you see a clear trend of repair costs increasing. Commons sense tells you that machine hours are a more reasonable cost driver for repair costs than manufacturing labor hours.

Juggling cost hierarchies and cost estimation issues

A cost hierarchy considers different levels of costs. (Take a peek at Chapter 5 for a review.) Consider the difference between a unit cost and a batch cost. Say your company makes auto parts. You produce products in batches. When you change from producing one auto part to producing another part, you incur setup costs (that is, the cost of labor to make changes to the equipment).

Here's the skinny: You need to match the batch cost (setup cost) with the batch-level activity (setup labor hours). Setup costs aren't allocated or traced to a unit; instead, the costs are allocated to a *batch*.

The work process is obvious. Make a batch of parts, stop and do setup, and then make a batch of a different parts. There could be 2 units in a batch or 200. In either case, the setup time would be the same, because the batch process drives it.

By contrast, metal costs for your product are a unit cost. You trace material costs to each unit. (And direct costs have been covered many times in this book.) You can picture each auto part produced using metal material. So you trace material costs at the *unit* level.

Exploring Nonlinear Cost Functions

In the section "Checking out the quantitative analysis method," earlier in this chapter, you saw a definition of the linear cost function. Moving left to right on the graph, a linear cost function is a straight line.

However (there's always a "however"), not all cost functions are linear. There are *nonlinear cost functions,* too. With a nonlinear cost function, the graph line isn't straight. You need to distinguish between linear and nonlinear cost functions.

Changing cost functions and slope coefficients

With a nice, tame linear cost function, *the slope coefficient is constant.* It may be fairly shallow (making copper ingots) or steep (making platinum door-stops). But here's the deal with a nonlinear cost function: At various points along the x-axis, *the slope coefficient changes.* The change might look like a curve, or it might be a dramatic jag. When you see examples, nonlinear cost functions make sense.

Understanding the impact of quantity discounts

Say you're buying material (metal) for your auto parts production process. Picture a graph with square feet of material on the x-axis and cost on the y-axis. From 0 to 10,000 square feet, you pay $5 per pound. The slope coefficient is a straight line. As you order more material, the cost increases at a constant rate. The cost function is a straight line.

When you order more than 10,000 square feet in a month, your supplier offers you a quantity discount. From 10,001 to 20,000 square feet purchased, you pay $3.50 per pound. Your slope coefficient has changed. The cost function line isn't as steep in the 10,001- to 20,000-square-feet range. If the discount got larger (say for material purchases between 20,001 and 30,000 square feet per month), the slope of the line would flatten even more.

And quantity discounts are common; they encourage customers to order more product. If you're a buyer, your average cost declines. If you pay for a portion of the metal at $5 per pound and then pay $3.50 per pound for more, your average cost is less than $5. Because the cost function line changes along the way, the cost function is nonlinear.

Assessing the Impact of Learning Curves

A *learning curve* is a cost function that measures how your labor costs per unit decline as production increases. Decline? Yes! That's because as your employees learn more about the tasks they're doing, they get better at doing them. They may take less effort, and the employees can perform them faster. When that happens, productivity increases and your labor cost per unit declines.

Learning curve may also refer to costly lessons that real life teaches. A friend of mine often says, "Nothing is wasted." Any experience in business — even one that seems awful — can be a learning experience. Even if your response is "I'll never do that again," you've still learned something.

"Experience keeps a dear [costly] school, but fools will learn in no other" (Benjamin Franklin, *Poor Richard's Almanac,* 1743). If possible, try to learn from *somebody else's* experience.

As a manager, you can improve your decision-making due to the learning curve. As production increases, you improve how you schedule your work. Maybe you realize that certain days of the week are busier due to customer demand. You start to schedule based on that demand pattern.

Some industries have days of the week when companies don't want product delivered. One of my clients distributes food products to grocery stores. He knows that his three largest customers don't want deliveries on Wednesdays, so he uses that knowledge to run his business more efficiently. On Wednesdays, he delivers to other, smaller clients.

A learning-curve model compares *labor hours per unit* with production levels. After that, you consider *labor cost per unit.* It's similar to the cost estimate analyses described throughout this chapter. You look at an activity level and then review the cost per unit.

Assume you make a high-end office chairs. You train your production staff on how to assemble a new, more complex type of chair. Early on, your employees take more labor hours than planned to assemble the chairs. As time goes on, they start to understand the process and they work faster. Your labor hours go down — and so do your labor costs.

As your workers learn how to make the chairs, your labor cost per unit decreases. Your labor cost per unit for the first chair is a lot higher than the labor cost for the 500th chair. If you average the labor cost for units 1 through 500, the average cost is less than unit number 1's cost.

The cost function changes as you produce more product. Because the cost function isn't a straight line, it's a nonlinear cost function.

Chapter 11

Making Smart Business Decisions with Relevant Information

A business owner makes decisions every day, some with far-reaching consequences. This chapter describes the decision model, the use of relevant information, and some choices that business owners may face.

In business, making a decision usually means cutting off one option and going with another. (Serendipitously, the word *decision* comes from the Latin word *decidere,* and it literally means "to cut off.")

In cost accounting, *relevance* means "connected to the matter at hand" (as it also does in real life). It's critical to focus on the most important data.

Your job is to define problems and determine which information (accounts, activities, costs) is most important. Then you decide what to do.

In this chapter, you see how to determine relevant costs and make decisions in an orderly way. You also look at special orders, opportunity costs, outsourcing, and capacity costs because they each have a big impact on your company's profit. Use this chapter to make smart decisions about your most critical business decisions.

Navigating the Geography of Relevance

Relevant costs and *relevant revenue* have an impact on your profit. You should pay the most attention to these numbers. Get these numbers "right," and you can be more profitable. You get numbers right by analyzing relevant costs and relevant revenue, using what's called a decision model.

In cost accounting, *relevant* means that you consider *future* revenue and expenses. Also, *relevant* means that a cost or revenue will change, depending on a decision you make. Past costs are water under the bridge, and if the costs or revenue remain the same no matter what you decide, they aren't relevant.

A relevant amount is not necessarily a *material* amount. If you were closing a factory, the cost you pay for trash removal at the factory location would be relevant. If the factory stays open, you pay for trash removal. If you close the factory, you no longer pay for the service. So your decision determines whether or not you have the trash removal cost.

While the trash removal cost is relevant, it may not be material. Materiality refers to the *dollar amount* of the cost. Most accountants determine a minimum dollar amount for materiality. Amounts below the minimum are ignored. If the relevant decisions for the plant closing total $1,000,000, a $600 decision about trash pickup may not be material.

It helps to define a term by explaining what it isn't. A relevant cost isn't a past or sunk cost. (Take a look at Chapter 3, if you need a refresher.) Sunk costs are done deals and are irrelevant moving forward. They're already paid, and you can't change them.

Say you make the lease payment on your factory on the first day of the month. Later, on the 15th, you make a decision about which product to produce for the rest of the month. Your lease payment is *important* (of course), but it's not *relevant* to the production decision. That's because the lease payment can't be changed for the remainder of the month.

Introducing the decision model

As you sort through and determine what's relevant to a decision, you can move on to using a great tool: the decision model. A *decision model* is a process for making important decisions. Most types of organizations (businesses, sports teams, and governments, to name a few) have a formal process for making choices. Some of this, of course, is common sense. Here are the steps in a typical decision model:

1. Define the problem.

2. Gather information.

3. Make assumptions about future costs. (This is called *forecasting.*)

4. Analyze alternatives, and select one.

5. Implement your decision.

6. Evaluate the outcome of your decision.

This process may seem obvious, but companies have to learn it. If fact, some companies hire consultants to come onsite to teach the principles.

Applying a model to an equipment decision

Say you manufacture Supperware plastic containers — simple items for storing food. You identify a problem: A piece of machinery has become inefficient. The machine breaks down frequently and requires a lot of repair and maintenance. You decide to consider replacing the machine.

Using the decision model, you define a problem. Now gather more information.

Determining alternatives

Your current machine has a five-year remaining useful life. After that, it will have to be scrapped. You can use the machine for five more years, but there are two problems. First, the repair and maintenance expense is much higher on the current machine compared to a new one. Second, the old machine produces fewer items than a new one. Fewer items produced may mean less revenue.

Now forecast — that is, make assumptions about future costs. If you buy a new machine, you have to borrow funds for the purchase. Like any loan, you need to repay the principal (the amount borrowed) and interest. Those payments are part of the decision.

Analyze alternatives, and select one. You perform an analysis on two scenarios. In the first scenario, everything stays as is. In the second scenario, you buy a new machine. (That also means that you sell the old machine, but it's not worth much, because the technology is very old.)

You analysis should include a comparison of the most expense and revenue data.

Your how-to book: An operations manual

The largest decisions a company makes — whether to sell the company or merge with another company, for example — can't be easily explained in a manual. That decision is very complex. For everything else, there's the operations manual. An *operations manual* is an internal company document that explains how you operate your business. It's not shared with the outside world. All the major tasks you perform (manufacturing, product delivery, bill payment, hiring, purchasing decisions, and so forth) should be explained in the operations manual. The purpose of an operations manual is to educate people in the company. I call it the "hit by a bus" document (not a very positive title, but it makes an impression!). If someone in your company leaves or retires (or is hit by a bus), another employee can pick up his or her work more quickly if the operations manual is up to date. When someone leaves your business, a certain amount of institutional knowledge goes out the door with him or her. Hopefully, a lot of that employee's company-specific knowledge is recorded in an operations manual. To ease the decision-making process, more companies have an operations manual.

Considering depreciation

Depreciation is an expense. Depreciation expense accounts for the decline of an asset's value. The decline occurs as the asset is "used up." You calculate depreciation expense using the cost of the asset, its useful life, and its salvage value. *Salvage value* is the sales proceeds you receive if you choose to sell the asset at the end of its useful life. When you buy a new car, you get cash by trading in your old car. That's the salvage value. Actually, the dealer uses the trade-in "cash" to reduce the cost of the new vehicle. (I drive cars until the wheels fall off, so I don't usually get much on the trade-in.) Most important, depreciation expense doesn't use "real" cash — the expense is on your books, but you don't write a check each year as your car depreciates. The car is just worth less. By the way, there are many ways to calculate depreciation. Some methods have more expense in early years and less in later years. Other methods assume a fixed amount each year. What you see in Table 11-1 is called *five-year straight-line*.

Table 11-1 provides an analysis, comparing "keepin' on keepin' on" with the old machine for five years versus buying a new machine.

Coming to conclusions

It might be surprising, but you're better off keeping the old machine for five years. Check out the bottom line of Table 11-1. The old machine's total is $20,000 higher each year ($125,000 versus $105,000).

Sure, you would earn a lot more revenue from the new machine each year. In fact, you could take in $100,000 more ($260,000 versus $160,000). However, you have to pay that $100,000 annual tab for the loan. Because it's a new machine (and almost certainly more expensive to buy), your depreciation expense is also higher.

Table 11-1	Machine Purchase Decision — Comparison	
Annual Expense	*Old Machine*	*New Machine*
New machine loan payments	N/A	-$100,000
Proceeds from selling old machine	$20,000	$0
Depreciation expense	-$30,000	-$50,000
Repair and maintenance expense	-$25,000	-$5,000
Subtotal: Annual expense	**-$35,000**	**-$155,000**
Annual production revenue		
Units produced (A)	80,000	130,000
Revenue per unit (B)	$2	$2
Annual revenue (A × B)	**$160,000**	**$260,000**
Revenue less expense	$125,000	$105,000

To be fair to the new machine, the numbers for the old machine look good only in Year 5 (shown in Table 11-1), when you take in $20,000 in salvage value. Ignore that, and both deals are even. Further, if production is trending up, the old machine will never keep pace, so you may want to seriously consider buying that new machine.

Connecting your decision to the balance sheet

You just analyzed whether or not to replace a piece of machinery. Machinery is an asset, because it's something you use up to make money in your business. This is a good point to go over the concept of a balance sheet.

Don't jump to another chapter simply to review what a balance sheet is. I sing "The Balance Sheet Song" here and now, once more with feeling. The balance sheet formula is equity = assets – liabilities. A company's true value is equity. If you sold all of the assets and used the cash to pay off all the liabilities, the remaining cash balance is equity, the true worth of the business.

If you were deciding to buy, say, a restaurant, your analysis of relevant information would include a list of assets: furniture, fixtures, ovens, dishwashers, and the like. However, you'd also want to see the depreciation listing. Here's the skinny: You want to know the *real value* of the assets you're buying. That value is called *book value,* and it's defined as original cost less accumulated depreciation. *Accumulated depreciation* is the sum of all the depreciation of an asset since it was purchased.

If the current restaurant owner bought an oven for $60,000 but has already recognized $55,000 in accumulated depreciation, the book value is only $5,000. That implies that the asset (the oven) needs to be replaced soon.

Book value cannot be seen as the replacement value. You typically can't replace a depreciated asset with a similar asset at the same price. Prices go up. Equipment models are discontinued. You will likely replace an old machine with a new, more expensive (and presumably better) model.

Considering relevant qualitative factors in decision-making

Qualitative factors don't involve numbers and financial analysis. Call them "people" factors. Decisions based in part on qualitative factors are relevant, even though you can't tie specific cost or revenue numbers to them. They can have a long-term impact on profitability, so you need to consider them. Qualitative factors should always be considered before making any business decisions.

The qualitative factor that has the biggest impact on your business may be employee morale. It's really an issue when there's bad news, such as a layoff. Layoffs, as a rule, don't improve employee morale. Employees are uncertain about their futures, even if they've been told that their jobs are secure. They may be skeptical, saying, "Yeah, and if you believe that, I've got a bridge I want to sell you."

On top of that, the remaining employees may have to take on the workload of people who were let go. The worst thing you can say to them is, "Work smarter, not harder." Trust me, employees have a BS meter that's always operating, and that statement is a 9.9 on a scale of 10.

There's a rule that's true far more often than not: When employee morale goes down, productivity goes down, too.

When companies reduce the workforce, the goal is, obviously, to reduce costs. Say a firm has 100 employees and cuts the staff to 80 people. You'd think profits would go up. After all, the company cut the cost (salary and benefits) of 20 people. The problem occurs with the 80 people who remain. Productivity (how much they get done) suffers, at least in the short term. Also, most people have an emotional reaction to the layoff. That emotion lingers and affects productivity.

There's another, bigger potential problem with layoffs: When you lay people off, some institutional knowledge leaves with them. Even the best operations manual can't cover everything. If a company lays off a great sales representative, personal relationships with customers may suffer, too. When other key people leave, those taking up their duties will make mistakes — that's almost unavoidable. Those mistakes can cost the company business, if the company isn't careful. In extreme situations, lost business (due to mistakes) costs more than the cost savings from the layoff.

You may not be able to *trace* the impact of a qualitative factor such as layoff effects to product costs, but you can *allocate* it. Doing so adds more lines to your decision-making analysis. It also requires you to make judicious estimates. For example, you might say, "I'm going to assume a 10 percent drop in productivity for three months."

If you happen to employ one of the most creative people of the 21st century, try not to lay him off. You might lose money. Link these two sentences together: "After losing a power struggle with the board of directors in 1985, Steve Jobs left Apple." "On July 9, 1997, Gil Amelio was ousted by the board of directors *after overseeing a three-year record-low stock price and crippling financial losses.* Jobs became the interim CEO and began restructuring the company's product line." Over 12 years, Apple got into trouble. When Jobs returned, he introduced the iPod, iPhone, and iPad — and incidentally caused Apple to have *more cash in the bank than all corporations and most of the nations of the world.*

The remainder of the decision-making process is simple but requires some detail work. First, implement your decision. Then evaluate the outcome of your decision. The results will tell you if you decided wisely. If you've made a mistake, you must make new decisions about how to fix it.

Special Orders Don't Upset Us, Do They?

You might remember the commercial jingle "Hold the pickles, hold the lettuce, special orders don't upset us." (I do, but then again, I remember having only five TV channels when I was in grade school.) A *special order* is a one-time customer order, often involving a large quantity and a low price. Hey! This is a chance to make money or lose money. Tough choice.

A special order requires you to make decisions using relevant information. You decide which costs and revenue are relevant. Based on your analysis, you make a decision designed to maximize your profit.

Keep the following points in mind when you're considering special orders:

- ✔ Because you are already in business to produce other goods, assume that your fixed costs are being paid for from your regular production. Assume that you've received other orders, completed work, and billed clients. That revenue allows you to cover fixed costs — like a building lease payment or insurance premiums.

- ✔ A special order can be filled only if you have excess capacity (see Chapter 9). You must have the ability to perform the work.

- ✔ Get ready for this: You can accept a *lower* sales price for a special order and still be profitable. Huh? Really, it's true. As you see in this section, fixed costs aren't relevant. The fixed costs have already been paid for with earlier production. They are past (sunk) costs, so you do not need to worry about covering them with your special-order revenue.

- ✔ Variable costs *are* a part of your special-order calculation. Variable costs are almost always relevant to a special order.

Say your company manufactures bath towels. Table 11-2 shows your results before you're approached about a special order.

Table 11-2	Towel Company — Before Special Order	
Units Produced: 300,000	**Per Unit**	**Total**
Sales (revenue)	$12	$3,600,000
Fixed cost		-$1,000,000
Variable cost	$7	-$2,100,000
Profit		**$500,000**

A customer wants to place an order for 50,000 towels. The customer is willing to pay only $8 per towel. Assuming you have excess capacity, would it be profitable to accept the order? Check out Table 11-3.

Table 11-3	Towel Company — Special-Order Proposal	
Units Produced: 50,000	**Per Unit**	**Total**
Sales (revenue)	$8	$400,000
Fixed cost		$0
Variable cost	$7	350,000
Profit		**$50,000**

Actually, the order *is* profitable. Because fixed costs were covered by your other production, there's no fixed cost related to this order. The variable costs per unit are the same ($7). At $8 per towel, the order generates a $50,000 profit. Think of anything above $7 as icing on the cake, because this is a sale that would not normally be part of your regular income stream.

Again, this order is a one-time deal. The 50,000 units in Table 11-3 aren't part of your normal production. Units in normal production incur fixed costs, and fixed costs are excluded from the special order. An $8 per-unit price wouldn't cover the *full cost* of the product in normal production. You exclude fixed costs from your special order because they're already covered by your regular sales; however, an $8 unit price wouldn't cover the full cost of the product in normal production.

![REMEMBER] Always think of fixed costs in total dollars. Although it's good to also look at fixed costs on a per-unit basis, per-unit fixed costs can be misleading and lead to mistakes in analysis. Why? Because fixed cost per unit is always changing, depending on how many units you produce. Always consider the *total* costs.

The goal is to generate enough revenue to cover (pay for) the entire dollar amount of fixed costs. That concept is in the definition of contribution margin (see Chapter 3). Contribution margin pays for fixed costs. Whatever's left over is profit.

You show a total dollar amount in your analysis because you're trying to cover a dollar amount of costs. In Table 11-2, you see fixed costs in dollars. The per-unit column is blank.

Certainly, you can analyze *variable* cost on a per-unit basis. That makes sense. You *trace* materials and labor to a unit. Fixed costs, on the other hand, normally are *allocated* as an indirect cost. Stick with the total fixed cost in dollars.

Deciding between Outsourcing and In-house Production

Outsourcing is defined as purchasing a good or service from an outside vendor rather than producing the good or service in-house (within your company). It's also referred to as a *make versus buy decision*.

A decision to outsource certainly considers reducing costs as a goal. If you can get the same (or virtually the same) product or service for less than it costs in-house, why not? So part of your analysis is reviewing costs, and you focus on relevant costs.

There's more to your outsourcing decision than just costs. You also must consider what you'll be giving up by losing some control over the goods and services. Think about the quality. Assume you create quality items with few flaws. Is the outsourced item just as good?

Anything you outsource should be delivered on time, just as it is when you make a product in-house. That means that the company you hire will need enough time, staff, and capacity to give you timely delivery.

The company taking over the process should also maintain confidentiality.

Look at two tables you can use to make an outsourcing decision. Table 11-4 is the "make" decision table. It shows the cost to continue making a product in-house. The product is towels (from an earlier example). Table 11-5 is the "buy" decision table. It assumes a purchase price from a supplier. The supplier will make the towels. You'll then add some finishing stitching and your company label. At that point, the towels will be ready for sale.

Table 11-4	"Make" Decision – Continue Production	
Units Produced: 40,000	**Per Unit**	**Total**
Variable costs		
Direct material	$2.00	$80,000
Direct labor	$1.00	$40,000
Variable factory overhead	$0.50	$20,000
Shipping and handling	$0.25	$10,000
Sale commissions	$1.00	$40,000
Total variable costs	**$4.75**	**$190,000**
Fixed costs, salary and benefits		$60,000
Other fixed overhead		$100,000
Total fixed costs		**$160,000**
Total costs		**$350,000**

You've seen some of the stuff in Table 11-4. Variable costs (material, labor, overhead) are described in Chapter 4. You also see shipping, handling, and sales commissions. These are costs to make the product, package and ship it, and sell it (sales commissions).

Your company incurs *other fixed overhead,* including depreciation in building and equipment, insurance premiums, and office costs. Finally, you incur $60,000 in fixed salary and benefits for a production manager, whose sole role is to manage your towel production during the year. The variable labor costs are for production workers. These employees are paid on an hourly basis, and their time is directly related to a unit of product. It's a direct cost and a separate expense from the production manager. The production manager's time can't be traced to an individual unit of product and is fixed.

So Table 11-4 is where you stand if you continue to produce the towels yourself. Then something interesting happens: A supplier offers to produce towels for you. Use the supplier's information to create Table 11-5.

Table 11-5	"Buy" Decision — Outsource Production	
Units Produced: 40,000	**Per Unit**	**Total**
Variable costs		
Direct material	$0	$0
Direct labor	$0	$0
Variable factory overhead	$0	$0
Purchase cost of towels – supplier	$3.80	$152,000
Shipping and handling	$0.25	$10,000
Sales commissions	$1.00	$40,000
Total variable costs	**$5.05**	**$202,000**
Fixed costs, salary and benefits		$0
Other fixed overhead		$100,000
Total fixed costs		**$100,000**
Total costs		**$302,000**

Say what? You save $48,000 ($350,000 versus $302,000 cost) by outsourcing. As you scan down Table 11-5 from top to bottom, here's what you find:

- Production-related variable costs (materials, labor, and overhead) are eliminated. In their place, you see "Purchase cost of towels – supplier." That's what the supplier charges to produce the product.

- Distribution costs (shipping, handling, and sales commissions) don't change. Your company will still perform those tasks and incur the costs.

- Other fixed overhead costs (depreciation, insurance premiums, and so forth) remain. Important point: When you consider outsourcing, some fixed costs *cannot be eliminated.* And that's the fact, Jack. By definition, they're fixed, and your company must continue to pay them.

- There's one final cost you can eliminate. Outsourcing assumes that you no longer produce the product. That means you don't need the production-manager position. That $60,000 fixed salary and benefit cost is eliminated. Because the outsourcing cost total is less than keeping production in-house, you should outsource.

Tables 11-4 and 11-5 show both relevant and irrelevant costs. You made your decision based on relevant costs — those that changed. Eliminating the variable production cost and the production-manager position saved money. The tables include all costs, so you can envision the entire process.

If you want to be able to live with yourself — and in your community — be very careful of creating a negative externality. In economics, an *externality* is a cost or benefit that isn't transmitted by prices. A *negative externality* is a cost that the creator of a problem (you) doesn't bear. "Nobody" pays for it, except that everyone pays for it. You could call it "playing for free." For example, if you lay off the production manager, he may go on food stamps, which everyone pays for. He may not be able to pay property taxes, which pays for the area schools. Further, the outsourcing company may not pay a living wage or health benefits. It may hire illegal workers. Does the deal seem so good now?

It may be that your best financial decision is to produce *at a loss.* On the surface, that sounds like a bad decision, but it might make sense if it allows you to pay for a fixed cost that you can't eliminate easily. Assume you're committed to make payment on a building lease. You signed a contract, which runs for two more years. You use the building for production. Your analysis indicates that you'll lose money if you keep producing. However, if you stop producing, you still have to pay that pesky lease payment. (You may want to use a stronger word than *pesky.*)

You have a choice. You can shut down production and lose the revenue — and *still* have to pay on the lease, or you produce at a loss. At the least, that generates some revenue to pay the lease. If the loss on production is less than the lease payment, keep producing. You'll lose less money.

Now, no one wants to tell people, "Business is great! I'm losing less money!" However, it may be the right decision. It allows you to cover at least some of the fixed cost. It's a short-term solution until you can get out of the fixed cost commitment. At that point, you can shut down production altogether.

Weighing opportunity costs

Opportunity cost is what you give up by making a decision to go in one direction rather than another.

Opportunity costs occur because all businesses have limited resources. For example, you only have so many machine hours you can use to produce goods. At some point, you have to decide how to use those hours to maximize profit. When you decide to concentrate on one product, you give up the chance to concentrate on another one, and that's an opportunity cost.

Table 11-6 shows an example of opportunity costs in a decision to outsource. Say you're losing money on a product, so you consider outsourcing it. On the left, you have the results of closing a company division. On the right, you see where you stand after the division is closed.

Table 11-6	Closing a Division — Financial Impact	
	Before Closing	*After Closing*
Sales (revenue)	$1,000,000	-$1,000,000
Less variable cost	-$550,000	$550,000
Equals contribution margin	$450,000	-$450,000
Less fixed cost	-$480,000	$370,000
Loss	**-$30,000**	**-$80,000**

The After Closing column is a little tricky. Here's an explanation: When you close the division, you lose $1,000,000 in sales (a negative). You also gain (by not spending) $550,000 in variable costs. The net result is that your contribution margin goes down by $450,000.

You also save the money you were spending on fixed costs; however, only $370,000 is added back in the right column. Just as in Table 11-5, not all of your fixed costs are eliminated. It makes sense, as many fixed costs (such as the building lease) are set up by contract. As long as the contract is in force, the company incurs the cost.

In the case presented in Table 11-6, you're *worse off* if you close the division. In fact, you lose $50,000 more than if you keep the division open (losing $80,000 versus losing $30,000).

The information in Table 11-6 suggests what to do: Keep operating until those fixed costs can be covered by another division or until the commitment to pay those costs ends. If the loss from the division staying open ($30,000) is less than the loss from the division closing ($80,000), keep operating. And who knows? You might be able to turn things around and make the division profitable.

Contemplating the carrying cost of inventory

Inventory can be a big cost in your business, and inventory issues may be a factor in a decision to outsource. If your company carries inventory, you have to consider the carrying cost of inventory. (See Chapter 4 if you need a review of inventory and the flow of manufacturing costs.)

In this section, you are a retailer who is buying inventory. In previous sections of this chapter, you looked at your costs from the point of view of a manufacturer. Now you're a retailer.

Carrying cost of inventory is the cost to hold and store your inventory. Carrying cost is also an opportunity cost. As a retailer, when you choose to purchase inventory, you're using an asset (cash) to buy inventory. Cash is an asset you could use for some other purpose. If you're a manufacturer, finished goods inventory represents "dead money" (stored cash). It's no good until you sell it.

Here are the primary factors to consider for carrying costs:

- ✔ **Interest cost:** Interest you pay on dollars borrowed to buy inventory. This factor can be stated another way. If you didn't have to borrow money to buy inventory, interest cost represents money you could have spent elsewhere or the interest you could have *earned* if you had invested the funds.

- ✔ **Ordering cost:** The cost charged by your supplier for each inventory purchase.

- ✔ **Quantity discount:** The percentage (or dollar amount) of discount you receive when you place a larger order for inventory.

Say you're the purchasing manager for a national chain of gift shops called Cuddly Puppies. You sell a line of scented candles that retail for $10. The candles normally cost you $5 each. Your supplier has called you to explain a new quantity discount program. If you purchase more candles in each order, you receive a discount on each candle. You're mulling over a decision: Should you take advantage of the discount and buy more candles? Table 11-7 lists the information.

Table 11-7	Carrying Cost Decision — Candle Purchases	
	Planned Buying	*Discount Plan*
Orders placed annually (A)	50	30
Candles per order (B)	2,000	3,400
Total candles (A) × (B)	100,000	102,000
Cost per candle	$5	$4.60
Total cost	**$500,000**	**$469,200**

Ordering candles at a lower price reduces total cost. Now consider the carrying cost factors, mainly the effect on cash. Assume that you can warehouse 3,400 candles just as easily as 2,000 candles.

Fortunately, your company has plenty of cash to operate. In fact, you're able to invest extra cash. (Extra cash — a great problem to have!) You currently earn 5 percent annually on the cash.

Consider the cash you would save. The quantity discount proposal (discount plan) would allow you to invest another $30,800 cash ($500,000 – $469,200). At a 5 percent annual rate, you'd increase your earnings on investing extra cash by $1,540 ($30,800 × 5 percent).

Ordering cost is $150 per order. Your total orders placed would decline from 50 per year to 30 per year — 20 fewer orders. Therefore, ordering costs would go down by $3,000 ($150 × 20 orders).

Consider the quantity discount. You will save $.40 per candle. Now, to make an apples-to-apples comparison, look at the first 2,000 candles you plan to buy. You save $800 ($0.40 savings per candle × 2,000 candles).

Here's the financial result, if you use quantity discount:

Total savings = interest earnings + ordering cost savings + price savings

Total savings = $1,540 + $3,000 + $800

Total savings = $5,340

Happy days are here again! You should take advantage of the quantity discount. But before you pick up the phone to call your supplier, consider one more issue.

Think about how long it takes to sell the 2,000 extra candles that you buy over a year. Because you were already buying 100,000 candles a year (2,000 a week for about 50 weeks), and the new quantity is 102,000, you're essentially buying an extra week's worth of inventory. Not a big deal — go ahead and take the quantity discount. The total amount ordered is only 2 percent more than you were purchasing before. You will probably be able to make these extra sales.

Maximizing Profit When Capacity Is Limited

When capacity is limited (and it always is), you have to make decisions. (See Chapter 9 for more about capacity levels.) In this section, you see how to make choices between two products when capacity is limited. Your goal is to combine the production of two products in such a way as to maximize profit.

You look at relevant costs and relevant revenue at the customer level.

Managing capacity and product mix

Product mix refers to the mix of products you produce. *Sales mix* refers to the mix of products you sell. They are broadly related. Every company deals with limited capacity, so smart decisions about product mix can greatly increase your profit. (And I hate to say it, but dumb decisions about product mix can greatly decrease your profit.) You just need to work out the most profitable product mix you can.

Say you produce furniture. The market you sell in is very competitive, so your profit margin (profit as a percentage of sales) is small. One step in your production process requires work to be performed by hand. The work is complex, and you don't have many people on your staff who can do it. Your capacity (labor hours) is limited, so you need to make sure that every hour worked is as profitable as it can be.

You need to allocate your production between two products: the Mellow Yellow chair and the Norwegian Wood chair. The challenge is that each product requires a different number of labor hours. Also, each product has a different contribution margin per unit. Recall that contribution margin equals sales less variable costs. You need to decide on the best mix.

To compare the two products, use contribution margin per hour. Table 11-8 lists the two products and the contribution margin per hour for each.

Table 11-8	Product Mix — Contribution Margin Per Hour	
Product Contribution Margin Per Unit	*Hours Per Unit*	*Contribution Margin Per Hour*
Mellow Yellow chair ($50 per unit)	2 hours	$25 per unit
Norwegian Wood chair ($57 per unit)	3 hours	$19 per unit

The Mellow Yellow chair has a higher contribution margin per hour. You should use your available capacity (labor hours) to produce as many Mellow Yellow chairs as needed. In other words, try to fill all of the Mellow Yellow orders, if possible. If there are hours left, use them to produce the Norwegian Wood chair.

Assume you have orders for 6,500 Mellow Yellow chairs. You have orders for 9,000 Norwegian Wood chairs. Now what? Table 11-9 details how production would look.

Table 11-9	Product Mix — Actual Production
Total Labor Hours Available	*31,000*
Mellow Yellow chairs	
Customer orders (units)	6,500
Labor hours per unit	2
Mellow Yellow hours used	-13,000
Remaining labor hours	**18,000**
Norwegian Wood chairs	
Customer orders (units)	6,000
Labor hours per unit	3
Norwegian Wood hours used	-18,000
Remaining labor hours	**0**

There's a two-step process in Table 11-9. First, you "max out" the Mellow Yellow chair production. You produce 6,500 chairs, and at 2 labor hours per unit, you use up 13,000 labor hours. That leaves 18,000 hours for Norwegian Wood chair production.

You couldn't fill all of the Norwegian Wood chair orders. There were orders for 9,000 chairs, but you had only enough labor hours left to produce 6,000 chairs (6,000 orders × 3 labor hours per chair).

You made the right decision. After you determined the best use of your labor hour time, you produced the product that created the bigger contribution to profit (contribution margin) first.

Business can be bizarre. Consider that you've limited production of the Norwegian Wood chair because compared with the Mellow Yellow chair, there's less profit in this item. In the minds of the retailers and customers, Norwegian Wood chairs are now back-ordered, because the manufacturer (you) just can't keep up with demand. Customers may perceive the Norwegian Wood chair as highly desirable and hard to get. Your limited production may have *increased* customer interest. (At some point, you might increase capacity or *raise prices.* The customers may eat it up. Then you'll be eager to do these calculations again.)

Analyzing customer profit and capacity

One more time, a cost object is anything (a product line, a unit, or a batch) that's used to accumulate costs. A *customer* can also be a cost object. This section looks at costs and profit per customer. That perspective helps you make good decisions about your limited capacity and customer profit.

Technology allows companies to analyze data for many customers. Computer programs can easily separate and review lots of customer data on costs and profits.

Small companies may not have the technology for complex analysis. If that's the case, customer analysis applies best to companies with a limited number of customers or those who have excellent homogeneous customer data.

Job costing versus process costing

Job costing collects data and analyzing costs by the job. It assumes that each job has a different combination of costs. Process costing assumes that each product is similar. In that case, you analyze costs by *process,* not by job.

With job costing, you see some customers who are more profitable than others, and that's what you're looking for. Job costing makes it easier to see key information. For example, the most expensive job — or the job that you didn't estimate accurately — becomes obvious. Just review your job cost sheets.

The ideal customer

Smart companies know who their *ideal customer* is. That's the customer who wants the product and is willing to pay a price that makes the transaction profitable. After the company figures out who its ideal customer is, it plans marketing, production, and pricing.

Say you sell mountain bikes. You've sold them for a while, and you've paid attention to your customers. You notice that the people who most often buy the bikes live in the Mountain West of the United States. The majority of your buyers are professionals in their 30s and 40s. They use the bikes on weekends for recreation. A smaller percentage of your business is younger people who ride the bikes to school and work.

Your ideal customer is the professional who rides on weekends. He (more likely a male) is willing to pay $2,400 for that little titanium-framed number in your product line. So you plan your marketing to target that group — male professionals who are weekend warriors. You price your product at a level you know they're willing to pay (probably a higher price than a younger person would pay). That's how you use your ideal customer profile to generate profit.

A large amount of indirect costs can create problems. Indirect costs are allocated rather than traced to the product. As you've seen several times so far, you need good customer data to properly allocate costs. If you don't have good numbers, you won't allocate costs accurately. This issue affects both job costing and process costing.

The point is simply that different customers have different levels of profitability.

Because you have limited capacity, you want to *do more business with the most profitable clients* and less business with the others. So come up with some criteria to decide which clients are the ones you *really* want. You already know in your heart (or gut) that it's true, and you just need to quantify it. Your most profitable clients are those that match the criteria you create.

Relevant cost and revenue

Connect the relevant cost and relevant revenue to the capacity planning. After all, capacity is limited. *Relevant,* of course, refers to the cost and revenue that makes a difference when you make decisions.

A friend of mine used to be a pastry chef. She created and delivered specialty desserts to local restaurants and had seven restaurants as clients. The type of product isn't relevant because each client got the same selection of desserts, but in varying quantities. (By the way, it's always great to go to her house for dinner, because the cooking is better than in any restaurant!)

With only seven restaurants, it's relatively easy to separate data about each one. If the products are identical for each client, there must be other cost and sale factors that could determine which clients are more profitable.

Research pays off. It turns out that five clients consistently placed their dessert orders a week in advance. This gave the chef time to plan ingredient purchases and production. She had two large commercial ovens at home, which allowed her to bake a large number of items at a time. Her production time was baking time, and normal production was a smooth process.

During her review, she noticed that two clients, the Blue Heron and the Lakeside Café, didn't give her as much notice. On average, they placed orders just three days in advance. As a result, she had to scramble. Her purchasing and production had to be changed.

There's a financial impact, and it's relevant. The chef had to buy additional ingredients (such as flour, milk, eggs, sugar, and specialty food items) at the last minute — all the time.

Also, she had to buy less than her normal amounts. And she had to make extra trips back to her suppliers to buy for the two late-ordering customers. The chef paid relatively more for smaller amounts of ingredients, and her driving cost was the same as for a normal buy.

She should have passed those higher costs on to the Blue Heron and the Lakeside Café. Being a diplomat, she would have explained the situation to them. Before she sent any invoice with higher prices, she should have explained that ingredient costs were higher because they ordered later than other clients. "If you order a week in advance, the product cost will be lower, Mr. Customer!" Maybe this explanation would have changed the client's behavior.

What type of restaurant would be the ideal new customer? One that orders one week in advance. Her policy would be to be clear up front about ordering, maybe saying, "If you can't do that, Ms. New Customer, I charge a 5 percent fee. I run up more costs by ordering materials later than planned. I'm sure you can understand that." If I heard that, it would sound perfectly reasonable to me.

If you know of customer behaviors that increase your costs, you can do something about it! You can actually coach or train your clients, so you don't have to pass on the additional cost to them. They can change their behavior and get a better price.

Managing a business requires you to make decisions. In fact, you are making a business decision when you choose to do nothing. As you gather and analyze data, focus on your relevant costs and revenue. Relevant costs and revenue will be different, depending on the decision that you make. When you consider relevant information, you can make a well-informed business decision.

Chapter 12

Making Smart Pricing Decisions: Figuring Total Costs

*T*urn to any chapter in this book, and you'll find topics about analyzing costs to reduce or eliminate them. Now, a logical next step is to use your total costs to price your product for a reasonable profit. Enter the fascinating world of pricing.

Managers make pricing decisions. They decide what to charge for their products or services. These decisions determine what and how much to produce. Ultimately, production decisions then determine spending.

In this chapter, you see how prices affect the buying habits of your customers (an inconvenient truth). This chapter defines *product costing* and *target costing.* You analyze whether a given cost adds value or if the cost flat-out isn't needed. The goal is that you come away with a better understanding of how to price your products or services.

Understanding Influences on Prices

As you consider a price for your product, keep in mind how outside influences impact the price. Suppliers affect the cost of your product based on the rate they charge you for materials or component parts. If you set your price too high, clients might consider buying from one of your competitors. A customer may not buy the product at all (from you or anyone else) if they consider the price to be a lot higher than the product's value. This section discusses influences on your product's price.

Customers

The old saying goes "The customer is always right." (Actually, the *real* saying is, "The customer may not always be right, but he or she is *always* the customer.") Think of it another way: Treat the customer with respect. When it comes to pricing, deal with customers fairly. If you don't, they'll leave you and take their business elsewhere.

Technology allows smart customers to do their homework. If customers feel they aren't being treated fairly, they're be on the Internet in an instant, and they can find someone else who can offer the same product or service. Constantly improving technology is the great equalizer. Everyone has access to the same basic information about products and price.

Competitors

Customers are an influence in your pricing decisions. You have other influences that affect price, too.

Competitors are likely to offer products that compete directly with your products (which is why they're called competitors). It can hurt when a competitor cuts prices or improves product design, and you need to decide how to respond. You might cut your prices. Maybe you can innovate an improved product and keep your price the same. It's okay; you can analyze the costs you incur for each of your options and make a decision.

Customer can use technology to compare products as easily as they compare prices. If your competitor makes changes, and you don't respond in some way, you can expect to lose business quickly.

 Every business has (or should have) a website. It's true for both retailers and commodity suppliers. Smart customers research their purchases. In fact, they even research where to get the best, cheapest, and fastest lunchtime burger. When you go out for lunch, if your local sandwich shop tells you it doesn't need a website, it's a safe bet that it's losing business to a shop that has a site.

Suppliers

A reliable supplier can have an excellent impact on your prices. Consider the supplier that ships you a quality product and does it quickly. You have a dependable pipeline for supplies (retail goods or manufacturing material, for example). If you know what you're getting and when you're getting it, you can confidently build supply costs into your product's price.

Special orders

Whether or not a customer order is a special order could have a big influence on the price you charge. That's because generally speaking, your costs are different for a special order compared with orders you normally take from customers.

A special order assumes you have *excess capacity* — production capacity you're not currently using. The concept also assumes that all fixed costs have already been paid through regular production. As a result, fixed costs are irrelevant and aren't part of the decision to take on a special order. (Take a look at Chapter 11 for a review.)

You may be willing to accept a lower sale price for a special order because you have fewer costs to cover; however, there are some additional variables for special orders. There are cases where you actually may need to cover some of your fixed costs for a special order. In some cases, the special order may create *more* fixed costs.

Finally, your special-order sales price may be driven by a competitor's market price. You might have to keep your sale price low to beat a competitor's price.

Say you make baseball gloves. Table 12-1 shows your sale price, cost, and profit for regular production.

Table 12-1   Baseball Glove Company — Before Special Order

Units Produced: 300,000	Per Unit	Total
Sales (revenue)	$90	$27,000,000
Less:		
Fixed cost		-$3,000,000
Variable cost	$70	-$21,000,000
Profit		**$3,000,000**

A client contacts you with a special-order proposal. He's willing to pay $74 per glove for 100,000 gloves, but the special-order glove requires some setup costs. You have to make changes to equipment to manufacture the new glove. You also need to load a different chemical in your machinery to spray waterproofing material on each glove.

The additional fixed costs for the special order total $300,000, and you consider these costs a one-time fixed cost for this special order. Your other fixed costs have already been paid, so they are irrelevant. The variable costs remain. You incur material and labor costs for any good you produce — that's always true for normal production or a special order. Table 12-2 shows your sale price, cost, and profit for the special order.

Table 12-2   Baseball Glove Company — After Special Order

Units Produced: 100,000	Per Unit	Total
Sales (revenue)	$74	$7,400,000
Less:		
Fixed cost		-$300,000
Variable cost	$70	-$7,000,000
Profit		**$100,000**

The special order is profitable, so you should accept it. The profit is only $1 per glove ($100,000 profit ÷ 100,000 gloves). That's not nearly as good as the profit from regular production ($10 per glove), but money is money, and it's a darned sight better than letting your equipment sit idle.

But say the client isn't 100 percent satisfied with a price of $74, the price they *said* they were willing to pay. Get ready: You're about to be low-balled. The client tells you he has a bid from a competitor to make the gloves for $72.50 each.

Don't touch this one. The order isn't profitable at $72.50. Take a look at this calculation:

Profit = sales - fixed costs - variable costs

Profit = $7,250,000 - $300,000 - $7,000,000

Profit = -$50,000

Your "profit" is a $50,000 loss!

Pricing for Profits Down the Road

A special-order decision is a short-term decision. The excess capacity exists only short-term, so shift your thinking, and consider long-run pricing decisions. Think about those clients who place orders every month (hopefully with your company), and you get into a whole different set of pricing considerations. As it turns out, long-term decisions may be more important.

Reviewing market-based and cost-based pricing

Market-based pricing sets the product price based on customer expectations and demand. You take a look at the customer's perceived value of the product. Based on the customer view, you estimate how much he or she would be willing to pay.

Companies that face high levels of competition use market-based pricing. Customers may not see much difference between your product and that of your competitors. Say you sell lawn mowers. You compete with similar products that are all priced around $300. If you price your product at $350, a customer may not see any difference between you and the competition. The customer buys a lawn mower priced at $300 from somebody else.

With market-based pricing, you start at the top — with the price. After you nail down a price, you then look at costs. You compare price less costs to see if the profit is reasonable. There's pressure not to raise your price; the only way to increase profit is to cut costs.

Cost-based pricing assumes that you can differentiate your product from your competitors. Think about the latest technology gadget. A certain number of people want to have a new device right after it's launched, and they're willing to pay quite a bit for that privilege. Those customers perceive a high level of product value, even if the value is only in its being The Next New Thing. In high tech, the mantra is "Time to market is *everything.*" When the customer buys a hot product from a competitor, you won't be selling to that customer.

Using cost-based pricing, you look at costs first. You then consider how high a price you can charge, based on your estimate of customer demand. This pricing method allows you to start at the bottom (costs) and work your way up to a price. You set that price as high as you reasonably can to maximize your profit.

Aiming at the target: Target costing

Target costing is a two-step process to determine the cost of your product. First, you estimate a target price — an estimated price you think your customer is willing to pay based on market conditions. You use the target price information to compute the target cost. You consider

- Customer perception of the value of your product
- Customer perception of your product compared with your competitors'
- Your ability to differentiate your product from the competition

The first point is about the customer's perception of your product. You can find what it is by *asking*. Talk to your customers; that's the easiest and perhaps the soundest method (and you'd be surprised by how many small businesses never ask). If you have a sales force, your sales reps can ask your customers about everything from perceived quality to perceived speed of delivery. Formally, you could conduct surveys and focus groups.

The second point considers how your customers compare you to the competition. Again, just ask and thou shalt receive. People *love* to be asked. You also might consider paying a firm to perform market research for you. The cost of hiring the firm may be worth the specific customer information it can provide. The more you know about your customers, the better you can serve their needs.

The third point is about differentiation in products. There are numerous ways to see the differences. You can always simply buy a copy of the competitor's product, but there's more. See the discussion of reverse engineering later in this chapter.

It's elementary, Dr. Watson: Gathering information from many sources

If you're willing to play detective, there are several great ways to learn about your competitors. The more you know, the better. You may start off just learning about the competition's product, but when you're done, you'll know a lot about the competitor's business processes and philosophy. That knowledge can make a big difference. The result is that you end up with information to make more accurate comparisons between your product and that of the competition.

You can get competitor information from customers, suppliers, and public information. There are less savory techniques (and you better believe that low-integrity businesses have used them), but we won't go there.

- **Your customers:** Ask your customers if they have done business with your competition. Find out about their whole buying experience: the price they paid, how they were treated, the service they received. That's great information, and they are likely to be willing to share.

- ✔ **Suppliers:** A supplier might be tougher, but it's still worth a try. Suppliers may keep information on *current* clients confidential, but you might be able to get some data on a competitor who is a *former* client. A supplier can tell you what your competitor bought, how much, and possibly for what price, and maybe why the competitor stopped buying from them. Essentially, you're getting data on your competitor's supply costs.

- ✔ **Company publications:** Companies publish information for a variety of reasons. In some cases, they provide information to comply with industry rules or regulations. Corporations publish a glossy annual report for shareholders. Publicly traded companies must file Form 10-K with the Securities and Exchange Commission (SEC). This report may contain data that's helpful to your analysis. Look online.

- ✔ **The print media:** Many companies issue press releases to announce new products and services. Information appears in the general press and in industry journals. CEOs give interviews, too.

- ✔ **The Internet:** The Internet is the print media "writ large." Read company websites. See what analysis, industry experts, and journalists have to say about the company.

- ✔ **Reverse engineering:** An excellent way to gather information about a competitor and their products is through *reverse engineering*. You get their product and literally take it apart to see how the product was designed and assembled.

  The auto and high-tech hardware fields do a lot of reverse engineering. The great added value to a car, computer, or a smartphone is the design, so the best way to keep up with your competitors is to pull apart their latest product and see how it works.

  However, you may find surprises that have nothing to do with design. You can see, for example, where printed circuit boards were made or that the product was assembled in China, Indonesia, or Vietnam.

- ✔ **Intelligent guessing:** My experienced clients can make very shrewd guesses about how competitors are cutting corners to lower cost. A lawnmower manufacturer may say, "Oh, I bet they're using a low-quality blade." A restaurant owner may say, "My guess is that they use salad mix from a big bag instead of tearing the lettuce." Use your experience.

All of the intelligence (also known as the G2 or the MI6, for ex-military folks) can help you price your product intelligently.

Implementing target cost and target pricing

Now use what you've learned to create a target price and target cost. All costs, fixed and variable, are relevant costs.

Here are the steps to create your target price and target cost:

1. Choose a target price per unit.

2. Decide on a target operating income per unit.

3. Compute a target cost per unit.

4. Use *value engineering* to reach the target cost, if needed.

The overall goal is to increase product profitability. If the price is driven by outside market conditions or competition, the only way to improve your profitability is to cut costs. But which costs do you cut? First, eliminate those costs that don't add value.

Value engineering is a process that separates *value-added costs* from *non-value-added costs*. A value-added cost is necessary to produce a product to fit your client's needs. A value-added cost enhances the value of the product or service, making the product more attractive. That's a good thing. Nonvalue-added costs are just the opposite, and that's not a good thing.

Essentially, value engineering is the process that asks, "Do I really need to do that?" If the answer is yes, value will be added when you incur the cost. Consider rework costs — repairing a product defect. The cost of rework doesn't add value. The idea (of course) is to make the product correctly the first time. A rework cost is a nonvalue-added cost.

After you find nonvalue-added costs, take steps to reduce or eliminate them. Activity-based costing (see Chapter 5) explains that activities drive costs (cost drivers). To reduce the nonvalue-added cost, reduce the related activity.

Table 12-3 shows the target price and target cost calculations for a lawn mower company.

Table 12-3 Lawn Mower Company — Target Price and Target Cost

Units Produced: 200,000	Per Unit
Target price	$290
Less target operating income	$29
Equals target cost (A)	$261
Current full costs (B)	$270
Cost to be removed (B – A)	**$9**

You decide on a target price of $290 per unit for your lawn mowers. Earlier in this chapter, you noted that many competitors sell a similar lawn mower for $300, so you price your mower slightly below $300 to maintain competitiveness.

Your target operating income is your profit. Your goal is operating income of 10 percent of the target price ($290 × 10 percent = $29):

> Target cost = target price - target operating income
>
> Target cost = $290 - $29
>
> Target cost = $261

Your current full costs are $270 per unit, $9 above your target cost ($270 - $261). Your goal is to squeeze $9 per unit of nonvalue-added costs out to reduce your full costs to the target cost.

Consider the design of your lawn mower. Your design team has installed a bigger, heavier flap that hangs off the back of the mower. It will provide better protection from debris flying up toward the user. Because this design change was made, you're committed to buying a larger plastic part for each mower. You haven't yet written the check, but you're committed to doing so.

Thinking about design decisions and cost

Good companies constantly innovate and change products. One reason is to meet changing customer needs. Your clients want product improvements, and you make design changes to accommodate them. Of course, design decisions can have a big impact on your costs.

Another reason to innovate (that is, to make design changes) is to remove nonvalue-added costs. It's a constant, ongoing process. Finding and removing costs helps you meet your target cost goals.

Think about design changes. You can reduce the number of moving parts. That would mean fewer parts to buy and assemble. It would also mean fewer parts that might break. Consider designing parts that are *easier* to assemble, too. You can reduce labor hours and machine time if you simplify the assembly process.

The automobile industry is always looking for ways to make cars lighter. Lighter cars get better gas mileage. This might mean using more of some types of material — such as aluminum or polycarbonate — and less steel. The goal is to address customer demand for more fuel-efficient cars.

So that's the news about good product design. Poor product design has the opposite effect. A faulty design change locks in an unneeded product cost. Maybe you decide to attach an umbrella to the top of each lawn mower; however, it doesn't sound like a design change customers want. The design change means you've locked in a cost (the umbrella) for each lawn mower. You haven't written the check yet, but you're committed to buying the umbrellas.

Arriving at a Reasonable Profit

The search for a reasonable profit often starts with *cost-plus pricing*. Cost-plus pricing is a *bottom-up* method that starts with costs and adds a markup. Also, because very few products maintain the same level of sales decade after decade, you look at the concept of product *life cycle*.

Cost-plus pricing can be used only if your product is significantly different from other products in the marketplace. That's because you're adding a profit to your cost (a markup) and asking customers to pay that total sale price. The sale price might be much higher than other products sold by your competitors. To attract customers, your product must be very different.

Using cost-plus pricing

Cost-plus pricing is a pricing method that starts with full costs (fixed and variable costs — the entire cost of your product). You then add a percentage markup (that is, a percentage of the costs). Here's the entire formula for cost-plus pricing:

Proposed selling price = cost base (full costs) + markup

Say you sell vinyl siding for homes. Your cost for a 10-foot unit of siding is $7. You compute a 10 percent markup: ($7 × 10 percent = $.70). Your proposed selling price is shown as follows:

Proposed selling price = cost base (full costs) + markup

Proposed selling price = $7 + $0.70

Proposed selling price = $7.70

Reducing your markup

If you have to cut your selling price, it's easier to reduce markup than to cut costs. So be flexible about that markup. If customers make a judgment that they can buy the same siding for $7.25 a unit, they may buy somewhere else.

You need to consider cutting your selling price and accepting a smaller markup. A $7.25 selling price would be made up of a $7 cost basis and a $.25 markup. That markup is 3.6 percent of cost rather than 10 percent. You're price-competitive, but at the cost of operating at a lower profit level.

Larger companies with sufficient assets (and especially big cash balances) sometimes accept breaking even for short periods of time. *Breakeven* means that revenue only covers cost. The product generates $0 in profit.

A friend of mine works for a large construction company. Its clients are corporations who need to build or renovate factories. During a difficult economy, his firm made the decision to accept work that would simply be a breakeven deal.

The company made a decision that let it stay in business long-term. It was able to maintain relationships with clients and keep employees paid. This was all good, because many other construction companies were closing their doors because of a poor economy.

Often, companies that make it through difficult times end up with *more* business when things improve. They get new clients — those that previously were dealing with companies that closed.

One of the most important things about being in business is *staying* in business.

Computing a target rate of return on investment

There are several methods to decide on your markup. Although customer judgments about price and competitor pricing can limit the markup, there's another view.

Target rate of return on investment is a method you can use to compute a markup. It's a rate of return on the assets (investment) that you've invested in your business. First, consider rate of return on investment (also known as *ROI*).

Recall that assets exist to make money. You should have some idea about a reasonable rate of return on those assets. After all, you have choices. You can use the same assets to make several different products or provide several different services. You could also invest those assets in other companies and earn a rate of return. For example, the owner of a men's and women's shoe store might wonder if adding a line of sport shoes would have a better ROI than adding a line of children's shoes.

Say you operate a combination pizza parlor and barbeque restaurant (which is not an impossible fusion). You've added $100,000 in capital (cash) to your business. You buy equipment and expand. You base your product decisions on how the $100,000 investment would generate the most profit.

You invest the asset (cash) in equipment, labor, and advertising, finding a good balance between pizza ovens and barbeque equipment. Good news! You earn an additional $10,000. Your incremental rate of return is 10 percent ($10,000 ÷ $100,000).

Now you need to consider whether 10 percent floats your markup boat. To determine a reasonable rate of return, think about the source of your $100,000 in capital. If you borrowed, and if the interest cost was 7 percent on a $100,000 loan, a 10 percent ROI would probably be reasonable. The rate of return is higher than the interest cost. If you've sold an ownership interest in your business, consider what rate of return your investors expect on their investment.

Selling pizza and barbecue together isn't the strangest restaurant concept in the world. In California, there's a hot two-store chain called Tex Wasabi's Rock 'n' Roll Sushi BBQ. How's that for giving customers what they want? It may sound like an odd combination of products, but the company is filling a customer need.

Weighing other issues with cost-plus pricing

Cost-plus pricing is an inexact science. It can be difficult to determine the amount of capital you need for your product, and how to best spend it. Consider the $100,000 in assets in the last section. Converting the $100,000 cash asset to different assets (such as equipment and labor) is an exercise in estimating.

One way to think through your decision is to consider different cost bases and different markups on each cost base. For example, maybe you use variable cost as a cost basis and add a 6 percent markup. Next, you can look at full cost and add a 3 percent markup.

By adding markups and cost bases, you come up with different prices. You can then decide which price is most realistic. By realistic, consider your competition and markup percentage.

In the end, product pricing is about balancing factors. Consider the cost-plus pricing method (cost plus a markup). Balance that against target pricing (setting a price and then estimating costs).

Using product life-cycle budgeting

In various chapters in this book, you plan cost and prices over a month or year. It's not easy! Now you move into an area where you plan cost and prices over a product's life. The time frame is longer, the total costs are higher, and there's more financial risk if your forecast isn't accurate.

More time, more financial risk

The father of a friend of mine has a doctorate in chemistry. He's one of a group of 12 people who patented the chemical compound for a major over-the-counter drug. (You see the product's commercials all the time.) I'm told that it took 13 years from the time the compound was discovered to get to the point where the product was on the shelf. So a major drug company paid chemists to find the compound and then spent another 13 years testing, getting government approval, and marketing the drug. Imagine the financial risk to the drug company.

Product life-cycle budgeting is a planning method used to determine if a product is profitable over the long term. All the assets you plan to invest in a product could be used somewhere else, and you don't want to make a poor decision. You'd miss the chance to invest in another product that would be more profitable. Product life-cycle budgeting may be hard, but it's not impossible, and many companies need to do it.

Assessing the risks of your product's life cycle

There can be huge risks over a product's life. Here are some examples:

✔ Large upfront costs unrelated to production

✔ Long time periods to implement nonproduction activities

✔ Large number of locked-in costs

✔ Need to track costs over multiple time periods

✔ Competition could beat you to market

Discovering drug compounds that can be approved for medical treatment is expensive. The main cost is *research and development* (R&D), the cost to staff a department that conducts research and experiments on new products.

A risk for a pharmaceutical company is spending years (and millions of dollars) on product ideas that aren't viable.

Research and development costs are expensed as they're incurred. Consider what you've seen on the matching principle (see Chapter 9 for more).

The idea of the matching principle is that you match the revenue generated with the expense related to that revenue. *Match* means that the expense and revenue are recorded in the same accounting period (month or year). Good idea, but it's hard to do with the long-term development of a product.

The issue with R&D is that you often can't easily know which expenses led to a product that created revenue. If you sell a product that started in research and development ten years ago, which costs would you match with the revenue? Which years of R&D would you expense?

The solution to the R&D issue is to apply the conservative principle of accounting (see Chapter 9 for more). When there's a need to make a judgment, err on the side that shows a less attractive financial picture.

If you can't match an expense with a source of revenue, expense the cost immediately. That way, your current year's financials will reflect the higher expense — and less profit.

Decisions about product design create locked-in cost. If you develop a product over years, you're accumulating the cost of many design decisions. That leads to more locked-in costs. The automotive industry is the prime example. A car design is made up of hundreds (maybe thousands?) of individual design decisions. Each of those decisions will lock in material costs, as well as labor and machine costs.

Considering pricing strategies and life cycles

How you price your product is critical to the long-term success of your product. Further, the price may change (with good reason) many times during the product's life. Your pricing strategy has a huge impact on long-term profit.

Your pricing is influenced by your competitor's behavior (mainly pricing, but other factors, too). The customer's perceived value of your product is also a factor.

Skimming the market is the concept of charging a higher price for a new product. Your target customers are those who really want to try your product to "be one of the first."

The best example is technology. Everyone knows someone who's a gadget-loving techie. That's the kind of customer you're trying to reach when you skim the market. When that target group of customers has made a decision on purchasing, you probably have to change your pricing. You then reach another target group who are thinking, "Oh, I'll buy one of those when the price comes down."

Customer life-cycle costs represent the total process your *customer* goes through. The customer considers your product, buys it, uses it, and then (hopefully) considers buying it again. There are costs throughout the life cycle. Some describe this process as the cost to buy and use the product until it needs to be replaced. Some call it *total cost of ownership*.

Think about a new car or any big-ticket-item purchase. There are three cost components the customer considers:

- ✔ The purchase price of the product
- ✔ The cost to operate and maintain the product
- ✔ The disposal value of the product

When you buy a new car, it's obvious that you are putting out cash. If you finance the car, you're making payments and paying interest on the loan.

The new car comes with an owner's manual that includes a maintenance schedule, so you know how often the car needs oil changes, tune-ups, and so forth. You know that there's a cost to maintain the vehicle. If you don't maintain it, it won't operate correctly.

With a car, the disposal value is the trade-in value. When you go to a car dealership to replace the car, you negotiate a value for the old vehicle. That value reduces the cost of your new car. If you add the costs related to the bullet points above and subtract the disposal value of the car, that's the total cost of the product — purchase price + maintenance — disposal value. (Of course, you can always sell your old car privately for cash, which still should be included in the formula above as disposal value.)

Some carmakers use low cost of ownership to justify a higher selling price. Essentially, they're saying, "Our cars are built better than the competition. You pay more now, but you save with the lower maintenance costs."

Price discrimination is the strategy of charging different customers different prices for the same product. Now, you might say, "That doesn't make any sense. Word will get around, particularly with all the information on the Internet. Why would one customer pay more than another?"

The reason price discrimination works as a strategy is that cost isn't always driving the buying decision. Consider buying tickets to a major sporting event, maybe the Super Bowl. What you see with price discrimination is that customer behavior can be very different from "normal" — maybe dramatically different.

Demand inelasticity exists when demand for a product doesn't change with the price. Some buyers are insensitive (or less sensitive) to price changes. Their demand for the product won't change much as price changes. Think of these customers as the "must have, must go" customers.

Corporations use tickets to big sporting events for several reasons. A ticket can be a performance reward for a company manager. And tickets are a goodwill gesture to reward a customer or a supplier.

Therefore, corporate buyers are less sensitive to ticket price changes. I've seen situations in which a company paid a huge premium to get tickets for a valued customer, and at the last minute, too. The focus is on the person who's getting the ticket, not the price.

Price elasticity (sometimes called *price elasticity of demand,* or *PED)* exists when buyers (such as ticket buyers) are sensitive to price changes. Think about a rubber band stretching and contracting. That's what happens to demand as prices change. When a big Broadway musical offers group rates, student rates, and special rates for buying at the last minute, customers sensitive to price will buy.

Big fans of a team love their team, and when the team makes it to the big game, they want to go. But there's a limit to what they're willing to pay for a ticket. (Often, another family member who pays the bills is driving that cost decision.)

You probably know people who are big fans. Many of these people say to themselves, "Well, I'll go to the city where the game is. If I can get tickets, great. If they're too expensive, I'll watch the game somewhere close to the venue. At least I'll feel like I'm there." For this group, if prices go up, demand goes down. If prices go down, the big fans will jump on any available tickets.

If you understand the price elasticity of the groups of customers who want your product, you have an advantage. You can offer different groups different prices. Again, you're selling the same product (such tickets, in this example). The result is your average price, and the sales totals are enough to generate a reasonable profit.

Peak-load pricing is the technique of charging higher prices for the same product when demand is peaking. Here's a simple way of saying it: "If you want the product now, Mr. Customer, you have to pay more for it. That's because *everybody* would like the product now."

The best examples are in the travel industry. Think about hotels near the ocean. They usually have a higher room rate when the hotel is in demand. That might be summer, or during a busy vacation period (December holidays, school spring break, and so forth). In fact, the hotels may use the terms *peak* and *off-peak* to describe room rates.

Consider using peak-load pricing in your business. If demand is high, charge a premium (higher) price. Remember that at some point, business may slack off. When that happens, you may have to offer a lower price for your product.

Pricing decisions and regulation

Every business has to deal with regulation to some extent. Regulators, in this case, protect consumers so they are treated fairly. They accomplish this by enforcing *U.S. antitrust law* (sometimes called *competition law)*. The laws that outline fair pricing practices are in place to ensure fair trade and to protect consumers.

If you have some awareness of these issues, you may be able to recognize a situation when a competitor is violating a regulation or law. This isn't a law book, but an overview will help your business.

I think any suspicions you have about pricing should meet the common sense test. An experienced businessperson (like you) can often see when a deal looks "off."

If a business is selling a product at a loss (and you see specifics in a minute) *that* is a regulatory red flag. Because no company can survive over the long term selling at a loss, there may be something shady going on.

Price discrimination is okay. If a company's goal is to maximize profit, no problem! That's perfectly reasonable and allowed. If a company is using price discrimination to *destroy competition,* that's a regulatory problem.

Consider how much a competitor is cutting prices. If you think it's to the point that there isn't a profit, ask yourself why. Some reasons are legitimate, and some aren't.

The company may view a product as a loss leader. A *loss leader* is a product sold at a loss to entice people into the store. The hope is that the same customer may also purchase another product that is profitable. The goal is to develop new customers and more revenue over the long term. That's a perfectly reasonable strategy.

There may also be a purpose with less integrity. It's called *bait and switch.* When the customer comes to the store, she sees that the product is so inferior that she buys a costlier model.

Circling with the vultures

Contrast price discrimination with predatory pricing. *Predatory pricing* is the act of setting a low price to eliminate competition. Now, that's far different from a loss leader.

Here are the key points about predatory pricing:

- ✔ The predator company charges a price below its costs.
- ✔ The prices are so low that competitors are driven out of business.
- ✔ Fewer competitors reduce the supply of product.
- ✔ The predator company raises prices, taking advantage of the decline in supply.

It almost sounds like the plot of a movie, doesn't it? But it happens in real life. In 1904, Standard Oil controlled 91 percent of production and 85 percent of final sales of petroleum. The federal Commissioner of Corporations studied Standard's operations and concluded "beyond question . . . the dominant position of the Standard Oil Company in the refining industry was due to unfair practices — to abuse of the control of pipelines, to railroad discriminations, and to unfair methods of competition in the sale of the refined petroleum products."

For the purposes of this book, predatory pricing is defined as selling a product below variable costs. With a special order, the assumption is that other production covers fixed costs. So a special order just has to be priced above variable costs, and you make a profit. That's okay. But if your selling price is below variable costs, that's a red flag to a regulator.

Dumping occurs when a non-U.S. company sells a product in the United States, and the price is below the market price in its home country. Dumping has an impact. It has an adverse effect on a U.S. company that sells a similar product. The U.S. company has to show that it was "harmed" or "injured," but that's a legal issue.

Collusion pricing (also known as *price fixing*) occurs when companies collude, or work together and agree to keep prices artificially high. Are you shocked? Companies collude to achieve two outcomes. First, they hope to set a price above a normal competitive price — the price that a customer would pay in a true free market. Second, they hope to *restrain trade*. Restraint of trade is simply some kind of agreed-upon provision that's designed to limit another's trade.

Predatory pricing, dumping, collusion pricing, and restraint of trade are tools used by unethical businesses. Some elements are designed to "game" the system, and others are designed to force out competitors. No competition, no problem, right?

Part IV
Allocating Costs and Resources

The 5th Wave   By Rich Tennant

"Yes, it's normally 'spoilage, rework, and scrap,' but we've got a crap surplus as well."

In this part . . .

After you make decisions, you then have to allocate costs. And that's what Part IV is all about. The all-important topic of profit is examined, as is how sales affect profit. This part also delves into support and common costs, joint costs, process costing . . . at all cost, read this part!

Chapter 13

Analysis Methods to Improve Profitability

Cost accounting analysis is a balancing act between costs and profit. It's not enough to produce a product or service at the lowest possible cost. To be profitable, you must perform analysis to compute a sale price that generates a reasonable profit. Finally, customers must be willing to *pay* your sale price. At this point, you need to spend some time on cost allocation, pricing issues, and sales analysis.

In this chapter you spend some quality time with sales and profits. The chapter starts by taking another look at cost allocation and how it relates to cost hierarchy, including allocating corporate costs — expenses you incur for the head office. And there's a section that adds to what you've learned about customer revenues and costs. The chapter wraps up with a detailed look at several sales-related variances. (See Chapter 7 for an introduction to variances.)

Processing Cost Allocation

The process of allocating indirect costs to a product involves judgment. Unlike direct costs (which are *traced*), indirect costs are *allocated,* and that requires estimates. The process isn't easy, but it's vital. You need to allocate indirect costs carefully to understand the cost of an object, such as a product or service.

Getting a handle on allocations may appear difficult, but you can master the subject and then apply it to support the assumptions you use for cost allocations.

Why bother? Purposes of cost allocation

You need to spend about two seconds deciding if the cost allocation process is necessary. Yes, it is. Consider whether or not your company will benefit by using the process. Yes, it will. You need to do it, and the information you create will benefit your company. Here are several reasons why cost allocation is important:

- ✓ The process helps you make economic decisions — for example, whether or not to accept a special order.

- ✓ The information helps you evaluate and motivate your staff.

- ✓ Cost allocation supports the costs you report to customers when making bids for jobs.

- ✓ The information is used in financial reports you send to external parties.

Over in Chapter 11, you can read that decisions (economic decisions) about special orders and outsourcing require indirect cost information — generated, of course, by cost allocations. You can't make a management decision about costs without allocating indirect costs.

Many companies reward employees based on company profit or by meeting other financial goals. It works like this: In order to forecast profit — and review the results — you need to allocate indirect costs. These indirect costs affect your bottom line. Careful allocation of indirect costs helps you calculate financial goals. You then use those goals to evaluate and reward employee performance.

Many industries sign contracts with customers, particularly for long-term projects. Say you're building a factory for someone. Your contract states that you receive payments based on a percentage of completion; for example, you're due a payment when the work is 25 percent complete. One way to measure completion is to calculate the costs you've incurred. (After all, if you've spent 25 percent, you must be 25 percent done, right?) Cost allocation supports costs you report to fulfill a contract requirement.

Finally, cost allocation provides documentation regarding costs you use for financial reporting. For example, Chapter 9 addresses costs for inventory. A portion of those costs is allocated to the product. When you report inventory on your balance sheet, you're using cost allocation.

Justifying cost allocation decisions

Justifying cost allocation decisions is important. Your justification verifies that you're selecting the method that allocates costs most accurately. If you can defend your choice of an allocation method, it's likely that you've selected the best one.

Consider these four criteria that support your cost allocation decisions. Most organizations use one of these four criteria to support their cost allocation decisions:

- ✔ Document the activity that caused the costs to be incurred.
- ✔ Identify the benefits received as a result of incurring the cost.
- ✔ Justify that the cost is reasonable or fair with the other party in a contract.
- ✔ Show that the cost object has the ability to bear the cost.

The cause-and-effect criterion relates to activity-based costing concept (see Chapter 5). Say you make several kinds of ovens. You pay labor costs to change machinery setups to switch from making one model of oven to making a different model. The activity (setups) is driving the cost (labor hours). You then allocate more cost to the model oven that requires the most machinery setups.

Consider who might benefit from your spending. Say your product engineers make design changes to the ovens you produce. As a result, you notice that oven repairs under warranty decrease, and that reduces your warranty expense (repair costs). The lower cost of the change should be assigned to the new products, because they benefited from the change.

Businesses might sign contracts with customers. Think about that factory-building contract earlier in this chapter. Every industry has cost levels that are considered reasonable or fair. We may assign costs to the customer based on these levels that typically occur in the industry.

Think about a fixed overhead cost for insurance. You pay insurance premiums to cover a job site against theft or damage. Every builder incurs that cost. So everyone in the industry has an idea about a fair and reasonable cost of insurance. That's how you can justify your cost to the customer.

The more revenue and profits your division generates, the more costs you can bear (incur). Say you're deciding how to allocate the cost of your corporate headquarters (building, insurance, and salaries of head-office staff) to each company division. You might decide to allocate costs based on the percentage of total profit each division produces. If, for example, the Midwest division generates 30 percent of the profit, it would get 30 percent of the head-office cost.

The biggest arguments I've seen in companies have been over indirect cost allocations. Compensation, bonuses, and promotions are calculated on costs and profits, so there's a lot riding on the cost allocations to a division or department. If a cost allocation is increased, the manager might miss a profit goal and take a hit on his own personal compensation. You can imagine the conversations. "Why should we get that large cost allocation? We're the ones who are carrying the company. You're punishing our division for being successful! What's the motivation for increasing revenue and profit — you're just going to allocate more costs." I've been in the room when those very words were said.

As an owner, you need to consider how you evaluate managers. In particular, how do you fairly judge the manager who gets a big allocation of head-office costs? You see more on head-office allocations later in this chapter, but the short answer is to evaluate the manager's profit *before* counting the corporate-office cost allocation. In that way, the division manager isn't "punished" for a large cost allocation based on his or her division's profit total.

Implementing Cost Allocation

Now it's time to use a cost hierarchy to implement cost allocation. Your goal is to allocate costs more accurately, and a cost hierarchy can help you accomplish that goal. Typical cost hierarchies are costs at the division, batch, or unit level (see Chapter 5 for more). As the book keeps emphasizing, the more specific you make your analysis, the better. Cost hierarchies help you get more specific about your costs. After cost hierarchies, this section moves on to allocating corporate costs to units produced.

Using cost hierarchy to allocate costs

Cost hierarchy is a methodology that allows you to allocate costs more specifically, and that's good. Think of it this way: you have a "bucket" of costs. When you start taking costs out of the bucket, where do they end up? Maybe they end up attached to a unit. Or it might be broader. You could attach the costs to a batch (a group of units), and that's often a more accurate way to allocate. You could expand the allocation even more broadly to an entire company division.

One theme is all over this book: The benefit of performing any cost analysis should be greater than the cost to obtain it. Cost allocations may become complex. Complexity costs more, and you need to educate managers on how the cost allocations were derived. The managers will be concerned about how the cost allocation impacts their performance. You need to be prepared to justify your cost allocations. (That's why the company chief financial officer makes big money.)

Say you manage a company that makes refrigerators. You have a residential division and a commercial division. Your commercial customers are grocery stores that need refrigeration. Each division sells three different models. You have determined the cost hierarchies and cost allocation bases for your three largest indirect costs (see Table 13-1). (Recall that a cost allocation base is the type of activity you use to allocate costs.)

Table 13-1	Cost Hierarchies and Cost Allocation Bases		
Activity	*Cost*	*Cost Hierarchy*	*Allocation Base*
Manufacturing	Plant utility cost	Unit level	Machine hours
Machine setup	Labor cost	Batch level	Setup hours
Administration	Head-office salary	Facility sustaining	Company-wide revenue

You could allocate your plant's utility cost (heating, lighting, and so forth) to each unit you produce. When you change from making one refrigerator model to another, you incur setup cost to change your machinery settings, so you'd likely allocate setup labor cost to batches.

Say you need the ongoing administrative services (such as legal and accounting) provided by the head office, and that suggests allocating the cost company-wide. However, you can likely allocate head-office administrative cost to divisions, based on each division's percentage of total revenue.

Ideally, all costs are eventually allocated down to a unit of product. After all, you don't sell batches; you sell *units* of product. So you attach all costs to a unit of product. When you sell a unit, you recover all of your product costs — as well as earn a profit.

Allocating all costs to a unit is not always possible. Keep in mind that *all* costs are totaled and posted to your financial statements. Whereas an individual unit may not absorb the cost, your overall company profit or loss is affected by the cost.

Allocating tricky corporate costs

Each division should probably bear some of the cost of the company's corporate headquarters. Why? Because without the work done by the divisions, there wouldn't be a need for the corporate headquarters at all. However, corporate (head-office) costs can be hard to allocate to divisions. You need to develop a formula you can justify. Here are some typical corporate costs that are allocated:

✔ Interest expense on company loans

✔ Salary, benefits, and other costs for human resources, accounting, and legal staff

✔ Salary, benefits, and other costs for administrative staff

✔ Head-office building costs: utilities, insurance, and maintenance

Keep in mind that each division has its own set of costs, too — both direct and indirect. Each one, presumably, makes a product and has direct costs. And each division has indirect costs of its own. Each one has production managers, whose salaries and benefits are allocated as indirect costs to products. Those costs are all separate from the corporate costs.

Thinking about allocation methods for corporate cost

Your decision about allocation boils down to three choices:

✔ Allocate the entire corporate cost to the divisions.

✔ Don't allocate any corporate cost to the divisions; use the corporate cost only to evaluate company-wide financial results.

✔ Allocate some of the corporate costs based on a method that justifies a partial allocation.

Say you determine that the head office exists entirely to support the divisions. To fully price each division's product, each division should receive a corporate cost allocation. You "capture" all of the costs to make your product (in this case, refrigerators).

The second choice is to not allocate any corporate costs. It argues that because the divisions have no control over the spending at corporate headquarters, they shouldn't get an allocation. Now, that doesn't mean that the costs disappear, of course, but this choice will make the division managers happy!

Here's how your financials would look if you decide not to allocate any costs to the divisions. Check out Table 13-2.

Table 13-2	Income Statement — No Division Allocation
Residential profit	$10,000,000
Commercial profit	$7,000,000
Subtotal	**$17,000,000**
Less corporate costs	$5,000,000
Equals company-wide profit	**$12,000,000**

Corporate costs are sometimes called *common costs*. Because these are costs that the firm as a whole incurs, you may not be able to readily assign them to a specific division, department, product, or unit. So you show the common costs at the bottom of your income statement. That way, readers of the profit and loss statement (P&L) can see that those corporate costs aren't directly related to either the residential or the commercial division. (See Chapter 6 for more on profit and loss statements. For this book, *profit and loss statement* and *income statement* mean the same thing.)

The final option is to allocate some of the costs. Essentially, any corporate cost you can justify allocating gets allocated. You justify the allocation by finding a cause and effect. See the section "Justifying cost allocation decisions" in this chapter for more on cause and effect. Any cost you can't justify allocating to the divisions remains an unassigned corporate cost. These unassigned costs are shown at the bottom of the income statement, similar to the costs in Table 13-2.

You can also consider allocating costs if the division has some control over those costs. For example, insurance costs for all company buildings are paid through the head office. However, say each division works with the insurance company. The division determines the amount of insurance coverage and policy details. Because the division has some decision-making ability, it's reasonable to allocate those costs to the divisions.

Considering pooling corporate costs

Cost pools are used to separate costs into groups. The pools are then used to allocate costs to a cost object. Again, the cost object is the reason you're incurring costs. A cost object can be a unit of product, a batch, or a department of your company. Notice how similar the terms *cost pool, cost hierarchy,* and *cost allocation base* are.

Consider cost pools and your corporate costs. Your goal is to create cost pools that have the same cause and effect on the cost object. The same activities should cause your costs to increase or decrease. In other words, the cost behavior is similar for all costs in the cost pool.

For example, combining vehicle repair, vehicle maintenance, and vehicle insurance into one cost pool makes sense. If you increase vehicle use (cause), you increase these costs (effect). So put them in the same cost pool. Then consider where in the cost hierarchy the cost pool belongs — unit, batch, division, facility, and so forth.

You've seen several types of corporate costs at the beginning of this section. What's the cost driver for these costs? Here's one example: More employees may mean a larger human resources department and more human resources costs. Legal costs are normally a head-office cost. Here's a cost driver for legal costs: If your company manufactures products that may be dangerous to use, you may incur more legal costs.

Estimating a product's litigation risk

Litigation risk is the risk that someone will sue you because they believe using your product harmed them. Well-managed companies estimate the dollar amount of this risk.

Years ago, I worked on an audit of a large company. Among its products, the company made garbage disposals for sinks. It also manufactured ladders for fire trucks and emergency vehicles. If these two products are used improperly, people can hurt themselves.

This company had a large legal department. They spent a lot of time considering their risk of litigation (lawsuits). As a public company, they were required to file periodic financial statements

for the public. Those reports included their estimate on the future legal expenses, due to litigation.

So they had a big spreadsheet. The sheet listed every case that was currently in litigation. It included the dollar amount of the lawsuit and the percentage likelihood that they would lose the suit and have to pay damages. They multiplied the dollar amounts by the percentages, added up the total, and reported that amount as their potential risk of loss.

There are many other legal risks of doing business, but they are not the focus of this book.

Allocating corporate costs to divisions

Say that you've thought about cost pools and the cause and effect relationships. (Keep your thinking cap on. Some of these ideas might occur to you while you're brushing your teeth or singing in the shower.) You decide that all head-office costs should be allocated to the divisions, because you determine that the corporate costs are incurred primarily to support each division's business activity.

Assume your firm took out a loan to finance machines. The cost pool is the interest cost on the loan. You decide to allocate the interest cost to each division, based on the percentage of the total loan proceeds each division received. Your logic is that if the residential refrigerator division got 60 percent of the loan proceeds spent on machines, it should incur 60 percent of the interest cost.

Machine costs can also be allocated to each unit produced. So you can relate the interest cost of the machines purchased to individual units.

You decide to allocate the interest cost using machine hours (activity). What you end up with is each product receiving an indirect cost allocation for interest.

Say $50,000 of your $5,000,000 corporate costs (see Table 13-2) is for interest. That could be a 5 percent annual interest cost on a $1,000,000 loan. The residential division used 60 percent of the loan proceeds for machines, so it gets 60 percent of the interest cost:

Residential division interest cost allocation = company interest cost × 60 percent of loan proceeds used for machines

Residential division interest cost allocation = $50,000 × 0.60

Residential division interest cost allocation = $30,000

Now you need to allocate the $30,000 interest cost allocated to each unit of product. You do that using machine hours. Assume 2,000 machine hours for the year:

Residential division interest cost per machine hour = interest cost ÷ machine hours

Residential division interest cost per machine hour = $30,000 ÷ 2,000

Residential division interest cost per machine hour = $15

If a unit of product requires less than 1 machine hour (say, 20 minutes of time — ⅓ of an hour), the interest cost for that product would be $15 ÷ 3, or $5 of interest cost. And there you are! Each unit of product has $5 more attached to the product cost due to the interest paid on the machines.

Because interest cost took a lot of effort, it's a relief to look at simpler items. Otherwise, you'll fall asleep with this book in your hands.

Say you make a judgment that $2,000,000 in salary and other costs for corporate legal and accounting staff is a facility-sustaining cost, needed to support the business company-wide. That means that the cost should be allocated on a broad basis, not by unit or by batch. Consider the divisions.

You decide to allocate the legal and accounting costs based on percentage of total profit. Table 13-2 indicates that the residential division generated $10,000,000 of $17,000,000 in profit (before allocating corporate costs). It turns out to be 59 percent (rounded). Here's the cost allocation to the residential division:

Residential division legal and accounting cost allocation = $2,000,000 × 0.59

Residential division legal and accounting cost allocation = $1,180,000

Interest costs and the legal and accounting costs were allocated. Each used a different level in the cost hierarchy. Some of the $5,000,000 in corporate cost still needs to be allocated, but you get the idea of how to allocate the costs.

Again, your goal is to allocate all costs down to a unit of product. If you can't do that, any costs not allocated to a unit should still be posted to your profit and loss statement.

Keeping track of customer revenues and costs

So far, this chapter has discussed allocating costs to units, batches, and company divisions. Now change your thinking. Consider allocating costs to *customers*. In addition to costs, you allocate revenue to customers and compute the profit you earn.

Customer profit comes up in Chapter 11. In that chapter, you define your ideal customer as a client who generates a profitable business for you, is willing to pay a sales price that generates a reasonable profit, doesn't make unreasonable demands, and doesn't create unnecessary costs.

Now for more detail about customer profit analysis. Kick it up a notch! Your goal is to determine who your most profitable clients are. When you know who they are, you can focus on getting more business from that group.

Boning up on profit analysis

Customer profit analysis states that if client A generates a higher income for you than client B, client A should receive a higher level of attention. This is good for profits, but it's easier said than done. To understand the profitability of each client, you need to understand the costs that they create for your business.

Here's a classic case of implementing customer profit analysis. In the last decade, many large investment management firms made pretty radical changes in how they do business. First, they identified the investment clients that are the most profitable. They considered current profitability and potential growth in profit.

Next, the firms changed the service level they offered clients, based on their profitability. For the more desirable (higher-profit) clients, not much changed. They still dealt with the same investment representative. Less profitable clients saw a big change in service. Their accounts were transferred to newer, less-experienced investment professionals, and got less skilled attention. Customers at the bottom of the profit pile were given an 800 number. They lost the ability to contact a specific investment rep. Is that cool, or what? NOT!

As you can imagine, many low-profit customers were angry. "Why don't I get the same level of service anymore?" the client might ask. "Well, Mr. Customer, the profit you generate doesn't justify the level of service we were giving you." Now, I doubt the customer service rep would say it in those words. That's the same as saying; "You ain't worth it to us, buddy!" That, however, is the reason that the service level went down for some people.

If you choose to change the level of service you provide, expect some fallout. When you change how you treat customers, you may lose some business. These large firms were perfectly willing to accept that risk. I heard that story from several friends who worked for them. In the end, they started spending more time with the most profitable clients. That's one goal of profit analysis.

Breaking down purchase discounts

A discount is a price reduction. It's used to encourage the buyer to increase purchases. A discount should be a rare and wonderful thing, so be careful how you use it.

Remember that when you offer a discount, you're reducing your revenue per unit sold. If you don't get an increase in unit sales (and that's the point), offering a discount decreases your profit over time.

Imagine a discount conversation between a salesperson and the chief financial officer (CFO). The salesperson explains that a new client will place an order if it can get a discount. The CFO asks, "Will the new client place orders down the road? How large a client will they be? Does the client currently order a lot of product from a competitor, and is it business that could come to us if we offer a discount?" That's the conversation that should happen before you approve a discount.

Isolating customer costs

Recall that you categorize customer costs by cost pools. For example, you've seen how vehicle costs (repair, maintenance, and insurance costs) are combined into a cost pool. Next, you *trace* or *allocate* the cost pool, based on a cost level (unit, batch, or company division). Finally, you consider the activities that lead to costs. Ultimately, your goal is to understand what activities are causing costs for the company. You use that knowledge to reduce or eliminate the activities that create those costs for you — not that you can always do this. Now let's isolate some of those activities and costs.

Say you own a catering business. (The two hardest-working people I know owned catering companies.) You're reviewing three clients who all purchased the same catering product in December — a dinner with dessert, served to 50 people. You charged $30 per person. Table 13-3 lays out three cost variables that differed among these customers.

Table 13-3   Catering Business — Isolated Costs and Activities

Activity	Cost Driver
Purchase discount	Judgment by owner
Food delivery	$3 per delivery mile
Staff at event	$30 per hour per person

Table 13-4 displays the dollar amount of costs for three customers.

Table 13-4	Catering Business — December Profit by Client		
Client	**A**	**B**	**C**
Revenue	$1,500	$1,500	$1,500
Food cost	-$1,000	-$1,000	-$1,000
Discount	-$75	$0	-$150
Delivery	-$60	-$120	-$75
Staff time	-$120	-$150	-$135
Profit	**$245**	**$230**	**$140**

Huh? What's happening? Client C received the largest discount (10 percent) but generated the least profit ($140). Start to pull apart Table 13-4. The revenue and food costs are the same for each client. That makes sense, because you're providing the same product (50 meals at $30 per meal).

Consider the discount. Client A received a 5 percent discount; Client C was given a 10 percent discount. Why? The salesperson's goal was to get the order from Client C — that's one reason. The other motivation is to get more (or larger) orders in the future.

You can't look at one catering event and determine if the discount paid off. Consider the whole year, or the next year. Does the client purchase more catering services (hopefully, yes)? Do those events generate any extra costs (hopefully, no)? These questions illustrate why offering a discount is a risk. You give up profit now in the hope that you'll make it up with more business down the road.

Your delivery cost is driven (no pun intended) by cost per mile. You can't control how far away an event is; however, consider whether or not you need to make any extra trips. If so, you need to coach or train your client in advance to be prepared for an additional cost. That can be explained and put into your catering contract. Something like "Any extra trips to the catering event will be assessed a cost of . . ." You get the idea.

You've determined that this type of event typically lasts two hours and requires two staff people to handle the catering. So you'd expect a staff cost of $120 ($30 per hour × 2 hours × 2 people). Two clients required more time. Again, ask, "Why?" Did the customer make unusual demands? (My catering friends tell me some clients expected them to perform light cleaning after events, even though that's not what the catering company agreed to.)

Labor cost is another opportunity to train your client in advance. Explain and document in the catering contract how you handle extra time incurred. At what point is a customer billed for that service? Can your staff stay an extra 15 minutes without charging? Thirty minutes? Think through all of this before you market to clients.

Client A was the most profitable. That client was given a small discount ($75). It happened to generate the lowest food delivery cost ($60). Well, it might just be luck that it was the closest location. Finally, it had the lowest staff cost ($120).

There's a lot of food for thought (again, no pun intended) in Table 13-4. Think about that discount issue and how to recover costs for extra delivery and staff time expense, with no "ups" and "extras."

Going Over Sales Mix and Sales Quantity Variances

Recall that a variance is a difference between your budget and your actual results. There are two basic reasons for a cost variance: You either *spent* more or less than planned, or you *used* a different amount than planned (see Chapter 7).

There's a third factor that produces a variance — a difference between your budgeted and actual sales. One of these sales variances is the *sales mix* variance. The *sales mix* is the percentage of each product you sell, compared to total sales. If you sell less of product A, maybe you can sell more of product B and still reach your sales and profit goals. (I seem to always use A and B, but I admit that they aren't very sexy product names.) Refer to Chapter 4 for more on sales mix.

Remembering variances and contribution margin

The challenge with sales mix is that each product is likely to have a different sale price and different costs. You need a tool to compare two products and their profitability. Contribution margin per unit should help. Then you're able to say, "Product A is a high-profit item, but product B isn't that big a deal."

For this section, you use contribution margin per unit because you'll undoubtedly sell a different number of units of each product, and taking a look at per-unit amounts eliminates the issue of selling different amounts of product.

There's another reason for using contribution margin. The amount represents what you have left to cover fixed costs. Whatever's left after paying fixed costs is your profit. (Yes, profit is "in there" somewhere.) So contribution margin is calculated *before* considering fixed costs. In fact, contribution margin is also called *contribution to profit.*

Sales and variable costs are attached to a product, with rare exceptions. If you're comparing product profitability, focus on sales and variable costs. They are the best way to judge an individual product's profit.

Getting the story about sales mix variance

Connect the sales mix concept to variance analysis. The goal is to use the completed variance work to improve your overall company profit.

Say you own a hardware store that sells two types of ceiling fans: a 52-inch bronze fan and a 54-inch pewter fan. You created an April budget for both products. The bronze fan's budget has a $180 selling price ($150 variable cost and $30 contribution margin) per unit. The pewter fan's budget is a $450 selling price ($350 variable cost and $100 contribution margin per unit).

Table 13-5 shows the budgeted contribution margin in dollars for both products.

Table 13-5	Budgeted Contribution Margin in Dollars		
Product	*Margin/Unit*	*Sales in Units*	*Margin in Dollars*
Bronze	$30	120	$3,600
Pewter	$100	80	$8,000
Total	**N/A**	**200**	**$11,600**

Note that Table 13-5 doesn't list a total contribution margin per unit (see N/A). That's because you consider contribution margin per unit *by individual product* (bronze versus pewter fans). Because the sales mix changes, you add each product's total contribution margin in dollars to get a total.

You budgeted to sell 200 ceiling fans and generate a total contribution margin of $11,600. Bear in mind that fixed costs aren't part of the contribution margin calculation. I'm just talking basics here.

Now you take a look at the April actual results. You sold 110 bronze fans (not so good) and 100 pewter fans (good). Table 13-6 shows the *actual* contribution margin in dollars. Note that the contribution margin per unit is the same as Table 13-5 for both products.

Table 13-6	Actual Contribution Margin in Dollars		
Product	**Margin/Unit**	**Sales in Units**	**Margin in Dollars**
Bronze	$30	110	$3,300
Pewter	$100	100	$10,000
Total	**N/A**	**210**	**$13,300**

Connecting sales mix to contribution margin

You sold ten more units in April than budgeted (200 versus 210). Your actual sales mix is also different than budgeted. Table 13-5 indicates that 60 percent of your budgeted sales were bronze ceiling fans (120 of 200 units). Your actual sales were 52.4 percent (110 of 210 units). Okay, so you sold fewer bronze fans, based on the percentage of total sales.

The difference (variance) in bronze fan sales is important, because bronze sales are less profitable than pewter fans. You just saw that contribution margin per unit should be used to judge profit, so you'll use that calculation. (The amazing thing is that people bought more of the costly pewter fan. Go figure!)

To fairly compare profit for both fans, take a look at contribution margin as a percentage of the sale price per unit. Contribution margin per unit doesn't change between budgeted and actual amounts. That means that the sale price per unit and variable cost per unit (the components of contribution margin) don't change.

Here's the contribution margin percentage for the bronze fan:

Bronze fan contribution margin in sale price = $30 ÷ $180 × 100

Bronze fan contribution margin in sale price = 16.7 percent

The contribution margin of $30 per unit, divided by the sale price per unit of $180, gives you the percentage. Here's another way to saying it: For every $1 of sales, about 17 percent (17 cents) of contribution margin is generated. Now compare that to the pewter fan:

Pewter fan contribution margin in sale price = $100 ÷ $450 × 100

Pewter fan contribution margin in sale price = 22.2 percent

Based on contribution margin as a percentage of the sale price per unit, the pewter fan is more profitable.

The investment management business generates some of the highest contribution margins of any industry. Think about this: How much more cost do you incur to move from $1 billion under management to $10 billion? Not much. With technology, you can perform analyses and make investment decisions without adding much cost. Better technology also allows you to generate client statements quickly. (One of the biggest marketing keys to an investment management firm is an easy-to-read customer statement.)

In an investment management firm, the largest cost of growth is adding staff to serve the clients. But if the same client base is adding investment dollars, you don't need to add many people. The contact person may be the same, whether he or she manages $10 million of investments or $50 million. Conclusion: Billionaires make the best investors.

Introducing the sales mix variance

You've seen the rest; now see the best! Look at the sales mix variance.

Recall from the last section that your actual sales mix was slightly different from budgeted. Note that the $13,300 actual contribution margin in dollars (Table 13-6) is higher than the $11,600 budgeted total (Table 13-5). Your sales mix shifted to the more profitable product.

The pewter product's contribution margin as a percentage of the sale price is higher than the bronze product (22.2 percent versus 16.7 percent). You saw in the previous section, "Connecting sales mix to contribution margin," that the bronze sale percentage declined (from 60 percent to 52.4 percent). That means that the pewter sales percentage increased (up from 40 percent to 47.6 percent). You increased sales of your more profitable product.

Here's the formula for sales mix variance:

Sales mix variance = actual units sold × (actual sales mix percent – budgeted sales mix percent) × budgeted contribution margin per unit

Yikes! That looks complex. Now pull apart some of the components, and you can make sense of it.

Consider the difference between actual and budgeted sales mix. For the bronze fan, that total is 52.4 percent – 60 percent, a 7.6 percent decline. Because the bronze fan went down 7.6 percent, the pewter fan's percentage increased by 7.6 percent.

Now multiply the sales mix difference by the budgeted contribution margin per unit. For the bronze fan, you have $30 × -7.6 percent, and that's -$2.28. The pewter fan is $100 × 7.6 percent, and that's $7.60. Finally, you can plug the calculations into the sales mix variance formula, as shown in Table 13-7. I don't know about you, but I definitely want an extra $7.60 each time I sell a product than an extra $2.28.

Table 13-7		Sales Mix Variance	
Product	**Actual Units**	**Mix Percentage and Contribution Margin**	**Variance**
Bronze	110	-$2.28	-$251
Pewter	100	7.60	$760
Total	**N/A**		**$509 favorable**

The Mix Percentage and Contribution Margin amounts were calculated in the paragraphs before Table 13-7. The table multiplies actual units by the mix percentage and contribution margin column to compute the variance.

A positive number for a sales variance is a good thing. It means that the contribution margin in dollars was higher than planned. So the $509 sales mix variance is a favorable variance. Because you sold more of the more profitable product, you generated more profit.

Calculating sales quantity variance

The sales mix variance focuses on the shift in sales mix. The percentage of sales of the pewter fan increased. The *sales quantity variance* reflects the difference between actual and budgeted units sold. Here's the formula:

Sales quantity variance = (actual units sold – budgeted units sold) × budgeted sales mix percentage × budgeted contribution margin per unit

Pull the formula apart to understand it, and use Tables 13-5 and 13-6. Actual sales of bronze fans were 10 units lower than budgeted (110 - 120). Actual sales of the pewter fan were 20 fans higher than planned (100 - 80).

Even if you kept the sales mix the same at 60 percent and 40 percent, the volume of each product sold had an impact on your profitability. Table 13-8 explains that impact.

Table 13-8 computes the sales quantity variance.

Table 13-8	Sales Quantity Variance		
Product	*Change in Units and Budgeted Mix*	*Budgeted Contribution Margin Per Unit*	*Variance*
Bronze	(110-120) x.60	$30	-$180
Pewter	(100-80) x.40	$100	$800
Total			**$620 Favorable**

The variance is favorable, which means more profit. The bronze fans sold went down by 10 units, but the pewter fan sales increased by 20 units. The increase in total units sold (going up from 200 to 210) had the biggest impact on the favorable sales quantity variance.

Last, consider *sales volume variance*. This variance measures how much impact a change in the number of units sold had on your profit and loss statement, either because the sales mix was different or the sale quantity in units was different. This variance is the sum of the sales mix variance and the sales quantity variance. Those amounts are listed in Tables 13-7 and 13-8. Here's the sales volume variance calculation:

Sales volume variance = sales mix variance + sales quantity variance

Sales volume variance = $509 + $620

Sales volume variance = $1,129 favorable variance

Both components of the sales volume variance are favorable variances. You improved your sales mix by shifting sales to the product with a higher contribution margin per unit. The sales quantity variance is favorable, because your actual sales were higher than budgeted. Favorable + favorable = favorable!

Chapter 14

Behind the Scenes: Accounting for Support Costs and Common Costs

· ·

In This Chapter

▶ Distinguishing between single rate and dual rate cost allocation

▶ Considering support cost allocation methods

▶ Allocating common costs

▶ Thinking about customer contracts

▶ Working with government customers and costs

· ·

Many vital business activities happen behind the scenes. These are known as *support activities,* and they reinforce the departments that make products or deliver services.

The work isn't visible to the customers, but it can make or break your business. If you perform this work poorly or overspend on the process, your business may incur a loss. Allocating the costs of these activities correctly is critical. The allocation affects accurate product costing and better product pricing.

There are several types of behind-the-scenes costs. *Support costs* are costs incurred for activities that assist other company departments. *Common costs* are costs shared by multiple departments. This chapter discusses methods for assigning these costs.

There's also a discussion of customer contracts. The issue of contracts comes up in several chapters of this book; in this chapter, you see how to handle contract costs. The chapter wraps up with tips on working with federal, state, or local governments.

A customer contract may dictate how you handle support costs and common costs. When you negotiate a contract with a customer, you need to understand how support and common costs affect your business.

Not Everyone Generates Revenue: Support Costs

Support costs are incurred to provide a product or service to a company operating department. An *operating department* is a department that makes a product or provides a service for customers — something for "the outside world." You may see the term *operating manager* or *line manager* to refer to someone who manages an operating department.

A *support department* exists to help operating departments. Support departments can also provide services to one another. That makes the cost allocation to the product or service that goes out the door a little more complicated. Your goal is to properly allocate costs, so you know the full cost of your product.

Introducing single rate cost allocation method

The concept of allocating a cost is in practically every chapter of this book, so you probably have bumped into it before. The *single rate cost allocation method* uses one cost rate to dictate the dollars that are allocated from a cost pool to a unit, batch, department, or division. In the case of support departments, the rate allocates dollars to another department or division.

The single rate method doesn't distinguish between fixed and variable costs. Now, if it strikes you that this kind of allocation doesn't seem very specific, you're right.

Of course, more specific cost analysis leads to more precise cost allocations (a recurrent theme in cost accounting). But for now, you use one rate to allocate costs. The principle is incredibly simple: When you compute the single cost allocation rate, *you multiply it by actual usage* (activity) to apply the cost to the cost object.

Check out the example in the following sections.

Figuring out the cost allocation rate

Say you manage an online tutoring business. Your instructors serve two markets — high school students and adult continuing education students — so your firm has a high school division and an adult ed division. Both company departments use technology in a big way. Your computer department (called *information technology,* or *IT)* installs software, trains staff, backs up data, and repairs computers.

The IT department has fixed costs that include the salary and benefits for five employees and the equipment (hardware and software) they use each day. The department also incurs variable costs, incurred when staff spends time working on technical issues (see Table 14-1). The variable expense can include hardware and software costs, as well as the expense of outside experts.

Table 14-1	IT Department — Budgeted Cost Pool	
Fixed costs		$2,000,000
Variable costs		
	Variable cost per hour	$200
	Budgeted hours	3,200
	Total variable costs	$640,000
Total cost pool		$2,640,000

Your single rate budgeted cost allocation rate is

Single rate budgeted cost allocation rate = cost pool ÷ budgeted hours

Single rate budgeted cost allocation rate = $2,640,000 ÷ 3,200

Single rate budgeted cost allocation rate = $825 per hour

The single cost allocation rate is $825 per hour.

Pulling apart the single rate cost allocation

Fixed costs should be viewed in total dollars. From the IT department's point of view, the job is to allocate $2,000,000 in fixed costs. But consider the high school division manager's view of the IT cost allocation rate. He sees that $625 of the $825 allocation rate is to cover fixed costs. If the manager uses the department for an hour, he is billed $825, and that's going to be upsetting.

In the high school division manager's world, the cost for computer services looks too high. The manager might consider going outside the company to get help at a lower price. Say the division manager gets outside computer help at $500 per hour. The division saves $325 per hour ($825 - $500).

Like many things in life, there's good news and bad news with such a decision. When a manager goes outside the company to save $325 an hour, he lowers costs of the division and increases divisional profit. However, the company as a whole must still cover the entire $2,000,000 fixed cost of the IT department. If both divisions go outside the company for computer help, overall company profit goes down. The company's still incurring a fixed cost for the IT department — a department that not being fully utilized.

As you might expect, companies have various policies to prevent this from happening. For example, they may tell the division managers they'll be charged for the fixed cost portion of the IT department, whether they use the services or not.

Sure, the division can use an outside service for computer support, but that decision may not make sense, because it still pays a share of the fixed cost of the IT department. If the manager adds the fixed cost plus the cost of an outside vendor, the division is worse off financially.

Looking at actual results

At the end of the year, you take a look at actual hours of use. The high school division used 1,300 hours. The adult education division used 1,800 hours. Table 14-2 applies the budgeted cost allocation rate to actual hours of usage.

Table 14-2	IT Department — Applied Cost Pool	
High school division		
	Allocated rate	$825
	Actual usage hours	1,300
	High school allocation	**$1,072,500**
Adult ed division		
	Allocated rate	$825
	Actual usage hours	1,800
	Adult education allocation	**$1,485,000**
Total allocation		**$2,557,500**
Total usage hours		**3,100**

The actual allocation is less than budgeted ($2,557,500 actual versus $2,640,000 budgeted), because 3,200 budgeted hours were more than the 3,100 actual hours.

Your actual results rarely agree with your budgeted amounts. The difference between budgeted amounts and actual results is called a *variance*. Stroll over to Chapter 7 for more. So variances are to be expected.

It's critical that you understand your costs and that you can explain the cause of any variances. That's because your division managers will ask you to justify your budgeted amounts — and explain any differences between budget and actual numbers. A manager's performance review and compensation are affected by these results.

Checking out dual rate cost allocations

The preceding section addressed the single rate cost allocation method. You saw that this method put your costs into one bucket for analysis. You noted that the cost information was more useful when it was separated between fixed and variable costs.

The *dual rate cost allocation method* categorizes cost into two types of cost pools: fixed costs and variable costs. You calculate a different cost allocation rate for each cost pool. A more specific review of costs leads to more precise cost allocations. (You can check out Chapter 5 for specifics.) The dual rate allocation method is more specific than the single rate allocation. See for yourself in a minute.

In the section "Pulling apart the single rate cost allocation," you see that the budgeted fixed cost allocation rate for the IT department was $625 per unit. Continuing that example, here's a two-step process to calculate the *dual* rate cost allocation of the IT department:

✔ Multiply the budgeted fixed cost allocation rate by the budgeted usage

✔ Multiply the budgeted variable cost allocation rate by the actual usage

Note that the cost allocation rates are multiplied by different usage amounts. Here's a way to keep the difference straight: It's possible that your budgeted fixed cost come in as planned. In fact, your fixed cost may involve a contract (lease agreement, insurance premiums) that *cannot change* after budgeting. That's a way of remembering that you use budgeted usage for fixed cost allocations.

Variable costs are harder to pin down in planning, so you use actual usage for the variable cost allocations.

Table 14-3 show the total budgeted fixed cost for the IT department.

Table 14-3   Dual Rate Allocation — Total Budgeted Fixed Cost

Fixed Allocation Rate	Budgeted Usage Hours	Budgeted Fixed Costs
High school division		
$625	1,500	$937,500
Adult education division		
$625	1,700	$1,062,500

The next step for a dual rate calculation is to compute the variable costs. Using the IT department example, you see the related info in Table 14-4.

Table 14-4   Dual Rate Allocation — Total Variable Cost

Variable Allocation Rate	Actual Usage Hours	Budgeted Fixed Costs
High school division		
$200	1,300	$260,000
Adult education division		
$200	1,800	$360,000

Using the dual rate method of allocation, the *total* IT department cost allocated to the high school division would be

> High school division IT department cost allocation = fixed costs + variable costs
>
> High school division IT department cost allocation = $937,500 + $260,000
>
> High school division IT department cost allocation = $1,197,500

The adult education division's cost allocation is $1,422,500 ($1,062,500 fixed cost + $360,000 variable cost). The data come from Tables 14-3 and 14-4. If you add the two allocations, you get $2,620,000, the total IT department allocation.

Table 14-1 shows budgeted costs of $2,640,000. No actual usage amounts were used. In Table 14-2, applied costs total $2,557,500. That table takes the $825 budgeted rate per hour and multiplies by the actual hours.

Consider why the dual rate cost allocation total is different from both Table 14-1 and 14-2. It's because the fixed portion of the allocation is based on budgeted information only. The fixed cost rate and usage are both budgeted amounts. You calculate variable costs as budgeted variable cost rate × actual hours of usage.

The dual rate method allocates your costs more precisely than the single rate process. That's because the dual rate method separates the analysis of fixed and variable costs. A more precise allocation means that your full product cost is more accurate.

Using practical capacity to determine cost allocation rates

Practical capacity is the maximum level of capacity you can handle, taking into account unavoidable delays. Unavoidable delays might include the facts that your production staff takes vacation and that you need to schedule repair and maintenance to maintain your equipment. After you account for those types of production stoppages, you can calculate practical capacity. Take a gander at Chapter 9 for more info.

The IT department example in the previous sections considered usage based on demand. The 3,200 hours of usage in Table 14-1 is based on demand. Practical capacity is different.

Practical capacity views your production level from the supply side — not the demand side. "What if my department had all of the work it could handle? How would that level of production look?" That's what you ask yourself when you're using practical capacity to determine cost allocation rates.

This section considers the impact of using practical capacity for single rate and dual rate cost allocations. There is some fallout, because cost allocations may change. Those changes may affect decisions your managers make.

Budgeting with practical capacity and single rate allocations

Say you operate a marketing company. You service clients in the financial services market and the medical market, and you have separate divisions to service each of them. The printing and web services department supports both divisions, providing all printed ads, marketing pieces, and websites designed for clients.

Costs are allocated based on each division's usage in hours. In planning, you determine that the financial services division needs 2,000 hours and the medical division needs 1,800 hours.

Table 14-5 shows the budgeted cost pool, using budgeted usage (hours).

Table 14-5	Marketing Support — Budgeted Cost Pool	
Fixed costs		**$2,500,000**
Variable costs		
	Variable cost per unit	$210
	Budgeted hours	3,800
	Total variable costs	**$798,000**
Total cost pool		**$3,298,000**

Your single rate budgeted cost allocation rate is

Single rate budgeted cost allocation rate = cost pool ÷ budgeted hours

Single rate budgeted cost allocation rate = $3,298,000 ÷ 3,800

Single rate budgeted cost allocation rate = $868 per hour (rounded)

Now consider just the fixed cost portion of the cost allocation. The cost allocation rate is $658 per hour ($2,500,000 ÷ 3,800 rounded).

Next, you take a look at the same calculation, using practical capacity in Table 14-6. You "put the pedal to the metal" by maxing out your available hours for providing marketing support. You determine that the financial services division can generate 2,500 hours, and the medical division can generate 2,000 hours.

Table 14-6	Marketing Support — Budget with Practical Capacity	
Fixed costs		**$2,500,000**
Variable costs		
	Variable cost per unit	$210
	Practical capacity hours	4,500
	Total variable costs	**$945,000**
Total cost pool		**$3,445,000**

Consider what's changed. The practical capacity hours are higher than budgeted hours (4,500 versus 3,800). It should make sense that the total variable cost goes up ($945,000 versus $798,000), because you multiply the variable cost per unit by the practical capacity hours.

Your single rate budgeted cost allocation rate is

Single rate budgeted cost allocation rate = $3,445,000 ÷ 4,500

Single rate budgeted cost allocation rate = $766 per hour (rounded)

Now consider just the fixed cost portion of the cost allocation. The cost allocation rate is $556 per hour ($2,500,000 ÷ 4,500 rounded).

The single cost allocation rate is multiplied by actual hours (usage) to apply costs to each division. Multiply the practical capacity rate of $766 by the actual hours used to calculate the cost allocation for each division.

What you've just seen is a reminder of the risks of looking at fixed costs per unit. The practical capacity fixed cost allocation ($556 per hour) is lower than the fixed rate at budgeted capacity ($658 per hour). Hey, I'll take it! Lower costs are always better. Keep in mind, however, that the only reason the fixed cost per unit is lower is because you're spreading the same dollar amount ($2,500,000 in fixed costs) over a higher number of hours. You have to cover your fixed costs, come what may. If you don't, you can't generate a profit.

Considering practical capacity and dual rate allocations

Recall that *budgeted hours* are used to calculate the dual rate cost allocation. In this section, the *practical capacity hours* are used. So the fixed cost rate is $556 per unit (see the previous section). Here's the first part of the dual rate cost allocation method:

Dual rate method, fixed cost portion = budgeted fixed cost per unit × budgeted hours

Dual rate method, fixed cost portion = $556 × 4,500

Dual rate method, fixed cost portion = $2,500,000

To finish the dual rate calculation, you need the $210 variable cost per unit from Table 14-6. Assume your actual hours used by both divisions total 4,200. Here's the variable cost for the dual rate method:

Dual rate method, variable cost portion = budgeted variable cost per unit × actual hours

Dual rate method, variable cost portion = $210 × 4,200

Dual rate method, variable cost portion = $882,000

Your dual rate cost allocation (to both divisions) is $3,382,000 ($2,500,000 fixed cost + $882,000 variable cost).

Is using practical capacity practical?

Yeah, these calculations are a lot of work, so it's good to ask yourself if the extra effort is worth it. Consider what, if anything, you gain by collecting more information. Well, there is a method to the practical capacity madness.

Walk through it in your mind one more time. If you use practical capacity, the hours (or any activity) will be higher. Again, practical capacity assumes your customers need everything you produce. Practical capacity spreads your costs over more hours, so your cost per hour declines.

Here's the benefit of using practical capacity: Because you're allocating a lower cost per unit, less gets allocated to each division. Using practical capacity helps you avoid overburdening. *Overburdening* is defined as allocating too much cost to a division (or to anything). The downside is that more costs aren't allocated — they stay at the corporate level.

Essentially, using practical capacity requires corporate management — not division management — to figure out whether the cost allocations are reasonable. Even more important, corporate management has to justify "keeping" the costs that aren't allocated to the divisions.

Once more, with feeling: You'd prefer to allocate all costs to a unit of product. If you can't, the cost ends up on your profit and loss statement.

Going Over Variance Analysis and Department Costs

A *variance* is a difference between budgeted and actual costs. See Chapter 7 for an extensive discussion. When you analyze variances, you learn from them. Understanding a variance can help you reduce costs and possibly eliminate them.

In this section, you perform variance analysis at the department level. Variance analysis will identify areas in each department where you can reduce or even eliminate costs. All of this effort can improve company-wide profit.

Passing the cost allocation buck

I once worked for a large insurance company. The company name is being withheld to protect the innocent (an old TV-show reference). One company division (tech division) was paid by another (sales division) to create software. The software was designed to help the sales division account for some very complex insurance data for clients.

The project went $5 million over budget. In fact, the software never worked correctly, even with an extra $5 million in spending. So who posts the expense? The CEO called both division heads to a 7 a.m. meeting. (He wasn't happy, which is why he had them meet so early.) He decided that each division was equally to blame.

The sales division didn't know what was needed well enough. In the CEO's view, it didn't give the tech division proper guidance. The tech division was blamed for mismanaging the project, when it should have been completed correctly. Each division had to take half of the loss.

Choosing budgeted versus actual rate of usage

A usage variance occurs when you *use* more or less of something (material or labor) than you planned. If your budgeted usage is different from your actual usage, you have a variance. You see an amazing discussion of variances in Chapter 7.

You have some choices about the usage rate (hours) that you use for budgeting cost allocation. For example, you estimate a level of usage in planning a budget. That estimate could be based on a sales and production forecast or based on the same level of production in the prior year. You can use that budgeted level of usage to allocate costs to divisions.

The production capacity level that you choose has an impact on your usage. Are you producing your product 24/7, or do you expect some downtime, due to a lack of orders? This section helps you consider the impact of the usage rate you choose.

Looking once more at practical capacity

Practical capacity generates a low cost per unit. That leads to a lower total cost allocation to each division. Less cost allocated to the division means more costs sitting in the head office — unallocated.

The company recognizes all the expense, whether it gets allocated to a division or not. Once the head-office managers decide on a cost allocation method, it should be fixed for the year. If the head office sets an allocation rate per hour that applies too little cost to each unit, it's stuck with it. It's unreasonable for the head office to ask division managers to take on more cost because the head office made a poor cost allocation decision.

If the head office uses budgeted usage for cost allocation, it's committed to those estimates. If there's an unfavorable variance (not enough expense allocated), that amount isn't passed on to the division after the fact. The head office incurs the cost. The divisions are not penalized for the head office's poor estimate.

Now, it's possible to use actual usage to allocate costs. It's a tricky process, however. By definition, none of the actual amounts are known until the *end* of the period. If you use this method, the division managers won't know their cost allocation until after the end of the period.

I don't know about you, but I'd prefer not to have surprises in my business — good or bad. It's better to manage your business with as much upfront planning as possible. A division manager would have to come up with some cost allocation number to budget at the beginning of the year anyway. But there would be a problem at the back end of the year. As a division manager, you may need to adjust your cost allocation expense number to match the allocation you get from the head office. This affects your divisional profits and likely your compensation at the end of the year. Therefore, you may conclude that using actual usage for cost allocations can lead to a lot of frustration.

Gaining or losing allocated fixed costs

If you use actual usage to allocate costs, one division's change in usage has an impact on another division's cost. If one division has higher or lower actual usage than budgeted, the cost allocations can change.

As a division manager, when you're dealing with actual costs, you're dealing with two unknowns. You won't know your actual cost until the end of the period. And your cost allocation may be higher or lower, depending on the actual usage of other divisions.

Now be a CEO or CFO, not a division manager. Say you manage a business with a residential and commercial division. You allocate all $1,000,000 of your actual shipping department fixed costs. The allocation is based on the percentage of total hours used by each division. Table 14-7 lists the shipping department fixed cost allocation for the *previous* year.

Table 14-7	Shipping Department — Fixed Cost Allocation, Previous Year	
Budgeted Usage (Hours)	**Percent Usage Hours**	**Cost Allocation**
Residential division		
1,500 hours	45.45	$454,545
Commercial division		
1,800 hours	54.55	$545,555
Fixed costs allocated		**$1,000,000**

Take a look at the residential division. That division's percentage of the total usage hours is 45.45 percent (1,500 hours ÷ 3,300 hours). The table then computes 45.45 percent of $1,000,000 in fixed costs, which is $454,545.

You decide to allocate fixed cost using actual costs this year. The residential-division manager needs some sort of cost allocation total to plan for the year. After all, the division manager can't price the product without knowing all the costs.

One of those costs is the division's cost allocation for the shipping department. After staring out the window for a minute, the division manager decides to budget using last year's allocation.

Now consider what would happen if the commercial division uses fewer shipping department hours than last year. At year-end, you determine that the commercial division used 1,200 hours. The residential division used 1,500 hours, the same as last year. The results are shown in Table 14-8.

Table 14-8	Fixed Cost Allocation — Current Year (1,200 Actual Commercial Hours)	
Budgeted Usage (Hours)	**Percent Usage Hours**	**Cost Allocation**
Residential division		
1,500 hours	55.56	$555,556
Commercial division		
1,200 hours	44.44	$444,444
Fixed costs allocated		**$1,000,000**

Over at the residential division, the manager pulls up the shipping cost allocation report — and nearly chokes on a breakfast bagel. The residential division's allocation is over $100,000 higher than last year! "Wait a minute. My division had the same 1,500 hours of usage as last year," the manager says (to no one in particular). Then he realizes what happened.

The entire $1,000,000 fixed cost is allocated between two divisions. The cost allocation is based on total actual usage for both divisions. If one division uses less (in usage hours), the other division is allocated more costs. At that point, the residential manager's blood pressure starts to go back down. He isn't any happier, but at least nobody's going to have a stroke.

Implications for the rate of usage selected

Using actual hours as the rate of usage for cost allocation causes problems. You're better off allocating costs using planned or budgeted amounts of usage. Again, if you use actual amounts, you have to wait until the end of the period to know what levels are.

So what to do? First, consider using a budgeted amount of usage cost allocations. Get input from your division managers. Ask them to estimate how much support (in hours) they will use. Use those estimates to create your budget.

Next, a little motivation can help. Provide a financial incentive for division managers whose actual usage is close to the budgeted level they provided. If those amounts are close, your company benefits. If each division actually uses the amount of support hours they budgeted, each area gets the cost allocation they expect.

Say the residential division manager's budget was for 45 percent of total support costs for the shipping department. If each division's actual use is close to budget, the residential division will get 45 percent of the cost actually allocated — which is what the manager expected. Everyone breathes a sigh of relief. Maybe there's a division-wide bonus for incurring the support costs that were budgeted.

As you sip your cup of coffee, consider this: Using budgeted amounts of usage to allocate costs can prevent a lot of heartaches.

Allocating to multiple departments

Every department in your business needs to budget to control costs. That rule applies, whether the departments create a product, provide a service, or support other departments.

When it comes to support costs, you should have a goal in mind. Figure out which departments exist to support other departments or divisions. Select a method to allocate the support costs to those departments. This section explains the methods you can consider to allocate costs to multiple departments.

Say you manage a chain of fast-food restaurants. (I'm getting hungry, so I thought I'd go with fast food.) The human resources department supports each restaurant. It does so by advertising open positions, performing background checks, and ordering drug testing for job candidates. The restaurants sell the product (fast food) to customers, so restaurants are an operating department. The human resources department is a support department.

Your company's legal department provides services to human resources. It assists with any potential legal issues that come up with employees (hiring, terminations, promotions, and so forth). The legal department is a support department providing services to *another support department.*

Now move on to allocating costs. Consider the fast-food restaurant example, and you may start to see some complications with support cost allocation.

The legal department provides support to human resources, but also to the restaurants directly. For example, the legal department reviews and negotiates contracts for the restaurants. You read earlier how HR supports the restaurants. All this makes sense, but you have to be prepared to slice up the cost allocation pie correctly.

The restaurant industry experiences high levels of employee turnover. *Employee turnover* refers to the process of losing employees (either voluntarily or through termination) and replacing them. In particular, the fast-food industry hires many young people, many of whom don't stay very long. It's a constant process of hiring. As a restaurant owner explained to me, "I'm not in the food business. I'm in the human resources business." Turnover is understandable, because there's not much future for fast-food employees, whose only bright moment is to ask, "Would you like a nice hot apple turnover with your order?"

Ideally, all support costs should be fully allocated to operating departments. That makes sense, because operating department costs get allocated to the products or services. If you don't allocate all support costs, those costs never get allocated to the customer (in the product price). Because all costs are allocated to the operating departments, any allocation method should zero out each support department's cost.

Kicking around the direct allocation method

The *direct allocation method* allocates support costs directly to each operating department. It's simple, because you allocate every dollar out of the support department to an operating department. Because all costs are allocated, none of the support costs remain at the head office. Ta-DAH!

Here's a direct allocation example. Say your human resources and legal departments support two operating departments: assembly and shipping. After some analysis, you conclude that 80 percent of your HR costs and 90 percent of your legal costs are incurred to support the assembly area. The remainder is allocated to shipping.

Table 14-9 shows that all support costs are allocated to the two operating departments. The assembly area gets 80 percent of the human resources cost ($100,000 × 0.80 = $80,000) and 90 percent of the legal costs ($200,000 × 0.90 = $180,000). The "leftover" support costs are allocated to shipping. Both support departments have a zero balance after costs are allocated.

Table 14-9	Direct Cost Allocation Example		
		Assembly	*Shipping*
Beginning balance	$300,000	$1,000,000	$75,000
HR cost allocation			
$100,000		$80,000	$20,000
Legal cost allocation			
$200,000		$180,000	$20,000
Total allocation	-$300,000	$260,000	$40,000
Ending balance	$0	$1,260,000	$115,000

There's a downside to this method, however. Direct allocation doesn't allow you to allocate support department costs to other support departments. That's likely to happen, depending on your business.

Consider an HR department and a legal department. Assume that all of the HR and legal department support costs are allocated to an operating division using direct allocation. So the bucket of HR and legal department costs is empty. All costs have been allocated out.

But (there's always a "but") during the same time period, human resources provides support for the legal department (it helps the legal area interview and hire an attorney). Naturally, some human resources costs should be allocated to the legal department. But the legal department costs have already been fully allocated to an operating division.

Consider where those new costs from human resources should go and *when* they should go. They need to be allocated to the legal department first, and *then* to an operating department. If the costs don't end up somehow allocated to an operating department, they never get attached to a product or service. The direct allocation method would be fairly inaccurate in this situation.

Moving to the step-down allocation method

The *step-down allocation method* allows support departments to allocate costs to each other — and ultimately to the operating departments. To accomplish this, the support departments are ranked. The ranking is often based on the percentage of costs that a support department incurs to support *other support departments.*

The support department with the highest percentage is allocated first. All of its costs are allocated out — whether to an operating department or to another support department. After that, the support department with the second-highest percentage is allocated. Step by step, the costs for each support department are fully allocated. In the end, the calculation "goes flat," because all costs are allocated.

To keep things simple, use the data from Table 14-9. Say $10,000 of the human resources cost is allocated to the legal department. Legal doesn't allocate any costs to human resources. So you rank the HR department higher than legal. That's because HR allocates support costs to another support department and legal doesn't. Table 14-10 shows that allocation.

Table 14-10	Step-down Allocation Example			
		Legal	*Assembly*	*Shipping*
Beginning balance	$300,000		$1,000,000	$75,000
HR cost allocation				
$100,000	$10,000	$10,000	$80,000	$10,000
Legal cost allocation	-$10,000			
$200,000 + $10,000			$189,000	$21,000
Total allocation	-$310,000		$269,000	$31,000
Ending balance	$0	$0	$1,269,000	$106,000

Note that the HR cost allocation shifted. In this scenario, $10,000 is allocated to the legal department for services provided by HR. The legal costs are now $10,000 higher, so you have to allocate $210,000 out of legal (not $200,000) to get an ending balance of zero. Ninety percent of the $210,000 ($189,000) is allocated to assembly, and the remaining 10 percent ($21,000) is allocated to shipping. It's important to note that the total dollars allocated to the two operating departments *are the same* ($1,375,000). It looks like more money was allocated ($310,000), but that's not true; it's just a matter of showing an "extra" $10,000 going into the legal department and going right back out again.

All good, except there's a drawback. This allocation method doesn't allow costs to be allocated between multiple support departments. For example, what if legal also provides services to the HR department? When you rank the support departments and allocate out the costs, you can't allocate costs back in. It's the same issue you saw with the legal and HR departments in the last section.

Exchanging services: the reciprocal method

Enter the reciprocal method. The *reciprocal method* of cost allocation allows you to allocate costs *between* support departments in full. You can allocate costs back to a support department that you've already addressed. Say that you allocated costs out of the HR support department. When you get to the legal department's allocation, you find that some of its support costs should be allocated to HR support. The reciprocal method can make that happen.

That's the good news. The bad news is that the process is so complex that it might not be worth using for your business. You're right back to the cost versus benefit discussion — a concept that comes up often in this book. How much analysis is worth doing? You may find that your time investment to separate and assign support costs just isn't worth the benefit you receive. The benefit, in this case, is a more precise allocation of your costs, but (as Mark Twain said) there's no point in being a darned fool about it.

To summarize the cost versus benefit issue: If you have multiple support departments, consider the reciprocal method. Then, if those support departments incur a lot of costs, by all means give the reciprocal method a shot. Finally, consider the complexity of your business and the dollars involved, and give it up if it's all too much.

Say you choose one of the other methods instead of the reciprocal method. And say you have a cost that needs to be allocated back to a support department. You can't allocate it back, but consider the dollar amount. If the amount doesn't significantly affect your total product cost, it's not worth switching to the reciprocal method.

The cost versus benefit discussion relates to *materiality,* a term that comes up in the auditing process. Go online and check out the annual report of any large company. The report almost always includes the audited financial statements for the year just ended. Scroll through the report, and read the auditors' opinion. It's the letter supplied by the CPA firm that performed the audit. In the audit opinion letter, you see a statement that the financial statements are "free of material misstatement." The language changes slightly over time, but that's the heart of it. A material misstatement is an error in the financials that would cause the reader to change her opinion about the company. The phrase "free of material misstatement" means "we didn't find any large errors that would change your view of this company's financials this year." Keep that in mind as a yardstick.

Focusing on Common Costs

Common costs are costs that are shared by more than one department. They are costs that can't be assigned completely to any one department. In Chapter 13, corporate costs (costs incurred for the head office) are defined as common costs.

It's difficult to distinguish between common costs and support costs, both of which were discussed earlier. Support costs focus on activities that assist other departments, other departments that are making products, selling, and marketing.

You can think of a common cost as a necessary evil. It's a cost you pay to be in business. You have to insure assets (buildings, equipment, for example). When you sell something, you have to ship it. Common costs aren't exciting and are harder to connect to a department's activity.

This section discusses two allocation methods for common costs. As always, you need to consider whether the time to implement a method is worth the benefit of more precise cost information. One method is simpler to use, and one is harder to use.

Mulling over stand-alone cost allocation

The *stand-alone cost allocation method* collects information from the users of a common cost. You assess how much of the total common cost is used by each entity and then you make the cost allocation based on how much each party uses. This is relatively simple.

Say your clothing company has two divisions — the department store division and the small shops division. You sell clothing to stores in both markets. The two divisions use the shipping department to get products to customers. Whenever possible, the divisions work together to put goods on the same truck for shipment. The cost for shipping is based on the weight of the product in the truck.

The department store was quoted $300 to ship 200 pounds of goods from St. Louis, Missouri, to Chicago, Illinois, in two days. The small shops division has a quote of $190 to ship 100 pounds of goods from St. Louis to Milwaukee, Wisconsin, in two days. The two destination cities are relatively close to each other. You can easily calculate the cost allocation. But wait! There's more!

The divisions combined their orders and asked for a quote from the shipping department. The combined quote was $420 to ship all 300 pounds to the two cities. (What the Dickens? I guess this is a tale of two cities. That's a savings of $70 — $490 versus $420). Consider how the stand-alone method would allocate the $420 common cost (check out Table 14-11).

This method says to allocate the common cost on the same percentage basis as the costs that would have been paid by each entity alone. For example, the percentage allocation for the department store division would be 61.2 percent ($300 ÷ ($300 + $190)). The small shops division gets an allocation of 38.8 percent (($190) ÷ ($300 + $190)).

Table 14-11	Stand-alone Cost Allocation Method		
Division	Percent Allocation	Common Cost	Cost Allocated
Department store	61.2	$420	$257.04
Small shops	38.8	$420	$162.96
Total Allocated			$420.00

Multiply the common cost ($420) by the allocation percentages, giving you the amount to be allocated to each division.

Pretty simple. Costs are shared proportionally based on use in terms of dollars. Anyway, your division managers will probably judge the allocation process to be fair.

Stepping up to incremental cost allocation

The *incremental cost allocation method* is more complex than the standalone cost allocation method. The method ranks users of the common cost by their use of the cost, or alternatively, uses other references to explain why users rank in order of *those most responsible* for creating the costs. Same idea: You establish a list of users by priority.

The *primary party* is ranked first. That user gets the first allocation of common costs. The first incremental user receives the next allocation, then the second incremental user (if needed), and so forth. Typically, the primary party gets the largest cost allocation.

Making a Commitment: Contracts

A *contract* may set guidelines for costs, outlining specifically which costs apply to the contract. The contract may also define which costs are direct and which are indirect. It might define the cost allocation base for allocating overhead.

The contract may (and often does) dictate payments. It may determine when a cost you incur can be billed and reimbursed. Normally, being reimbursed for a cost requires written evidence that the cost was incurred. That information is used to justify partial payment (a *progress payment)* for the work completed.

Contracting with the government

Many companies generate a majority of their business through *government contracts* (contracts with federal, state, and local governments). It can be a consistent and profitable business, but if you want to contract with the government, you need to educate yourself on the process.

There are several methods for computing the price of your product or service, which are billed to the government. The price may be the cost you incur, plus a markup or fee to allow for a profit (a *cost-plus contract).* If that's the case, it's critical to understand what costs are allowed and reimbursable. If the government has purchased the product or service before, you should be able to find data on the costs other companies incurred. Say you're contracted to build a municipal swimming pool. Because such projects are fairly common, you could research the costs incurred by other companies who've built pools.

If the project is new or unique, there's a bigger risk. If you can't find comparable projects, it may be hard to know what costs should be included. That makes it hard to negotiate which costs should be in the contract. You might miss some costs. Maybe it's difficult to estimate the labor cost for the project, as would be true if no one else has done it before.

There are other methods for pricing government work. See the section on markups in Chapter 12. Your price may also be a fixed price contract, which is a price driven by market competition. Finally, your price may include a share of cost savings generated.

Say you build a solar building for a city. Your compensation might include some of the energy savings. The city calculates the energy cost savings for the new building and then pays some of that to the builder. Such payments are for a fixed time period.

Thinking about reasonable and fair costs

To consider what may be a reasonable and fair price, you need to consider the cost for the product or service you provide. That's your starting point: Consider whether or not the costs are fair. After you and the other party agree, you can discuss a fair profit and price.

Many government entities require *competitive bidding*. That means that multiple vendors provide confidential bids for the work. The government then selects a vendor to perform the work.

The party selected normally is the low bidder; however, there may be other factors that affect the selection of the vendor. The government usually wants an experienced vendor who can meet a deadline. The contract likely requires vendors to provide references. So the lowest bid might not necessarily be selected.

Competitive bidding is most appropriate for work that's *not unusual or unique.* There are a few reasons why. If the work is common, the government is able to find multiple bidders. Also, bidders have enough data from other work to submit well-planned bids.

In the case of the municipal swimming pool, the city or state should be able to find multiple bidders. The work is fairly common. The bidders (also called *vendors)* likely have all built municipal pools before.

Things get tougher for both parties when the work is unusual or unique. Say the federal government wants bids on a manned spaceship to fly to Mars.

There aren't many companies that have the staff and expertise to build spacecraft, much less a vehicle that could go to Mars. Even having built a spacecraft that can go to the Moon won't provide all the experience needed for a Mars mission.

There's a lot at risk for a potential bidder. It is difficult to know all the costs that need to be incurred. After all, you can't go to the web and research other companies that have built a similar product. Given the dollar amount involved and the uncertainty, companies may not be willing to bid.

Ultimately, both parties need to agree on what's reasonable and fair. For common work that goes through competitive bidding, there's historical data to determine what's reasonable and fair. For unique work, the process is harder. If you could take time negotiating, you can nail down your definitions of reasonable and fair costs and prices. The trouble is that sealed, competitive bids don't allow for negotiating. At best, there is a "question and answer" process, where all bidders' questions — and the answers — are available for all bidders to see.

Chapter 15

Joint Costs, Separable Costs, and Using Up the Leftovers

- -

In This Chapter

▶ Distinguishing between joint costs and separable costs

▶ Finding the splitoff point

▶ Determining costs and product values at splitoff

▶ Thinking about stopping or continuing production

▶ Understanding byproducts

- -

Different products may go through the same production process, making it difficult to differentiate costs among products early in production. During this stage, your firm is incurring *joint costs*.

At some point, however, the products in production become separate and distinct from one another. For example, when you drill for oil, you eventually separate the crude oil from the other materials you take out of the ground. Then you apply costs to each product to better compute a sale price and your profit. Accountants call this the *splitoff point*. After splitoff, you consider each product's costs separately. Then you work with *separable costs*.

Ultimately, most production processes have some output that's a *byproduct*. It's not the primary product you produce — it's a "leftover" — but it might have some value to a customer. Smart business owners, like my parents, try to make use of the leftovers.

This chapter takes a look at these costs and what can be done with any byproducts.

Working with Joint Costs

You can imagine many products that start off in production together. If you make three models of blue jeans, you may cut and sew the same type of denim at the beginning of production. For a while, the three types of jeans look the same. You're in joint production, and you're incurring joint costs.

At some point, you separate production. One model of jeans can be distinguished from the models. As you produce jeans separately, you incur costs separately.

This section starts to explain joint costs.

Explaining joint cost terms

It's time to connect three terms. *Joint costs* are production costs incurred in creating two (or more) products. The *splitoff point* is the point when the costs of two or more products can be separately identified. After splitoff, each product incurs *separable* (or independent) *costs.*

Figuring a product's total cost

When your production involves some joint costs, you need to change your thinking about total costs. To compute total costs, you use a before-and-after process. The product's total cost are a portion of the joint costs (incurred before splitoff point) plus the separable costs (incurred after splitoff point).

Say you make two types of leather purses. Both purses go through the same production process. Each product incurs a portion of the joint costs of production. But the process doesn't end there. In this case, you'd expect to have costs after splitoff.

Sure, both purses go through a process to treat and shape leather — that's in joint production. But they each have different straps and different metal pieces added. That work (the separable costs) occurs after splitoff. To price both purses, you need to add the joint costs incurred to the separable costs.

It's possible that two products incur no additional costs after splitoff. At first, that may seem unlikely, but it happens all the time. In food production, for example, joint production costs can stop at splitoff. A dairy farmer milks cows. The raw milk can generate cream and skim milk. The same input (raw milk) creates two outputs. After the products reach the splitoff point, production and costs stop. The farmer has two products to sell.

Setting the sales value of a byproduct

In the cost accounting world, a *byproduct* is a product that is produced during joint production. It's something produced while you're making something else. Call it an *extra* or a *side effect* of production. Even though producing the byproduct isn't your main goal, it shares joint costs with the real product.

A byproduct has a lower *sales value* than other products in joint production. Sales value? Here's how to calculate a product's sales value:

Product sales value = Number of units produced × sale price per unit

You can tell a byproduct because it isn't the primary reason you're running production. The revenue produced (product sales value) is typically so small that you wouldn't run production for just the byproduct. But the sales value of the byproduct (just like any other product) can change. Over time, your byproduct's revenue may become more attractive. (Well, it can also become less attractive, too.)

Appreciating the importance of allocating joint costs

In addition to computing a product's total cost, there are other important reasons why you spend time figuring and allocating joint costs:

✔ **Financial reporting:** Joint costs need to be computed and allocated for inventory and cost of goods sold. *Financial accounting* is the process of creating financial reports for external users (for example, shareholders, creditors, or regulators). Of course, there are standards of financial reporting — rules of the road for explaining financial results — and many books have been written about them.

✔ **Product pricing:** Joint costs are used to compute total product costs. Product costs are then used to determine a profit and a sale price. You need to calculate joint costs to calculate *inventoriable costs.* Those costs are attached to inventory and expensed when the product is sold. Check out Chapter 9 for more on the concept. So you need joint costs to calculate inventory values and the cost of goods sold. This information ends up in your financial reports, too.

It's a mantra you may grow tired of hearing: You need total product costs to decide on a profit level and figure out a sale price. If you have joint production, you need the joint costs to compute total product costs.

- ✔ **Contracts:** Joint costs are part of cost reimbursement under contracts. Contracts come up in Chapter 14. Under many contracts, you need to justify your costs and document them to receive reimbursement. Essentially, you're proving that your spending met the guidelines in the contract. If you have joint costs, they need to be part of this process.

- ✔ **Insurance settlements:** Insurance settlements for damage claims include joint costs. If you file an insurance claim regarding damaged assets, you need to document each asset's value. Say you produce inventory using a joint production process. And say some of that inventory was damaged when your warehouse was hit by a storm. To justify the inventory cost for your insurance claim, you need details on the joint costs in that inventory.

- ✔ **Regulated products:** A regulated product or service may require joint cost allocations to compute a price. Some industry prices are set and controlled by federal or state regulation. Utility companies are the best example. Because it's a process of justifying costs, you need to provide your total costs (including joint costs) to the regulator.

- ✔ **Litigation:** Litigation documentation and support may require joint cost allocations. Unfortunately, litigation is a cost of doing business. Every company, to some extent, has to deal with litigation. Whether your company is initiating a legal action or defending itself against an action, you need good documentation.

   Often, the issue in corporate litigation is a product or service. The value of the product must be determined so that the court knows the dollar amount in dispute. If you use joint production, you need to include the joint costs in your total.

Considering joint cost allocation methods

The *matching principle* matches revenue with the expenses related to it. You tie the revenue from selling a unit to the cost of making a unit. The concept pops up throughout the book, and it's also used to allocate joint costs.

You can allocate joint costs based on the revenue the units generate. Accountants refer to this as the *market-based approach*. *Market* refers to the market value (sales value) of the product. The section "Setting the sales value of a byproduct" defines product sales value. Use that formula to allocate joint costs. The two market-based methods you see are the *sales value at splitoff method* and the *net realizable value* (NRV) *method*. You also see the *physical measures method* of allocating joint costs.

The sales value at splitoff method

One method of allocating joint costs is to allocate costs based on the benefits received from the expense. Take a peek at Chapter 13 for more info. Revenue is a benefit received from incurring joint costs. That's the basis for using a market-based approach.

In the section "Figuring a product's total cost," the dairy-farmer example doesn't include any costs after splitoff. The farmer uses joint production and then has two products (cream and skim milk) to sell. So you allocate costs using the relative sales value of each product.

Say you own a lumber company and mill. Your crews cut down trees and produces two types of lumber for the construction industry. Both types are two-by-fours (two inches by four inches by eight feet in length). Winter Pine is the more expensive product; the all-year-use two-by-fours are cheaper. Table 15-1 explains how to allocate $208,000 in joint costs using the relative sales value method.

Table 15-1	Joint Cost — Relative Sales Value at Splitoff		
	Winter Pine	**All-Year-Use**	**Total**
Production	10,000	16,000	26,000
Unit price	$12	$8	
Relative sales value	**$120,000**	**$128,000**	**$248,000**
Percent sales value	48.39	51.61	100
Cost allocated	**$100,645**	**$107,355**	**$208,000**
Cost per unit	$10.06	$6.71	

A product's relative sales value is unit price × production. The total sales value for both products is $248,000, and about 48 percent of the sales value is for Winter Pine. The joint cost allocation for Winter Pine is $100,645 (48.39 percent, or 0.4839 × $208,000). To check your work, add the two joint cost allocations and verify that they sum up to $208,000. Here's the cost per unit for Winter Pine:

Cost per unit, Winter Pine = cost allocation ÷ units produced

Cost per unit, Winter Pine = $100,645 ÷ 10,000

Cost per unit, Winter Pine = $10.06

The physical measure method

The *physical measure method* allocates cost by the weight, volume, or some other measurement of the product that's produced. It's a contrast to relative sales value. In this case, assume that the weight or volume for each two-by-four is the same. (Well, yeah. They are both two-by-fours.) So you allocate joint costs based on the *number of units* produced. Check out Table 15-2.

Table 15-2	Joint Cost — Physical Measure at Splitoff		
	Winter Pine	*All-Year Use*	*Total*
Production	10,000	16,000	26,000
Percent production	38.46	61.54	100
Cost allocated	**$80,000**	**$128,000**	**$208,000**
Cost per unit	$8	$8	

Winter Pine's 10,000 units of production are 38.46 percent of the total. The cost allocated is $80,000 (38.46 percent or 0.3846 × $208,000). The all-year-use product gets the rest, $128,000. The total cost allocated sums up to $208,000. The new version of cost per unit for Winter Pine is

Cost per unit, Winter Pine = cost allocation ÷ units produced

Cost per unit, Winter Pine = $80,000 ÷ 10,000

Cost per unit, Winter Pine = $8

In Table 15-2, the cost per unit is the same for both products. That's because the joint cost allocation isn't related to cost because it uses the physical measure method. Because you're allocating based on number of units, the cost attached to all units is the same. You're not weighting the cost allocation based on sales value.

Continuing Production: Computing Separable Costs After Splitoff

Separable costs are incurred after you pass the splitoff point. In many cases, the product won't be sellable at splitoff, because the product isn't finished yet. In the section "Explaining joint cost terms," you see a mention of leather purses. At splitoff, the purses aren't complete; you need to add straps and metal accessories to complete the product for sale.

Because many products require production after splitoff, it's important that you review two of these methods: the *net realizable value method* and the *constant gross margin percentage method.*

Exploring the net realizable value method

The *net realizable value method* allocates joint costs on the basis of the *final sales value* less separable costs. Final sales value is simply the price tag — the price paid by the customer. That price is paid after all production costs, whether they are joint costs or separable costs incurred after splitoff.

What you *realize* on a sale is usually your profit. You see this term used many times in business. But in this case, realizable value means sale price less separable costs. That doesn't equal profit. You have to subtract joint costs from the subtotal to get profit. It's not a perfect comparison, but it's close.

Computing total costs and per unit amounts

Use the leather-purse example for working through the net realizable value method. Say you sell two types of purses: The Sassy purse line is more expensive than the Everyday model. The separable costs per unit for Sassy purses, as you see, are higher than those of Everyday purses.

Table 15-3 calculates the net realizable value for each product.

Table 15-3	Joint Cost — Net Realizable Value Calculation		
Purse Type	**Sassy**	**Everyday**	**Total**
Production	20,000	24,000	44,000
Unit price	$50	$35	
Sales value (A)	**$1,000,000**	**$840,000**	**$1,840,000**
Separable costs (B)			
Per unit	$12	$10	
Total	$240,000	$240,000	$480,000
Net realizable value (A – B)	**$760,000**	**$600,000**	**$1,360,000**

Work your way down the Sassy purse column. The sales value of $1,000,000 is based on the production multiplied by the unit price (20,000 × $50). Then here's the separable cost calculation:

Separable cost = units produced × cost per unit

Separable cost = 20,000 × $12

Separable cost = $240,000

The net realizable value is the $1,000,000 sales value less $240,000 separable costs = $760,000. Next, you use net realizable value to allocate joint costs. Take a gander at Table 15-4.

Table 15-4	Joint Cost — NRV Cost Calculation		
	Sassy	*Everyday*	*Total*
Net realizable value (NRV)	$760,000	$600,000	$1,360,000
Percent of NRV total	55.88	44.12	
Joint cost allocation	$502,941	$397,059	$900,000
Total costs			
Separable costs	$240,000	$240,000	
Joint costs		$502,941	$397,059
Total costs	$742,941	$637,059	
Cost per unit	$37.15	$26.54	

Table 15-4 starts with the net realizable value (NRV) amounts from Table 15-3. The *Percent of NRV total* is the percentage of the total NRV for each product. The $760,000 of NRV for Sassy purses is 55.88 percent of the total of $1,360,000. Then you multiply $900,000 in total joint costs by the percentage, and that allocates joint costs to each purse. Simple, no? No.

What about separable costs? Table 15-4 displays the separable costs from Table 15-3. Add the separable and joint costs to get total costs. It makes sense that Sassy purses have a higher total cost per unit ($37.15). The Sassy's per unit separable cost of $12 (from Table 15-3) is higher than that of the Everyday product ($10), so the Everyday unit's cost is $26.54. The $502,941 joint costs allocated to the Sassy in Table 15-4 are also higher than the joint costs for Everyday purses.

Mulling over issues with the NRV method

One issue with the *net realizable value* (NRV) method is that amounts may change. For starters, your production process after splitoff may change. Hopefully, you're able to review variance results and improve the process. (Variances are brilliantly explained in Chapter 7.) If you change your production after splitoff, your separable cost totals change.

You may not be able to price your product until after production ends. And in a market with heavy competition, to maintain your sales levels, you have to keep your price competitive (for the Sassy purses, say $50 per unit or lower). If your total costs come in lower than expected, maybe you can price the product lower than $50, and that might increase sales.

If you can't determine a sales price in advance, you can't calculate relative sales value.

Introducing the constant gross margin percentage NRV method

The *constant gross margin method* expands on the NRV method. Before you get there, consider gross margin. *Gross margin* is defined as sales less cost of sales. You might recall that cost of sales isn't total cost, but the cost to make the good. Gross margin is the price of the asset less the cost to make it. There are other costs (marketing and sales, for example) that aren't part of the gross margin calculation. They come up later.

You can express gross margin as a percentage:

Gross margin percentage = gross margin dollar amount ÷ sales × 100

For example, if your gross margin for a pair of shoes is $10 and your sales price is $80, your gross margin percentage is 12.5 percent ($10 ÷ $80 × 100).

The constant gross margin method assigns joint costs after assigning each product the same gross margin percentage. It's a method that *works backward.* Here are the steps for using the constant gross margin method:

1. Compute the gross margin percentage for the entire company.

2. For each product, compute sales less gross margin as a percent of sales for the entire company to compute cost of goods.

3. Deduct separable costs from cost of goods for sale to calculate joint costs.

4. Subtract total costs from sales value to get gross margin.

5. Verify that the gross margin percentage calculation is correct.

Here's what working backward means: Normally, you use sales and cost of sales to compute gross margin. This new method uses a desired gross margin percentage to compute cost of goods available for sale. The reason the process uses cost of goods available for sale is that you don't know how much of the production will be sold. You know sales *value* but not actual sales.

Starting with total gross margin percentage

Assume you manufacture leaf blowers. Your two products are heavy-duty blowers and yardwork blowers. You start by computing the gross margin percentage for both of your products together. Total gross margin is $428,000 ($3,440,000 in sales value less total costs of $3,012,000). Here's the gross margin percentage:

Gross margin percentage = gross margin ÷ total sales value × 100

Gross margin percentage = $428,000 ÷ $3,440,000 × 100

Gross margin percentage = 12.442

The gross margin percentage is 12.442 percent.

Calculating goods available for sale by product

Now that you have the gross margin percentage for the whole company, you can calculate the gross margin percentage for each product. That amount allows you to come up with the cost of goods available for sale. Table 15-5 has the details.

Table 15-5	Goods Available For Sale by Product		
	Heavy-Duty	*Yardwork*	*Total*
Sales value (A)	$2,000,000	$1,440,000	$3,440,000
Gross margin (B)	$248,837	$179,163	$428,000
Cost of goods available for sale (A – B)	$1,751,163	$1,260,837	$3,012,000

The gross margin for each product equals the sales value multiplied by the gross margin percentage of 12.442 percent. For example, the heavy-duty blower's gross margin percentage is $248,837 (2,000,000 × .12442 ÷ 100 with a small rounding difference). Heavy-duty then subtracts the $248,837 gross margin from $2,000,000 sales value to get $1,751,163, the cost of goods available for sale.

Your cost of sales is sales value less gross margin. The formula in Table 15-5 rearranges the components. Again, you use cost of goods *available for sale* — at this point, you're only planning results.

Figuring out joint cost allocations

Cost of goods available for sale represents the product's total costs. One more time: Total costs have two components — joint costs and separable costs.

Assume the separable costs are $1,200,000 for the heavy-duty blower and $912,000 for the yardwork blower. If you know the separable costs and the cost of goods available for sale, you can compute the joint cost allocation. Table 15-6 shows the process.

Table 15-6	Joint Cost Allocation		
	Heavy-Duty	**Yardwork**	**Total**
Cost of goods available for sale	$1,751,163	$1,260,837	$3,012,000
Less separable costs	$1,200,000	$912,000	$2,112,000
Equals joint cost allocation	**$551,163**	**$348,837**	**$900,000**

Each company division provides the separable costs. So altogether, Table 15-6 gives you a joint cost allocation.

Verifying the gross margin percentage

You need multiple steps to get from a gross margin percentage to a joint cost allocation. This is tough stuff — a fairly complex process. So you should check your work. That's the purpose of Table 15-7. The goal is to use the traditional formula for gross margin. This last step lets you see if the gross margin percentage is really correct.

Table 15-7	Verifying Gross Margin Percentage		
	Heavy-Duty	**Yardwork**	**Total**
Sales value (A)	$2,000,000	$1,440,000	$3,440,000
Total cost (B)	$1,751,163	$1,260,837	$3,012,000
Gross margin (A − B)	**$248,837**	**$179,163**	**$428,000**
Gross margin percentage	12.442	12.442	

The sales value comes from Table 15-5. The total cost is the cost of goods available for sale from Table 15-6. The gross margin percentage is the gross margin divided by the sales value. For each product, the gross margin percentage is the same (12.442 percent) as the company's overall gross margin.

Here's the point of Table 15-7: The table uses the traditional formula to compute gross margin and gross margin percentage. The table verifies that the calculations in Tables 15-5 and 15-6 are correct. You gotta admit that there are a lot of numbers flying around in these tables. It helps to have a tool to verify the calculations, which is what Table 15-7 is supposed to do.

Go back through the tables, and take a look at some overall trends in the data. In Table 15-5, the heavy-duty product has the higher sales value. As a result, it ends up with a higher gross margin *in dollars* than the yardwork product. However, both sale values are multiplied by the same gross margin *percentage*.

Both products have a gross margin of about 12.5 percent (rounded). That means that about 87.5 percent of sales value represents cost of goods available for sale.

The difference between the products occurs with separable costs. Take a spin (or a slog) through Table 15-6. The "Cost of goods available for sale" number comes from Table 15-5. To make the company-wide gross margin percentage hold true, the total costs have to be $3,012,000.

Reducing separable costs

Assume that the heavy-duty blower division is able to sharply reduce its separable costs to an amazingly low $500,000. Table 15-6 listed heavy-duty separable costs of $1,200,000. Consider what now happens to heavy-duty's joint cost allocation. Take a look at Table 15-8.

Table 15-8 Cost Allocation — Less Heavy Duty Separable Costs			
	Heavy-Duty	**Yardwork**	**Total**
Cost of goods available for sale	$1,751,163	$1,260,837	$3,012,000
Less separable costs	$500,000	$912,000	$1,412,000
Equals joint cost allocation	**$1,251,163**	**$348,837**	**$1,600,000**

Heavy-duty's joint cost allocation *increases* to $1,251,163 (from $551,163). That doesn't seem right. The point throughout this book is to analyze costs to reduce or eliminate them. If you do, supposedly you increase your profits.

In this case, the heavy-duty division's reducing separable costs *increased* its joint cost allocation. There doesn't seem to be a benefit to operating more efficiently.

Here's an explanation: The gross margin percentage method *locks in* total costs as a percentage of sales value. If the gross margin is about 12.5 percent of sales value, it means that costs must be about 87.5 percent of sales value. For heavy-duty, that 87.5 percent total cost number is $1,751,163, like it or not. Those costs are either separable or joint costs. If one increases, the other decreases.

The heavy-duty manager may (may?) have a problem with this process. The manager works hard (using good old cost accounting) to lower the separable costs. The manager's "reward" is a higher joint cost allocation. The heavy-duty division has lowered costs but doesn't get any savings in total costs.

The constant gross margin percentage method clarifies the revenue and profit calculations company-wide. This method eliminates some of the variation between company divisions. Although some managers may complain, each division has the same gross margin percentage. The process makes managing company profit easier.

This is one of those "Here's why the chief financial officer (CFO) makes the big bucks" moments. As CFO, you explain the gross margin percentage method to the heavy-duty division manager. The goal is to allocate joint costs so that each product maintains the same gross margin percentage of about 12.5 percent. If a division reduces separable costs, it *must* get a bigger joint cost allocation — *otherwise, the gross margin percentage would increase.* Now heavy-duty's manager should be evaluated based on the successful cost reduction. The manager had a success, and you want to encourage more cost savings. Although the gross margin percentage process requires a bigger joint cost allocation, that must not take away from the manager's good performance.

Choosing a Joint Cost Allocation Method

You want to select a method to plan and budget for joint costs. This section considers the costs and benefits of different joint cost allocation methods.

Choosing a method helps you know where you stand during joint production. You can assess if your actual joint costs are on track with your budget. If you're off track, you can make changes.

Making the case for sales value at splitoff

Allocating joint costs using sales value at splitoff may be the most effective method for planning and budgeting for joint costs. Here are several reasons why:

- ✔ The method relates the benefit of production (revenue of sales value at splitoff) to the related expenses.
- ✔ No information on separable costs is required.
- ✔ The sales value at splitoff may be the best comparison of the products. At that point, you're making an apples-to-apples comparison.

Sale value at splitoff isn't affected by other production or costs after splitoff. A product's sales value after separable costs have been incurred may be very different. If you spend time and money after the splitoff point, you charge a higher price to recover those costs. So it's fair to say that the sales value at splitoff method is simple, compared with the others.

Falling back to other joint costing methods

There's a possibility that sales values aren't available at splitoff. The product's production may not be far enough along to come up with a price. If there's no price, you can't compute sales value. In that case, consider a different method.

The next best method may be the *net realizable value* (NRV) method. In the "Considering joint cost allocation methods" earlier in this chapter, you see how this method uses final sales value (the price tag on the product) less separable costs. The NRV method also does a good job of matching the benefit received (final sales value) with the costs incurred (separable costs). The calculation happens at the end of all production. Contrast that with sales value at splitoff. The difference is a matter of timing.

Making a calculation after production ends has some other benefits. The NRV method accounts for all separable costs, regardless of how much higher or lower they are than your plan. NRV also handles any change to the final sales value (price tag) due to a change in market conditions. NPV captures any changes to costs and sale price that might occur as products are produced separately.

The other methods have their challenges. The constant gross margin percentage method assumes that each department has the same level of profitability. The gross margin percentages and total costs (as a percentage of sales) are the same for everything produced. In the real world, different products produce different levels of profit.

Finally, the physical measure method doesn't relate revenue to expenses at all. You may find that this method is the least useful.

Many manufacturers make a big array of products. Two classic examples are automobiles and computer printers. Each manufacturer in each industry offers many makes and models in order to reach slightly different buyers, usually through different price points. Some products are "high volume/low margin," while others are "low volume/high margin." To give you a food analogy, you can make money selling 3,000 $1 hamburgers per day or 100 $30 filet mignon dinners per night. Same sales revenue.

Deciding to sell or process further

A *sell or process further* decision is a decision to sell a product "as is" at the splitoff point, or to process it further. There are two criteria you use to justify further processing (and more costs):

- ✔ If the product has a sales value at splitoff, maybe it's better to sell it.
- ✔ If the incremental revenue from further processing is greater than the incremental cost of further processing, maybe it's better to continue processing.

You saw in the preceding section that some products simply don't have a sales value at splitoff. The product's production isn't far enough along for it to be sold yet. No customers (or not enough customers) would consider buying the product at splitoff. Think about selling blue jeans without zippers or belt loops; it's probably not a good idea.

If you can't calculate a sales value at splitoff, there's no "sell or process further" decision to make. To have a viable product to sell, you need to keep processing.

But wait! There are times when a partially completed product at splitoff has value to *someone*. Say you make cabinets. You've run production on two types of products, and you're now at splitoff. Neither type of cabinet is ready to be sold to a customer because you have to complete the sanding and finishing on the wood. You also have to install metal handles.

The product is clearly not ready for a regular customer (likely a retail store that sells to the public). However, another business may ask you for a price quote for the partially completed goods. Maybe another cabinetmaker is having trouble filling a large order. It might be willing to buy your partially finished cabinets. In that scenario, you essentially become an industry supplier.

Keep your thinking cap on! Maybe you can build a business selling unfinished cabinets without hardware to the do-it-yourself (DIY) market. In that case, there *is* sales value at splitoff.

Joint costs are irrelevant for your "sell or process further" decision. Those costs are the same, whether you sell the product at splitoff or process further. In this case, joint costs are sunk or past costs. They've already been paid. Slip and slide on over to Chapter 3 for more on past and sunk costs.

Incremental revenue is the additional revenue you get from selling one more unit that has been processed further. *Incremental cost* is the additional cost. If you spend $5 more per unit, and earn $7 more from selling that unit, your incremental revenue is $2 higher than the incremental cost. *Incremental,* in this case, refers to the production from splitoff to a completed product.

Holding a Garage Sale: Making the Most of Byproducts

Byproducts are produced during the joint production of other products (see "Setting the sales value of a byproduct," earlier in this chapter). The byproduct's sales value is usually less than that of the "real" products in joint production; however, don't underestimate the value of a byproduct, because the revenue from byproduct sales may be used to reduce total joint costs.

When you consider byproducts, visualize a garage sale. The money you make from the garage sale isn't (hopefully) your primary source of income. However, that revenue can be used to cover other costs — maybe the month's air conditioning bill. (I know people love garage sales. When I ride my bike early on weekends, I have to weave my way around the cars parked at garage sales.)

There are two methods to account for joint costs that include a byproduct:

- ✔ The *production method* recognizes the byproduct in the financial statements when it's produced. The production method deducts the byproduct revenue from cost of sales at the time of production.

- ✔ The *sales method* delays recognition of the byproduct until it's sold. The sales method adds the byproduct revenue to the main product revenue. Revenue is slightly higher using the sales method. The net cost of sales, however, is also higher. In fact, the higher revenue is offset by the higher cost of sales.

Gross margin is defined as sales less cost of sales. The total gross margin in dollars is the same using both methods. Using the sales method, the slightly higher revenue is offset by an equally higher increase in cost of sales.

Chapter 16

Tracing Similar Products with Process Costing

*P*rocess costing is a costing methodology that traces costs as they move from one process or stage of manufacture to another. Along the way, you need to track the partially completed units — and the costs they incur. Process costing can be a big challenge, but in this chapter, you see several methods of tracking both the units and the costs.

You use process costing when the products you produce are similar or identical.

Process costing has the same goal as other types of costing in this book: to help you understand what is driving costs. In this chapter, you focus on the value of your inventory and computing cost of sales. You also use that info to generate financial reports, which educate the "outside world" (shareholders, creditors, regulators) about what's going on in your business.

Good costing helps you manage costs and assess performance. The goal is to cut costs and *improve profitability,* which is the big reason you go through the blood, sweat, and tears of using process costing.

Process Costing: Presenting the Basic Approach

You need to *trace* or *allocate* all of the costs attached to a product so you know the full cost of the product. After you know the full cost, you can compute a reasonable profit level and set a sale price for the product. That's easy to say, but getting it done takes a little work.

To fully price the product, each unit must absorb material, labor, and overhead costs. Because the goods are identical, the costs you eventually assigned to each unit are identical. Note the word used was *eventually*. As this chapter shows you, the process takes time.

Process costing is all about moving costs from one production department to another. Take a peek at Chapter 4. That part of the book discusses the flow of manufacturing costs.

Say you manufacture blue jeans. Denim material goes to the cutting room and is cut from patterns. The cut material then goes to the sewing department. After the blue jeans are sewn, they move to the dyeing department to add color. As the blue jeans move, so do the costs accumulated along the way.

So as you can see in the blue-jeans example, as a product moves through production, it accumulates costs. Now consider *when* the costs are incurred.

Leading off with direct material costs

In most cases, material costs go into production *before* labor and overhead costs. You need material before you can perform most of your work. The employee can't run the sewing machine if there isn't any denim to sew. At any point in production, you'll probably see a higher percentage of material costs incurred, compared with labor and overhead costs.

Material costs are often incurred all at once. Consider the blue jeans. You decide to put all the denim you need into production at once. Because the first production area is the cutting department, all of the material cutting happens as soon as possible. If the denim is brought into production gradually, the cutting department may have to stop and wait for more denim. That would slow up your production, and you're unlikely to do that.

Material costs lead most of the time, but not all of the time. Keep your eyes open for exceptions. For example, auto bodywork is labor-intensive. So's the work of plumbers. Service businesses, of course, sell services.

Following up with conversion costs

Conversion costs are all costs other than material costs. They are costs you incur to "convert" material into a final product. So labor and overhead are conversion costs.

Also, keep in mind that conversion costs are put into production gradually. Maybe your product moves through several stages of production. If you make baseball gloves, for example, you have a department that cuts the leather for the baseball gloves and another department that sews the leather. Because there are workers and machines in each department, you add costs as the product moves through production — gradually.

Sitting on the Factory Floor: Dealing with Work in Process

When you open the door of your factory on the first day of the month, you may see partially completed goods sitting on the factory floor. Those goods are considered *work in process* (WIP). The goods are partially completed, so you've incurred some costs, but not all costs.

Your *finished goods inventory* affects process costing. The costing process becomes more complicated when you have inventory. Both WIP inventory and finished goods inventory may have a beginning balance. Each account may also have an ending inventory balance.

A manufacturer doesn't usually start the month without partially completed products or end the month with all products sold. It can happen, but generally, it's expected that manufacturing is a continuous process. So most firms always have a work in process balance (costs posted to the account).

This chapter uses the term *percentage completed,* which means work completed and costs incurred.

It's a given that WIP at different stages has incurred different amounts of costs. Here are scenarios that may be in play:

- Say your items in April beginning WIP inventory are 10 percent complete. During April, you complete them. This means that you spend the remaining 90 percent of their costs during April. Beginning inventory WIP has a different amount of costs to complete (90 percent to go) than items *started during the period* (100 percent to go), which are 0 percent complete and may or may not be complete when the period ends.

- ✔ If you start and complete an item in April, it accumulates 100 percent of its costs of production during the month, and that's that.

- ✔ When you lock the factory doors at the end of April, any partially completed items are considered ending WIP. There's bound to be WIP, because an efficient manufacturer usually starts making new units as soon as the machines and staff free up. Your April ending inventory is also the *beginning inventory* for May. Say the April ending inventory has incurred 30 percent of its costs. To complete the goods in May, you need to spend another 70 percent in costs.

Using Equivalent Units to Compare Apples to Apples

Products at different stages of production require different amounts of costs to complete them. The *total* product costs are (eventually) the same for each unit because the goods that use process costing are usually homogeneous (or all the same).

The section "Counting the units for equivalent units" shows that you may start a period with WIP, start and complete some product 100 percent during the period, and end a period with WIP. In two out of three scenarios, the work done on the units is spread over *two periods*.

The costing process seems complicated, but it's not. It's just that when you transfer units from one department to another, you're dealing with varying quantities. And units leaving different departments have a different amount of costs incurred to date. This is not a good thing for costing. You need an apples-to-apples comparison.

Enter *equivalent units of production*, a solution! Equivalent units of production is a calculation computed by multiplying each unit in production by its percentage of completion. In that way, all units are comparable, and there's your apples-to-apples comparison.

Counting the units for equivalent units

The first step in calculating equivalent units is to correctly account for the units. When you have the movement of units figured out, you can attach costs to the units. Table 16-1 displays an accounting for units.

Table 16-1 Equivalent Units — Physical Flow of Units (April)	
	Units
Work in process, beginning inventory (4/1)	50
Units started during April	100
Units to account for	**150**
Completed and transferred out during April	120
Work in process, ending inventory (4/30)	30
Units accounted for	**150**

It's simple. Start with beginning WIP units (50 units). Add units you start during April (100 units). The total (150 units) amounts to the "units to account for."

Now, those units you worked on end up in one of two places. Look at the next two lines in the table. When you finish units, they're transferred out (120 units). They move to finished goods inventory, and are ready to be sold to a customer. Units that aren't yet completed are in ending inventory WIP as of April 30th (30 units). The "units to account for" equal the "units accounted for."

To account for the units correctly, this formula must hold true:

Beginning inventory WIP + units started during the month = units completed and transferred out + ending inventory WIP

At this point, it isn't possible to determine which items (beginning inventory WIP or units started during the month) *were completed in April.* You get an answer to that question later.

Hunting down the total costs of production

You need to add costs to complete production on the units. Material costs are generally easy, but a department will add conversion costs. For example, you pay labor costs to an employee, so the worker will operate a sewing machine. That's labor, and there's overhead as well.

The goal is to isolate the costs added during the period. After you do that, separate the cost total between direct material and conversion costs.

You've seen percentage completion several times in this chapter. As a manager, you need to estimate the percentage of work completed on each unit.

Deriving direct material costs

Estimating direct material costs is easier than estimating labor and overhead costs. In fact, it may be an exact figure, because you probably know how much material you moved into production. Say you make men's cotton dress shirts. Your records indicate that you've moved 125 linear yards of cotton fabric into production. You know how much fabric you use in each shirt, and you also know the number of shirts in production.

With that info, you can compute the percentage of completion for units in production. Assume that 100 shirts are in production, but the cotton fabric moved into production will make only 50 shirts. At that point, you're 50 percent complete (50 shirts ÷ 100 shirts) in terms of direct materials.

Figuring out labor and overhead costs

Labor and overhead percentage completion estimates are harder. That's because there is less hard data to grab and analyze. Also, the labor estimate typically drives the overhead allocation.

You can estimate labor completion based on the percentage of total tasks complete. If you're making blue jeans, you have production departments to dye, cut cloth, sew, finish, and package. You can judge your percentage completion by adding your estimates for each department in the production process. If dyeing is 10 percent and cutting is 20 percent, the product is 30 percent complete when it arrives in the sewing department. If work in the sewing department is 40 percent of the process, the product is 70 percent complete before it goes to finishing.

A level of activity usually drives overhead allocations. (Jump over to Chapters 4 and 5 for more info.) Those levels of activity are usually based on labor hours or machine hours. If sewing the jeans amounts to 40 percent of the labor, you can usually use the same percentage for overhead costs.

Estimating by percentage completion requires your experience, as well as math. It's both an art and a science.

Putting units and costs together

After you count the physical units and figuring a method of costing them, put them together. You use equivalent units to assign real dollar costs to products.

Laying out physical units and total costs

Say you're a candy manufacturer. You make inexpensive pieces of candy that sell for 20 cents each. So a piece of candy is your product unit. Table 16-2 displays the movement of physical units for a period.

Table 16-2 Candy — Physical Flow of Units (September)	
	Units
Work in process, beginning inventory (9/1)	400,000
Units started during September	800,000
Units to account for	**1,200,000**
Completed and transferred out during September	600,000
Work in process, ending inventory (9/30)	600,000
Units accounted for	**1,200,000**

The formula is

> Beginning inventory WIP + units started during the month = units completed and transferred out + ending inventory WIP

The total units to account for agrees with the total units accounted for. (And it's a good thing all the WIP candy went out the door, because candy doesn't improve with age.)

If the formula for units to account for doesn't balance, stop your analysis and find the error. Otherwise, there's no point in attaching dollar amounts to the units.

Here are the costs of making candy for the period:

> Total costs = cost of beginning inventory + costs added during the period
>
> Total costs = \$48,000 + \$53,800
>
> Total costs = \$101,800

Computing equivalent units

Equivalent units are the units in production multiplied by the percentage of those units that are complete (100 percent) or those that are in process. That covers everything.

If a unit is completed and transferred out, *it's 100 percent complete.* Now, that may seem obvious, but it's a point that gets lost when accountants start this analysis. Your approach to complex analysis should be to account for the easy stuff first. The completed and transferred out units are easier to address than work in process.

Say you've mixed enough sugar to make 600,000 units. Assume that ending work in process is 25 percent complete for all components of production (material, labor, and overhead). Table 16-3 shows the computation of equivalent units.

Table 16-3	Equivalent Units of Production		
	Units	*Complete*	*Equivalent Units*
Completed and transferred	600,000	100 percent	600,000
Work in process, ending	600,000	25 percent	150,000
Equivalent units			**750,000**

Although 25 percent of the units are unfinished, in "equivalent unit talk" you can treat them as 150,000 *completed* units. Add them to the really completed units to get 750,000 units, which represents the number of *equivalent whole units* you have produced. It's a lot easier to talk about a whole unit than some whole units and some partially completed units.

The next step is to compute the *cost per equivalent unit.* Take the total costs of $101,800, and divide by the number of units. Remember that the total costs are the sum of the beginning inventory cost ($48,000) and the costs added during production ($53,800):

Cost per equivalent unit = total costs ÷ number of units

Cost per equivalent unit = $101,800 ÷ 750,000

Cost per equivalent unit = $0.1357

The calculation goes to four decimal places, because when you're making candy that sells for 20 cents per unit, and you're producing hundreds of thousands of units, every tiny fraction of a dollar counts.

Now assign the cost per equivalent unit to the completed work and the WIP. Table 16-4 shows the calculation (costs are rounded).

You've assigned costs to both completed work and WIP. Congratulations! Maybe you should eat a pound or two of candy to celebrate.

Table 16-4	Assignment of Costs		
	Units	*Cost/Unit*	*Cost Assigned*
Completed and transferred	600,000	$0.1357	$81,440
Work in process, ending	150,000	$0.1357	$20,360
Equivalent units			**$101,800**

Seeing different percentages of completion

Material costs typically enter the production process before conversion costs. Flip back to "Following up with conversion costs" for more. You usually need to have material before you pay people to make a product with it. So material costs accumulate sooner and faster than conversion costs.

Different conversion costs occur at different points in production, and the percentage completion changes, too. This section walks through an example with different percentage of completion amounts for material and conversion costs.

Say your company makes high-end men's dress shoes. Your cost analysis runs through the same steps to compute equivalent units that you saw earlier. See the section "Computing equivalent units." However, there are a few extra twists that complicate the process.

Let's get physical: Physical units

First, you track down your units; then you account for the physical flow of units. After that, you can apply costs to each unit. Finally, you move on to computing equivalent units.

Table 16-5 displays the physical flow of units.

Table 16-5	Shoe Company Physical Flow of Units (November)
	Units
Work in process, beginning inventory (11/1)	0
Units started during November	600
Units to account for	**600**
Completed and transferred out during November	400
Work in process, ending inventory (11/30)	200
Units accounted for	**600**

The total inputs (units to account for) must equal the outputs (units accounted for), and they do. Good! Next, calculate equivalent units.

Going over equivalent units

Table 16-6 calculates equivalent units. There's something new here: The table separates percentage completion for material and percentage completion for conversion costs. Why? Because materials are all added at the beginning of the process and are 100 percent complete right away. Conversion costs, however, are added gradually and are not entirely finished at the end of the period.

Table 16-6	Shoe Company — Equivalent Units of Production		
	Physical Units	**Equivalent Units**	**Equivalent Units**
		Material	Conversion
Percent completed in WIP		100 percent	60 percent
Units completed and transferred out	400	400	400
WIP, ending	200	200	120
Equivalent total		**600**	**520**

It's no surprise that material percentage completion is higher than the conversion figure. Equivalent units are computed by multiplying physical units by percentages for *both material and conversion*. The total equivalent units is the sum of both calculations. Note that the physical units still can't be transferred out until all of the material *and* conversion costs are 100 percent complete.

No equivalent unit calculation will ever produce a number higher than the number of physical units. That's because you never multiply the physical units by a number greater than 100 percent. Keep this in mind, because it's a way to check your work as you go.

Putting in costs

The costs you incur are separated into material costs and conversion costs. In the shoe example, there's no beginning work in process. All of the costs are started during the period. Here are the costs:

Costs added during the period = material costs + conversion costs

Costs added during the period = $30,000 + $20,000

Costs added during the period = $50,000

You divide costs by equivalent units to compute cost per equivalent unit. This time, however, you compute two costs (material and conversion) per equivalent unit. To allocate the two types of costs (material and conversion), you need two cost rates. Table 16-7 displays the details.

Table 16-7	Shoe Company — Cost Per Equivalent Unit	
	Material	*Conversion*
Costs added during the period (A)	$30,000	$20,000
Equivalent units (B)	600	520
Cost equivalent units (A ÷ B)	**$50.00**	**$38.46**

The two cost rates are $50.00 per equivalent unit for material and $38.46 per equivalent unit for conversion. In other words, a completed single unit would cost $88.46 ($50 for material and $38.46 for conversion cost). Now, that's a completed *whole* unit, one that has incurred all the necessary costs to be complete.

You wrap up cost for equivalent units by allocating costs to completed goods and ending WIP. You multiply the equivalent units (Table 16-6) by cost per equivalent units (Table 16-7).

This process is a bit complicated, because you've separated material and conversion costs. Look at Table 16-8.

Table 16-8	Shoe Company — Assignment of Costs		
Material Costs	*Units*	*Cost/Unit*	*Cost Assigned*
Completed and transferred out	400	$50/unit	$20,000
Work in process, ending	200	$50/unit	$10,000
Conversion costs			
Completed and transferred out	400	$38.46/unit	$15,385
Work in process, ending	120	$38.46/unit	$4,615
Total costs assigned			**$50,000**

The total costs assigned ($50,000) agree with the "costs added during the period" calculation at the start of this section. That's good!

Using the Weighted Average Method for Process Costing

You've seen two issues that make process costing complex. One issue is dealing with beginning and ending work in process (WIP). The other issue is dealing with different percentage completion rates for material and conversion costs.

The *weighted average method* includes both of these variables. Yikes! Don't worry; you'll get through it. In fact, going over this method reinforces your understand of the prior concepts in this chapter.

In accounting, taking a weighted average is thought to be an easier method than other choices. You add up all of the cost, divide by a number (like inventory units), and that's your weighted average. You use that rate to apply costs to everything.

Consider inventory valuation. For inventory, weighted average method is easier than the first-in-first-out (FIFO) method or the last-in-last-out (LIFO) method. Jump over to Chapter 9 for more on inventory methods. The same is true with process costing — the weighted average method is easier.

The *weighted average method for process costing* calculates equivalent unit costs for *all work done to date.* Work done to date means all work performed (and costs incurred) so far on the units, regardless of when the work occurred.

So here's a practical example. Assume you have units in production. Material costs for the units were incurred in October and November. The weighted average method includes the work and costs from *both months.*

October and November costs are included in the calculation of equivalent units. Here's the cost per equivalent unit for the weighted average method:

> Cost per equivalent unit = total costs for all work done to date ÷ total equivalent units

Material costs generally go into production before conversion costs. The percentage completion for material is almost always higher than the percentage completion for conversion costs. It might remains the same, but it won't go lower. That holds true whether you're looking at beginning WIP or ending WIP.

Handling beginning work in process

Work done to date is the beginning work in process. This month's beginning WIP is *last month's ending work in process.*

Say you make men's bow ties. (If I knew how to tie a bow tie well, I'd wear one. But because I don't, I wear standard ties.) You've decided to use the weighted average method to compute costs for process costing in February.

To start the analysis, you need to review ending work in process from January. That data is listed in Table 16-9.

Table 16-9	Tie Company — Cost Assigned to January Ending WIP (100 Physical Units)	
	Material	*(100% Complete) Conversion (60% Complete)*
Equivalent units (A)	100	60
Cost per equivalent unit (B)	$60	$45
Total cost assigned	**$6,000**	**$2,700**

You have all the data you need for your beginning work in process for February. The flow of physical units (see Table 16-10) uses the *actual* units for February beginning WIP (100 units). I'm just pointing out again that *actual units* may be different from *equivalent units.* The January ending WIP costs are included in the total cost calculation for February.

Continuing with equivalent units

The next step is to figure the physical flow of units for February. See Table 16-10.

Table 16-10 Tie Company — Physical Flow of Units (February)

	Units
Work in process, beginning inventory (2/1)	100
Units started during February	600
Units to account for	**700**
Completed and transferred out during February	400
Work in process, ending inventory (2/28)	300
Units accounted for	**700**

Beginning WIP units (100) comes from Table 16-9. That's where you see the ending WIP from January, the previous month. Now calculate equivalent units of production. Take a look at Table 16-11.

Table 16-11 Tie Company — Equivalent Units of Production

	Physical Units	*Equivalent Units*	*Equivalent Units*
	Material		**Conversion**
Percent complete in ending WIP		100	60
Completed and transferred out	400	400	400
WIP, ending	300	300	180
Equivalent units total		**700**	**580**

The percentage of completion numbers are for completed goods and ending work in process. *You've already addressed beginning work in process.* Table 16-9 used the data from January's ending WIP. That data included equivalent units — which uses January percentage completion data. When you use the prior month (January) data for beginning work in process (February), you don't need anything more.

Also note that Table 16-9 (January's ending WIP) and Table 16-11 (February's ending WIP) use the same percentage completion amounts. Each table uses 100 percent completion for material and 60 percent completion for conversion costs. The percentage completion amounts may be different for each month.

You're making progress! Now that you've calculated total equivalent units, you assign costs. Your cost amounts come from two sources: beginning work in process and costs added during the month. The costing process is similar to Table 16-7, with one extra step. Look at Table 16-12.

Table 16-12	Tie Company — Cost Per Equivalent Unit	
	Material	*Conversion*
Beginning work in process costs	$6,000	$2,700
Costs added during the period	$30,000	$20,000
Total costs incurred for units (A)	$36,000	$22,700
Total costs — material, conversion		**$58,700**
Equivalent units (B)	700	580
Cost equivalent units (A ÷ B)	**$51.43**	**$39.14**

The beginning work in process costs ($6,000 and $2,700) come from Table 16-9. Costs added during the period are new, of course. Those are your costs for February ($30,000 and $20,000). Cost equivalent units (700 and 580) come from Table 16-11. Now you calculate the dollar amount of costs to assign to each unit ($51.43 and $39.14). Hang in there, because there's only one more step! Put it all together, as shown in Table 16-13.

Table 16-13	Tie Company — Assignment of Costs		
Material Costs	*Units*	*Cost/Unit*	*Cost Assigned*
Completed and transferred	400	$51.43/unit	$20,571
Work in process, ending	300	$51.43/unit	$15,429
Conversion costs			
Completed and transferred	400	$39.14/unit	$15,655
Work in process, ending	180	$39.14/unit	$7,045
Total costs assigned			**$58,700**

The total cost assigned agrees with the total cost for materials and conversion in Table 16-12, and that's what you need to see. You did it! You've assigned costs using the weighted average method for process costing.

Introducing the First In, First Out Method of Process Costing

FIFO, FIFO, it's off to work we go. The first in, first out method of process costing treats beginning and ending inventory costs differently. The term *first in, first out* is used with inventory (see Chapter 9). For inventory, FIFO means that you sell the oldest units of inventory first. Your cost of goods sold starts with the oldest units sold and then adds newer units sold.

Here's the process for the first in, first out method of process costing:

1. **Determine the physical movement of units** (units to account for and total units accounted for).

2. **Divide the completed and transferred units into two groups.** The first group is all the units that were completed, which came from beginning WIP units. All the remaining units are considered started and completed during the period.

3. **Compute ending work in process.** Treat ending WIP the same way you've seen previously. It's what's left on the factory floor after most units are completed and transferred out.

4. **Calculate total equivalent units.** Add completed and transferred equivalent units to ending WIP equivalent units.

5. **Assign costs.** Assigning costs uses is the same process you've seen before. Divide the current period costs by the equivalent units to compute cost per equivalent unit. Multiply each cost per equivalent unit by the applicable number of equivalent units.

As usual, and as always, start by calculating the physical flow of units. Table 16-14 shows the physical flow of units, using February as the month analyzed.

Table 16-14   FIFO Method — Physical Flow of Units (February)

	Units
Work in process, beginning inventory (2/1)	100
Units started during February	600
Units to account for	**700**
Completed and transferred out during February	

	Units
From beginning work in process	100
Started and completed in February	300
Total completed and transferred out	**400**
Work in process, ending inventory (2/28)	300
Units accounted for	**700**

Notice that completed and transferred items are split into two categories. Of the 400 completed items, 100 units are "from beginning work in process." The 100 units in beginning WIP are considered to be *completed first.* After that, the remaining 300 completed items are started during the month.

That's why this is called the FIFO method. Beginning WIP items are considered to be completed first. First-in units are the first units out. No, nobody's going to go to the factory floor and tag each unit to track its age. It's theoretical, and it works.

TIP

Imagine you open your factory doors at the beginning of the month. You note that 100 units are partially completed (beginning WIP). If you're cranking up production for the month, you probably complete those WIP items first. That's the fastest way to get more finished goods. Instead of starting an item from zero, finish up those that are partially completed.

Scan down Table 16-15. The completion percentages for beginning WIP (0 percent material and 40 percent conversion) are percentages completed in the current month (February). Again, percentage completed really means work completed and costs incurred. For example, if 80 percent of the material was added in January, you add 20 percent in February (the current month).

Table 16-15   FIFO Method — Equivalent Units of Production

	Physical Units	Equivalent Units Material	Equivalent Units Conversion
Completed			
From beginning WIP		0 percent	40 percent
	100	0	40
Started in period		100 percent	100 percent
	300	300	300
Total completed (A)	**400**	**300**	**340**
		100 percent	60 percent
WIP, ending (B)	300	300	180
Total (A – B)		**600**	**520**

The units completed and transferred out are allocated between beginning WIP (100 units) and units started in the period (300). The 300 units started and completed in the period are 100 percent complete for material and conversion costs.

Total equivalent units are the completed units plus ending WIP. Material costs amount to 600 equivalent units; conversion costs amount to 520 equivalent units.

Finish the FIFO method of cost assignment by computing all of your costs. Those costs are divided by equivalent units to get cost per equivalent unit. Then you end by multiplying the equivalent units by cost per equivalent unit. The result is your cost allocation. (I'd put the calculations here, but you've seen them before.)

Comparing Processing Costing Methods

You've plowed through some very complex examples of process costing. Some methods calculate separate percentages of completion for material and conversion costs; others don't.

If your process costing includes work in process (beginning or ending), your cost allocations will change. This section considers how your process costing method affects your profit.

Mulling over weighted average and FIFO methods

The weighted average method will very likely result in different cost allocations than the FIFO. The best way to digest the differences is to consider how weighted average and FIFO differ when you value *inventory*, as opposed to manufacturing process costs.

Kicking around inventory costing methods

In Chapter 9, you see the impact of a selected inventory costing method on profit. You use a few assumptions and two inventory methods:

- Assume the prices rise over time.

- Say you don't have any beginning inventory, but you make two purchases of 100 units each to stock up.

✔ You paid $6 per unit for the first purchase on the first of the month, and $8 per unit for the second purchase on the 15th.

✔ You sell 50 units on the 25th. You need an inventory costing method to compute cost of sales (for 50 units) and ending inventory (for 150 units).

The *weighted average method* price is $7 per unit (($6 + $8) ÷ 2). You sell 50 units. Your cost of sales is $350 ($7 × 50 units). What remains in ending inventory is 150 units with an average cost of $7. Your ending inventory value is $1,050.

The FIFO method assumes that the oldest units are sold first. You sell 50 units with a cost of sales of $6 per unit. Your cost of sales is $300 ($6 × 50 units). Ending inventory is 150 units. In this case, you have 50 units that remain at $6 per unit and the additional 100 units purchased on the 15th at $8. Your ending inventory using FIFO is $1,100 ($300 + $800).

And that's how inventory valuation methods affect the cost of goods sold.

There's a reason why an inventory cost of goods sold (COGS) calculation appears here. The cost behavior in this example is the same behavior you see with the weighted average and FIFO process costing methods. Here's what you'll notice:

✔ **FIFO sells cheaper units:** Prices generally increase over time (due to inflation), but FIFO sells the cheapest units first. That's because the cheapest units are the *oldest units.* By contrast, a weighted average cost will be an average. The average will be a combination of the cost of older and newer items.

✔ **Cost of sales and ending inventory:** Selling the older FIFO items first will generate a lower cost of sales in earlier periods than weighted average. Because the newer, more expensive inventory items remain in FIFO inventory, FIFO's ending inventory will be more expensive.

✔ **FIFO profit:** The FIFO method creates a lower cost of sales than weighted average. As a result, FIFO profit must be higher than weighted average profit.

✔ **Profit in future years:** Over time, the newer, more expensive FIFO inventory is sold. It follows that FIFO's cost of sales *in the future* is higher, and profits are lower. Because weighted average uses the same unit cost throughout, the weighted average profit calculation will be the roughly the same each year. (Don't worry. In real life, whether you're stocking inventory for a store or buying material for manufacturing, future purchases are likely to be even higher than your current numbers.)

> ✔ **Total profit on all units:** When all units (200, in this example) are sold, the total profit and total cost of sales *are the same* over time, regardless of which method you choose. This can affect your profit and therefore your pricing: If you use the FIFO method, remember that higher costs are coming down the road. Eventually, you have to sell the more expensive inventory items.

These concepts are the same whether you're analyzing inventory methods or process costing methods.

Checking on standard costs and process costing

Standard costing can be used with process costing, just as it is with other costing methods. *Standard costs* are budgeted or planned costs that are estimated at the beginning of the year. You compare standard costs to actual costs and compute a *variance* (which occurs when actual results differ from your plan). Take a peek at Chapter 7 for an amazingly clear discussion of variances.

Until now, this chapter has discussed actual costs. You compiled those actual costs, divided them by equivalent units, and computed cost per equivalent unit. But wait! There's more! It's a good bet that you used your cost accounting skills to come up with some very good standard costs. You have some budgeted amounts in mind for material and conversion costs.

Seeing a variance is pretty straightforward. Backpedal to Table 16-7. There, you use actual costs added during the period to calculate a cost per equivalent unit. You could replace those total actual costs ($50,000) with your standard cost total.

After you plug in your standard cost total, you can calculate a standard cost per equivalent unit. You know by now that you multiply cost per equivalent unit by the number of equivalent units. Those physical units *don't change*. The same units move in and out, regardless of what costs you apply to the units.

If you have a difference between your standard costs and actual costs, you have a variance. You can investigate the variance in order to make better decisions to reduce your costs. And that's the name of that tune.

Debating transferred-in costs

Transferred-in costs are costs transferred from one department to another. That should make sense, because most businesses need more than one department to complete a product. As the product moves through each department, the costs incurred to date move along with each unit. Each department treats an incoming cost as a cost incurred at the beginning of the period.

If you use standard costing to transfer costs between departments, the accounting is easier. Your costs won't be a moving target. You plan your standard costs in planning meetings, and they remain the same throughout the year. You accumulate standard costs in department A, and those costs move through department B with the units that are partially complete.

On the other hand, using weighted average or FIFO costing may make the accounting more complex. (May? It will!) As you've seen, those two methods require you to track different percentage completion amounts, and different units in beginning and ending WIP. The goal is for you to find a process costing method you can live with — and stick to it.

Financial statements that are generated for the "outside world" have a set of rules. One rule is that if you change an accounting method, you must disclose the financial impact of that change. It's a heads-up to the statement reader. So if you change a process costing method (for example, changing from the weighted average method to the FIFO method) that affects the cost of sales in your income statement, you need to declare it.

Part V
Considering Quality Issues

"Do you want the variable cost figures with or without the shark tank overhead?"

In this part . . .

Customers want products that work. If you don't sell a quality product, customers may not buy from you again! Quality has an effect on the cost of your product. Part V revolves around quality, and the costs associated with quality. Chapter 17 deals with spoilage, rework, and scrap. The chapter is all about minimizing waste in your production. Ordering costs are covered in Chapter 18, and you see an overview of quality in Chapter 19. Selling a quality product keeps customers coming back.

Chapter 17

What a Waste! Getting the Most from Spoilage, Scrap, and Reworked Products

*S*poilage is a term that describes units you produce that don't meet your production standards. There may be defects (errors) in production, or in the case of food, at some point in time the product will no longer be wholesome. Either way, you won't be able to sell substandard units to customers.

No production process is perfect. Every manufacturer ends production with stuff that's left over and not used. Accountants refer to leftover material with a low sales value as *scrap*.

Sometimes, you can repair a defective product so it meets your production standards. At that point, you can sell it to a customer. Those units are considered *reworked*.

No production process "works" all the time, so there's usually some scrap, spoilage, and rework. That costs you something, and you need to account for those costs. Allocating these costs generate an accurate total product cost. You use the total product cost to price your product and generate a profit.

Accounting for Waste

In a perfect world, there would be no waste in manufacturing and retailing. (In a perfect world, there'd be no earthquakes or hurricanes, and French fries wouldn't make you fat.) In the real world, however, some material is flawed, some products are made wrong, and items bought for retail sale get broken. This section shows you how to account for the waste in manufacturing, retailing, and craft services.

Determining the inspection point

The *inspection point* is the stage in production when you inspect the units produced to determine if they meet your standards. If so, they are units you can sell to a customer. If not, you consider whether the units can be reworked and sold later. The inspection point is also the time when you determine if any spoilage is avoidable or unavoidable.

Consider the timing of the inspection. Ideally, units should be inspected at each stage of the production process. Cost accountants assume that the spoilage occurs at the completion of a particular production stage, and that that's when the goods are inspected. So, for example, if your company bakes 200,000 cookies per day, the inspection point would be when the cookies exit the oven. Then it's obvious that any spoilage happened in the baking department.

Understanding spoilage and scrap

The *matching principle* (a term made popular throughout this book and a fundamental accounting principle) matches the costs incurred to produce a product with the revenue generated from selling it. The problem with the cost of spoilage and scrap is that you can't directly *trace* it to a product you've sold. You have to *allocate* it.

Spoilage and scrap are *not* the costs making a single finished unit. Just the same, the units you sell must absorb some of this costs. So although spoilage and scrap don't relate directly to finished units, they do relate *indirectly*.

If it's any consolation, you may be able to sell scrap as something else — a different product with a lower sales value. For example, beef processors (also known as slaughterhouses) sell any usable scrap, edible or not, to a rendering plant. That decision allows you to increase the revenue you earn from your production process.

Even though the additional revenue is great to have, the revenue produced by scrap isn't revenue from the primary product. They aren't (and you aren't) running production to generate scrap revenue.

A *factory second* is an item that's spoiled, in that it failed quality inspection and doesn't meet your standards. But with a factory second, there's nothing intrinsically wrong with the product. The finish on an electric guitar might have a blemish (a "blem"), but the guitar plays fine. A garment might have a "holiday" in the fabric, or a seam isn't perfectly sewn. Still, it's a wearable garment. And bread sold at a big bakery's retail outlet (a "bakery thrift shop") may be day-old bread, but it's still good. The point is, you may be able to make money by selling so-called spoiled items.

Differentiating normal or abnormal spoilage

Not all spoilage is created equal. As you look at your production results, you need to distinguish between *normal spoilage* and *abnormal spoilage*.

Normal spoilage occurs even in the best of production environments. No matter how efficiently you work, you still incur normal spoilage. That's because there are limitations to any production process. For example, if you're baking 200,000 cookies per day in a continuous baking oven, consistency is vital. The trouble is that even with the best of ovens, there's spoilage you can count on. It could be as simple as cookies breaking when they leave the belt, and that situation might be costly to fix. If the vast majority of cookies are coming out fine, the breakage is considered to be normal spoilage.

The *matching principle* connects your production costs to production revenue. You include the cost of normal spoilage as part of cost of goods manufactured. That makes sense, because some normal spoilage is inevitable. It's a normal part of the production process.

Because normal spoilage always shows up, you spread the cost over the *good units* you sell. Good units are those that meet your standards — items that are sellable to a customer.

Abnormal spoilage is spoilage beyond what you normally expect in production. Accountants also define the term as spoilage that wouldn't happen if you operated efficiently. If you have spoilage you can avoid, you have abnormal spoilage.

As a business owner, you're probably starting to think about your staff and machinery. Consider just how well your operation is running. If machines aren't kept in good working order, they won't operate correctly, and the goods they produce may be defective. These are costs that can be avoided.

Assume again that you're baking 200,000 cookies per day in a continuous baking oven. You can overbake or underbake if the heat distribution is wrong, or if the wheels and pins in the chain aren't well lubricated. Some cookies won't meet the standard. The defective units generate abnormal costs. Some machine problems are unavoidable, but the lack of proper maintenance *is avoidable*.

Keep your thinking cap on!

You may be able to turn costs you "can't recover" into a profit center. For a classic case of cost recovery, consider world-famous Jelly Belly jelly beans, a favorite of President Ronald Reagan. Jelly Bellys have their share of normal spoilage, because the company makes 14,800,000,000 jelly beans per year. So what do you do with out-of-spec Jelly Bellys? You sell them as Belly Flops. The official website says, "Belly Flops are no less flavorful, or lovable, than regular Jelly Belly jelly beans; they just come in wild shapes and sizes. You may find one that's round, one that's square, or you may even find a bunch stuck together."

If you bake cookies in batches, you cut the dough as precisely as you can, but the dough surrounding the cookies be left over. (Come to think of it, this book is all about leftover dough. That's a little cost accounting humor for you.) Anyway, the excess dough is neither avoidable nor unavoidable spoilage; it's scrap. "Donut holes" were scrap until someone figured out that they could be a product.

If an employee isn't properly trained, he or she may make mistakes, and those errors may produce a defective product. For example, an employee who isn't trained properly to monitor baking oven temperature may cause overbaking or underbaking. That would produce defective units and avoidable (hence, abnormal) costs.

Accountants post the cost of abnormal spoilage to a "loss for abnormal spoilage" account. The loss isn't related to cost of goods manufactured. Instead, abnormal spoilage is a separate cost that you can't recover.

Expiration date: A special kind of spoilage

When a product reaches its expiration date, it no longer meets your standards. The product can't be sold to a customer. Say you own a grocery store; consider milk that goes bad. When that milk expires and can't be sold, you incur a cost. Even worse, you don't generate any revenue from that stale milk.

Grocery stores have to be precise about when they order products that are perishable — and how much they order. They need to be aware of expiration dates and plan to remove expired product from their shelves.

Spoilage and process costing

Process costing assumes that all units produced are identical — that's the assumption you make throughout this book. Step on over to Chapter 16 for more on process costing.

When spoilage creates costs in a process-costing environment, you apply the methods in this section to account for them.

Breaking out abnormal spoilage

Accountants post the cost of abnormal spoilage to a "loss for abnormal spoilage" account. The loss isn't related to cost of goods manufactured. Instead, abnormal spoilage is a separate cost that you can't recover.

As a result, abnormal spoilage isn't included as a product cost. So break it out first. Your accountant will put the cost in a loss account separate from costs of manufacturing. When you determine that a cost represents abnormal spoilage, you recognize a loss — and you're all done with that part.

Shifting to normal spoilage

Costing normal spoilage takes a little math. You add spoilage costs to cost of goods manufactured. Now consider how costs are assigned using process costing.

As units move from one production department to another, the costs move along with them. Process costing uses equivalent units to account for units that are partially complete. The percentage of completion for material cost might be different from conversion costs, and vice versa. (Recall that for a lot of products, most material costs are incurred at an early stage of production.) Equivalent units even things out. The goal is for each *equivalent unit* to have the same amount of costs attached to it.

Some of your equivalent units will be spoiled. Maybe you're running production of 10,000 magazines. As you inspect the magazines for defects, you notice that 10 magazines have pages that were printed incorrectly. Those magazines aren't sellable to customers. Because you expect some spoilage (due to the limits of your machine's capability), the ten magazines are considered normal spoilage. Normal spoilage adds costs to your goods.

So you have a choice when accounting for normal spoilage. You can include the spoiled units in your calculation of physical units and equivalent units, or you can exclude them.

Presenting normal spoilage methods

Get ready to see two costing methods for normal spoilage. You calculate equivalent units *including* spoiled units first. Then you look at the results when you *exclude* spoiled units from equivalent units.

Say you manufacture men's leather belts. Consider this information for the example:

- ✔ Material costs enter production at the beginning of the process. There is no beginning inventory for this month (January).

- ✔ Because material costs are incurred at the beginning of the process, assume that the units are 100 percent complete for material costs. So material equivalent units equal physical units. Other costs (like conversion costs) may not be complete. This analysis considers only material costs.

- ✔ You produce 6,000 units during January. Of these, 5,800 are good units that can be sold to customers. The other 200 units are spoiled. The spoilage is about 3 percent of total production (200 spoiled units ÷ 6,000 units produced × 100). Based on your experience and knowledge of the process, a 3 percent level of spoilage isn't unusual. You consider the defective units to be normal spoilage.

- ✔ Spoiled units are treated as completed goods that are transferred out.

- ✔ Ending work in process is 2,000 units. Good units completed and transferred out are 3,800 units (5,800 good units – 2,000 ending work in process).

- ✔ The total material costs to be allocated are $150,000.

Table 17-1 is the calculation of equivalent units with spoiled units included in the calculation. It calculates cost for *material only*.

Table 17-1	Equivalent Units — Spoiled Units Included		
	Units	Cost/Unit	Cost
Costs incurred to date (A)			$150,000
Equivalent units (B)	6,000		
Cost per equivalent unit (A)/(B)		$25.00	
Assignment of costs			
Units completed, transferred out	3,800	$25.00	$95,000
Add spoiled units	200	$25.00	$5,000
Goods transferred out	**4,000**		**$100,000**
Work in process, ending	2,000	$25.00	$50,000
Costs accounted for	**6,000**		**$150,000**

Work your way from the top of the table toward the bottom. Cost per equivalent unit is the total cost to date ($150,000) divided by the 6,000 equivalent units cited in the text. Jump over to Chapter 16 for more detail on calculating equivalent units.

Any goods you work on during the period (whether in work in process or started during the period) end up in one of two places. They are goods completed and transferred out to finished goods inventory, or they are considered work in process. Keep in mind, however, the actual spoiled units aren't transferred to finished goods. Spoiled units aren't sellable. Finished goods are units that can be sold to a customer.

In Table 17-1, there are 4,000 units transferred out, 3,800 of which are good units (units you can sell to a customer). You treat the 200 spoiled units as completed, too. They're bad units, and you can't sell them to a customer — but you are finished working on them.

This costing method for normal spoilage equivalent units assumes spoiled units are completed. It makes sense, if you assume there's an inspection at the point of completion, and some units are spoiled.

Defective units could be reworked and sold as good units. That's not always the case, but it's possible. To be clear, the Table 17-1 and the following Table 17-2 don't take reworks into account. Check out the "Reworking a product to recoup some profit" section later for more on reworked products.

In Table 17-1, the work in process units (2,000 units), plus the completed and transferred-out units (4,000 units), total the 6,000 equivalent units at the top of the table. You've accounted for all of the units. Finally, the cost accounted for ($150,000) at the bottom of Table 17-1 agrees with the costs incurred to date at the top of the table.

So you just calculated equivalent units and accounted for normal spoilage. Table 17-1 assumes that spoiled units were *included* in the equivalent unit calculation. Now give it a try with spoiled units *excluded* from equivalent units.

Table 17-2 excludes the spoiled units. All the other variables are the same.

Table 17-2	Equivalent Units — Spoiled Units Excluded		
	Units	**Cost/Unit**	**Cost**
Costs incurred to date (A)			$150,000
Equivalent units (B)	5,800		
Cost per equivalent unit (rounded) (A)/(B)		$25.86	
Assignment of costs			
Good units completed	3,800	$25.86	$98,276
Add spoiled units	0		$0
Goods transferred out	3,800		**$98,276**
Work in process, ending	2,000	$25.86	$51,724
Costs accounted for	**5,800**		**$150,000**

Here's how Table 17-2 differs from the first calculation of equivalent units:

- ✔ There are 5,800 equivalent units. You get that number by taking 6,000 total units produced and subtracting 200 spoiled units.

- ✔ Your total material costs remain at $150,000. You're spreading the same cost over *fewer equivalent units.* Your cost per equivalent unit is $25.86 ($150,000 total cost ÷ 5,800 units). The cost per equivalent unit is $0.86 higher than the cost per equivalent unit in Table 17-1.

- ✔ The good units completed are the same as Table 17-1 (3,800 units). However, no spoiled units are added to the total goods transferred out. So those same 3,800 units are transferred out (instead of 4,000 in the previous example).

- ✔ Work in process (2,000 units) is the same as in Table 17-1. The total units accounted for are 5,800 (not 6,000, as in Table 17-1).

- ✔ The costs accounted for is the same $150,000. That agrees with the cost incurred to date at the top of the table. You assign the same cost to 200 fewer units than you did in Table 17-1, because the cost per equivalent unit is higher.

Choosing a method to cost normal spoilage

Think about which method you want to use to account for normal spoilage. Consider an issue that recurs throughout this book: You go through the effort of cost accounting to identify areas where you can make improvement. Ideally, you prefer a system where a problem generates a red flag — it gets your attention so you can fix it.

Those spoiled units need to get your attention. Because most companies inspect goods periodically during production, you eventually identify the spoiled units. If you identify spoiled units sooner instead of later, however, you can evaluate your production method and make changes faster.

Normal spoilage is considered unavoidable. Normal spoilage occurs because even the best machines can break down and even the best employees can make some mistakes.

Improvement includes changing production to reduce *any* spoilage, including normal spoilage. Because you need to evaluate production constantly, you need an accounting system that identifies spoilage cost every month, quarter, or year.

The better method, according to the matching principle, to use for normal costing is to *include* spoiled units in the equivalent unit calculation. Look at the inspection process once again:

✔ The inspection process occurs when units are 100 percent complete. (That's not always the case. Many companies inspect goods more frequently than just at the end of production.)

✔ If you include spoiled units in the equivalent unit calculation, spoiled units are considered completed (and transferred out).

✔ Excluding the costs of spoiled units for the equivalent unit calculation "pushes" costs into ending work in process (WIP). In Table 17-2, the cost of ending WIP is $51,724. That's higher than the previous ending WIP cost of $50,000 (in Table 17-1). When the costs are pushed into WIP, they are not yet expensed. Because WIP is an inventory account, moving costs into WIP delays the recognition of cost of goods sold.

Table 17-2 assigns the same $150,000 in cost as Table 17-1, only to fewer units.

Including spoiled units in the equivalent unit calculation is the better choice. It allows you to identify spoiled units sooner. The spoiled units act as a much-desired red flag, too. Hopefully, you analyze the spoiled units and find ways to improve your production process.

Reworking a product to recoup some profit

The good news is that you can sometimes rework a defective product to make it right. The bad news is that you incur a cost to rework it. For example, if the lining in a felt hat needs to be resewn, you incur labor and material costs to make it right.

Here's where rework differs from spoilage and scrap: Rework revenue is generated from producing the primary product (felt hats). You didn't *intend* to generate rework costs. Your intention is that all hats are made to meet your standards.

Obviously, if you do have defects, the rework cost reduces your profit on each reworked felt hat you sell, but that's better than not having the hat to sell.

Applying Process Costing Methods to Spoilage

This section uses the two great process costing methods — *weighted average* and *first-in first out* (FIFO) — to account for spoilage. You find those concepts in Chapter 16. Swing, dance, or bounce over to that chapter, if you need to.

Weighing in on the weighted average costing method

You use the *weighted average costing method* to calculate costs in a process-costing environment. Now incorporate weighted average analysis into calculating spoilage costs.

To get super-psyched for the weighted average method, keep these points in mind:

✔ To keep it simple, you analyze only the material units and material costs for a product.

✔ Assume that material costs go into production at the beginning of the period. Material is 100 percent complete in any ending work in process.

✔ The weighted average method calculates units and costs on work done to date. The cost includes work performed in the *preceding* period (beginning WIP) and in the *current* period.

Here are the steps you take to implement process costing:

1. **Account for the physical units you produce.**

2. **Compute equivalent units, based on percentage of completion.**

3. **Total your costs and then calculate cost per equivalent unit.**

4. **Multiply your equivalent units by cost per equivalent unit.**

In this section, you're going through the same process. You're simply adding in the impact of spoilage.

Accounting for physical units

Say you manufacture an electric kitchen wall oven. Your total production cost is $1,500 per oven. A portion of that cost is for materials (plastic, steel, and aluminum). You use the weighted average method to account for costs, including the cost of spoilage. As you start the analysis for May, consider these factors:

✔ You *include* normal spoilage units as completed units. That means that normal spoilage units will be part of the equivalent unit calculation.

✔ Normal spoilage is expected to be 5 percent of production. That percentage is based on past production results and your product knowledge.

✔ The cost of *abnormal* spoilage won't be attached to the product. Instead, those costs are posted to a "loss for abnormal spoilage" account. Abnormal spoilage isn't part of the cost of goods manufactured.

Just as in Chapter 16, start by accounting for the physical units. Check out Table 17-3.

Table 17-3   Weighted Average — Physical Flow of Units (May)

Material Cost Analysis	Units	Equivalent Units
Work in process, beginning inventory (5/1)	100	
Units started during May	600	
Units to account for	700	
Completed and transferred out during May	400	400
Normal spoilage (5 percent of good units)	20	20
Abnormal spoilage (2.5 percent of good units)	10	10
Work in process, ending inventory (5/31)	270	270
Units accounted for	700	700

For these high-end ovens, material is introduced at the beginning of production. For your analysis, assume that material costs are 100 percent complete. As a result, the equivalent units are equal to the physical units. The 700 units for which you need to account equal the 700 units accounted for.

Attaching costs to equivalent units

Here are the material costs for making ovens for the period:

Total costs = cost of beginning inventory + costs added during the period

Total costs = $80,000 + $400,000

Total costs = $480,000

To calculate equivalent units, divide total costs for the period by the total equivalent units. Here's the calculation:

$480,000 total costs ÷ 700 equivalent units = $685.71 cost per equivalent unit

Table 17-4 assigns the $480,000 total cost to units produced. The table multiplies equivalent units by the cost per equivalent unit ($685.71).

Table 17-4	Weighted Average — Equivalent Units (May)		
	Equivalent Units	*Cost Per Unit*	*Total Cost*
Completed, transferred	400	$685.71	$274,286
Normal spoilage	20	$685.71	$13,714
Cost of good units	**420**	**$685.71**	**$288,000**
Abnormal spoilage	10	$685.71	$6,857
Work in process, ending	270	$685.71	$185,143
Totals	**700**		**$480,000**

Note in Table 17-4 that the cost of good units includes both units transferred out and the normal spoilage. The total units (700) agree with the total in Table 17-3. The total costs assigned ($480,000) agree with the total cost calculation in Table 17-4.

Normal spoilage cost ($13,714) is attached to cost of goods manufactured. Abnormal spoilage cost ($6,857) is recognized as a loss — not attached to the cost of goods.

You've assigned total material costs to the units you worked. To complete costs for the full product, you perform the same analysis on conversion costs. You finish up by adding material costs to conversion costs. That total is your full product cost for the ovens.

Doing the FIFO Hokey Pokey: Put your first in first, take your first out first

The FIFO method for process costing treats beginning work in process differently from the weighted average method for process costing.

The FIFO method divides completed and transferred units into two groups. One group is the beginning WIP units that are completed during the period (they often have a lower cost). All other completed units are considered *started and completed* during the period (they reflect current cost). Ending WIP is treated in the same way as the weighted average cost calculation; nothing special happens to it.

The equivalent units process for the FIFO method is different from the weighted average method. Consider the beginning WIP units. Equivalent units for beginning WIP include the percentage to be completed in the *current period* only (May, in this case). So here's the formula for beginning WIP's equivalent units:

> Beginning WIP's equivalent units = Beginning WIP physical units × percentage to be completed during the period

The equivalent unit calculation drives the costs assigned. Beginning WIP costs incurred during May are included in the FIFO cost calculation. Therefore, you are including the work done in May and matching it with the costs incurred in May.

Beginning WIP costs *before May* are excluded from the FIFO cost calculation. Because the costs are excluded from the cost calculation in May, so is the work you completed in the preceding period.

The scenario is basically the same as in the section "Accounting for physical units." This time, however, you use the FIFO method for process costing.

Table 17-5 shows the physical flow of units, using the FIFO method. It's similar to the format used for weighted average in Table 17-3. The one big difference is that goods "completed and transferred out during May" are split into two groups. Some completed goods were originally beginning WIP and have different costs from the goods started and completed during the period (May). Of course, Table 17-5 includes the number of spoiled units during the period.

Table 17-5	FIFO — Physical Flow of Units (May)	
Material Cost Analysis	***Units***	***Equivalent Units***
Work in process, beginning inventory (5/1)	100	
Units started during May	600	
Units to account for	**700**	
Completed and transferred out during May		
From beginning work in process	100	0
Started and completed during May	300	300
Total units completed, transferred out	**400**	
Normal spoilage (5 percent of units)	20	20
Abnormal spoilage (2.5 percent of units)	10	10
Work in process, ending inventory (5/31)	270	270
Units accounted for	**700**	**600**

The 700 units accounted for equal the 700 units you need to account for. Be reminded that for these high-end ovens, material is introduced at the beginning of production, and material costs are 100 percent complete in beginning work in process. As a result, the equivalent units are equal to the physical units. (Remember that the product has not been completed because there are likely some conversion costs that are not yet finished.)

The FIFO method generates different equivalent units for beginning WIP:

- ✔ Beginning WIP units are assumed to be 100 percent complete for material costs. Because all material was added in the preceding period, no material (0 percent) needs to be completed in the current period.

- ✔ The material costs for WIP were incurred in the *preceding period*.

- ✔ The 100 physical units for beginning WIP are multiplied by 0 percent completion (in the current period) to yield zero equivalent units for May. So you're costing 600 total equivalent units versus 700 in the weighted average analysis used in Table 17-3.

- ✔ Note that units started in May (600) does not equal units started and completed during May (300). That means that 300 units (600 – 300) were started during the period but don't yet count as completed.

- ✔ Ending WIP is 270 units. That's different from the number of units started during the period and *not finished* (300). The difference is 30 units with normal and abnormal spoilage. Yes, they're considered finished, but they're no good. So they're not in ending inventory.

To calculate equivalent units, divide current costs for the period ($400,000) by the equivalent units (600). Here's that calculation:

Cost per equivalent unit = $400,000 ÷ 600

Cost per equivalent unit = $666.67

Table 17-6 multiplies the FIFO equivalent unit counts by cost per equivalent unit.

Table 17-6	FIFO — Equivalent Units (May)		
	Equivalent Units	*Cost Per Unit*	*Total Cost*
Completed, transferred			
From beginning WIP	0	$666.67	$0
Started and completed	300	$666.67	$200,000
Normal spoilage	20	$666.67	$13,333
Cost of good units	**320**	**$666.67**	**$213,333**

	Equivalent Units	Cost Per Unit	Total Cost
Abnormal spoilage	10	$666.67	$6,667
Work in process, ending	270	$666.67	$180,000
Totals	**600**		**$400,000**

Job Costing for Spoilage, Reworked Products, and Scrap

Job costing assigns costs based on a specific job or customer. You use job costing when each customer sale incurs a different level of costs. Stroll on over to Chapter 4 for more about job costing.

People who work in "the trades" (plumbers, carpenters, and roofers, for example) use job costing. Say you own a plumbing company and work with homeowners and small commercial buildings. You're reviewing your plumbing supply costs for the week, and you notice that some brackets you used on pipes were defective.

You have several decisions to make about the defective part. You need to decide whether the spoilage is normal or abnormal. You also need to decide whether the cost should be assigned to a specific job or to *all* jobs.

The first section covers how to handle spoilage costs in a job costing environment. Later, I address job costing reworked products and scrap as well.

Making adjustments for normal and abnormal spoilage

Normal spoilage is expected under the best of circumstances. The cost is included in cost of manufacturing, and it's part of job costing. On the other hand, abnormal spoilage produces more defects than you would expect from normal production. Those costs are posted to a loss account. Abnormal costs aren't part of the cost of manufacturing or completing a customer job. They are a loss you take (which you might describe as "eating it" or "taking it in the shorts").

Assume that the defective brackets are normal spoilage. You have a good supplier for your plumbing supplies (a good supplier being a critical issue for anyone in the trades). You know from industry experience that 2 percent of the brackets you purchase may be defective because after all, they're only cheap stampings. The trouble is, you use a lot of them.

At this point, maybe you're asking, why not just go back to the supplier for a refund? Maybe that's not a good idea, because maybe you asked too much from the brackets. Specifically, you've used the brackets in such a way that they sometimes fail. It might simply be that your plumbers are putting too much stress on them (such as bending them more than the cheap metal can take). So a 2 percent failure rate isn't really based on the bracket maker's faulty production. It's based on how your plumbers use the part.

Adjustments are accounting entries posted to make corrections. Spoilage accounting entries may require adjustments. For example, you may have already moved the bracket cost (material) into work in process. When you inspect and find the abnormal spoilage, you may need to remove the cost from work in process and move the costs into a loss account. That entry is an adjustment.

You see an adjustment below for normal spoilage posted to all jobs. To keep things simple, I show the other two spoilage entries as if they were *posted correctly the first time*. Those entries don't show any adjustments, because that would make your brain explode. This approach should make the discussion more clear.

Pinning the normal spoilage on all jobs

The bracket defect isn't unique to one job. The defect could happen on any job, particularly because you use the bracket frequently. To allocate the normal spoilage to all jobs, the cost needs to be posted to *manufacturing overhead.* Those overhead costs are then moved to the work in process. Overhead costs, by definition, can't be traced to a specific product.

The bracket, however, is first considered a material cost put into production. When you write the check for the bracket, you debit (increase) material control and credit (decrease) cash. (You may also credit accounts payable instead of cash.)

The work in process account is assigned material, labor, and overhead costs that are put into production. (For an overview, take a peek at Chapter 4's flow of manufacturing costs.)

If you consider the bracket defect to be normal spoilage, you add the cost to production. Here are the accounting entries:

- ✔ Debit (increase) manufacturing overhead control and credit (decrease) material control. The cost of the brackets was originally posted to material control. This entry moves the cost into an overhead account.

- ✔ Debit (increase) work in process and credit (decrease) manufacturing overhead control. This entry allocates the cost of the brackets to production.

Now consider that if the bracket is defective, you replace it (true especially if you're using a lot of them on every job). When you buy the replacement bracket, you debit (increase) material control and credit (decrease) cash. One cost is the defective item (normal spoilage), and the other is a material cost for the job.

Posting the normal spoilage to one job

If the bracket defect is considered normal spoilage for *one particular job*, the cost should be added to production. Here are the accounting entries:

- When the brackets are purchased, debit (increase) material control and credit (decrease) accounts payable or cash.

- Debit (increase) work in process and credit (decrease) material control. This entry allocates the cost of the brackets to production *for a specific job*.

Dealing with abnormal spoilage

Unlike normal spoilage, which you expect, abnormal spoilage is a defect you don't expect. The normal spoilage for brackets is 2 percent. That rate assumes that your plumbers are using the bracket for normal use. In fact, you see the phrase *normal use* on packaging for many products.

Abnormal spoilage can happen when a part is used incorrectly. Say that a plumber uses the bracket in completely the wrong way. Not surprisingly, the defect rate (failure rate) of the part is much higher — call it 30 percent. ("Aw, these brackets keep breakin' when I try to turn them into hanging straps." "Well, Joe, they're not supposed to be deformed like that.")

One more time: Abnormal spoilage cost for job costing is posted to a loss account. The idea is that you recognize the expense (loss) immediately. Here are the accounting entries:

- When the brackets are purchased, debit (increase) material control and credit (decrease) accounts payable or cash. This is an entry you make for just about any purchase.

- Debit (increase) loss from abnormal spoilage and credit (decrease) material control by the cost of the abnormal spoilage. This transaction allocates the cost of the spoiled brackets to a loss account.

"Writing down" abnormal spoilage is consistent with the accounting *principle of conservatism*. The conservative approach is to recognize losses as soon as possible. Those losses will make their way into the financial statements. The financial statement reader will see a better picture of business activity.

Reworking and selling a product

Rework is defined as product that is produced, inspected, and found to be defective. The units are then reworked (fixed) and sold as acceptable products to a customer. Other sources define rework as repairing a non-conforming item.

Accounting entries for initial production

Say you manage a home remodeling business. Your production includes materials, labor costs, and overhead.

When you write checks for material, labor, and overhead costs, you debit a control account (material control, for example) and credit cash or accounts payable. As you move costs into production, the work in process is increased (debited), and the control accounts are decreased (credited). You can go over to Chapter 4 for a review of manufacturing costs.

The rationale for job costing is that each job has a different set of costs. So it makes sense to track each separate job on a *job costing sheet.* That sheet is a running list of the material, labor, and overhead you incurred so far for one customer job. See Chapter 4.

Even though each job has a job costing sheet, the cost accounts in your accounting system will be for *all jobs.* For example, labor costs for all jobs will be posted to a labor account.

There are accounting systems that allow you to segregate account balances by customer or job. When you put together your financial statements, the cost account balances will reflect all the jobs worked during the period.

If your accounting system doesn't have job/project management integrated, there are third-party software applications that very likely tie to your accounting software.

Assigning rework to a specific job

After inspecting your job sites, you find some normal spoilage. No front-page news. So you might allocate the cost of rework to a specific job.

Say you're putting up a special wallpaper. The wallpaper is used only for one job. It's not unusual for different remodeling jobs to have completely different material and labor costs. After all, a bath remodel requires different materials from a new kitchen, and even two bathrooms won't be exactly alike.

The wallpaper is 20 inches wide and comes in a 60-foot roll. After putting up the wallpaper, you find that a 3-foot-long area is discolored. The defect is 5 percent of the total roll of wallpaper (3 feet ÷ 60 feet × 100).

Based on your industry experience, you expect a 5 percent defect rate in a typical roll of the wallpaper. You also know the product well enough that you can treat the discolored area with chemicals and fix the color. It takes an employee 30 minutes ($15 of labor cost), and the chemicals (material) cost $50. Here's the journal entry for the rework costs:

> Debit (increase) work in process $65, credit (decrease) material control $50, and credit (decrease) labor control $15

Allocating rework to all jobs

If you determine that normal spoilage should be allocated to all units, the cost of rework should be charged to manufacturing overhead. Overhead can then be allocated to all products, based on the overhead allocation rate.

Say your remodeling business uses two-by-four treated lumber for many jobs during a particular month. You inspect the lumber for knots and other flaws before you use it in production. During the month, you find that about 3 percent of the lumber is defective. Given your industry experience, that defective rate is expected. You judge the defects to be normal spoilage.

Fortunately, your work crews have the experience to rework the lumber so it's usable. Workers sand the wood and fix flaws in its shape or appearance. Your rework cost is labor cost.

Because nearly every job uses some type of two-by-fours, you allocate all normal spoilage for two-by-fours to all jobs.

The good news is that you were able to rework the lumber and use it in production. You incurred more costs, but it's better than investing the time and money to get replacement two-by-fours and incurring the cost of the unused pieces of lumber.

When labor is assigned to a job, you debit work in process and credit either cash or wage payable control. Labor cost for rework is handled differently. When you compute the rework cost, you make this accounting entry:

> Debit manufacturing overhead control, credit wage payable control

There's a final step to get the rework costs into production. The rework costs are in manufacturing overhead control. You allocate overhead cost based on a predetermined overhead rate. You determine a budgeted overhead rate in planning. For more, take a gander at Chapter 8.

If you really want a gold star on your report card, consider budgeting for rework costs when you plan your overhead rate. Huh? Well, bear with me.

As a remodeler, you know that a 3 percent defect rate is acceptable for two-by-fours. You also have some idea of the cost to rework the two-by-fours. Because two-by-fours are allocated to all jobs, you know that the rework cost end up in a budgeted overhead account.

Your knowledge allows you to budget more precisely. Consider the normal spoilage rate for as many costs as you can. Then consider the rework costs for as many costs as you can. You can add the total dollar amount to your budgeted overhead for the year.

Making allocation decisions about scrap

Scrap is defined as material that's left over after production. Scrap has a low sales value, if it has any value at all. You sell scrap "as is." No costs are added to scrap before you sell it to someone. Keep in mind that if you add any costs (by performing more work) on an item, the unit is considered a byproduct.

Typically, the buyer will be another business — a company that can use the scrap to make a different product. The customers who buy your "real" completed products probably won't be in the market for your scrap.

An experienced manager should have some idea about how much leftover stuff a production run generates. But there's a difference between spoilage and scrap.

Again, spoilage has to do with a defective product. Scrap isn't a product at all. Instead, scrap is leftover pieces of items that were used to *make* a product. That's why your normal customers aren't interested in buying scrap. Accountants don't make a distinction between normal and abnormal scrap — it's all scrap.

You need to make decisions about allocating costs and revenue for scrap. Like spoilage, you can allocate scrap to a specific job, but you can also allocate scrap to all jobs.

Accounting for scrap is similar to accounting for inventory. (Head to Chapter 9 for more information.) You need to track where the scrap is — where it is *physically.* You do physical inventory count to verify where all the inventory is located. There's a similar process for scrap.

Track where the scrap is, and protect it against theft. After all, scrap usually has some sales value. You also need to account for any scrap cost and revenue in your accounting records.

Consider the timing of your accounting entries for scrap. Say you finish a production run for leather purses, and you have leftover scraps of leather. One option is to post accounting entries after *production*. Another option is to record the scrap accounting activity when the scrap is *sold*. Say a maker of leather baseball gloves shows up and buys your leather scraps. You could record the accounting activity when the sale occurs.

Chapter 18

Making Smart Ordering Decisions

· ·

· ·

*1*nventory is usually the largest investment for a business. When you consider how you use assets (cash, in this case), it's likely that your inventory requires a big investment. If you're a retailer, you probably spend a lot on money to stock the store. If you're a manufacturer, you have significant materials costs to manufacture your product.

You have other costs for inventory, besides the goods. You incur a cost to *order* inventory as well, and when you receive the goods, someone needs to verify that you received what you ordered. Then (if you're a retailer) you have to stock the shelves and put the rest of the inventory somewhere. That requires investing in space to hold stock. Oh, and don't forget to protect your inventory from theft!

This chapter introduces the concept of *economic order quantity,* a formula that helps you determine how often to buy inventory and how much to order. You mull over *just-in-time purchasing,* and you finish the chapter by looking at the *supply chain approach* to inventory management and the impact of customer demand on the inventory process.

The topics in this chapter are tools to help you manage ordering costs and carrying costs. You use these tools to figure out when to order, how much to order, and how to move costs through production efficiently.

Considering the Costs of Inventory

There's a lot riding on inventory choices. The cost of purchasing inventory may be your largest expense. And when you pay for inventory (which should be done within a reasonable amount of time whether the inventory moves off your shelves or not), the purchase reduces your available cash balance. This section provides cost accounting principles that may help you make good inventory decisions.

Consider the costs you incur for inventory. You know the basic principle: Stuff costs money. However, inventory is more than just writing a check for the items you put on the shelf. If you mull over the following costs, the need for tools and techniques to *control* the costs make more sense:

- **Purchasing cost:** This is the cost of an inventory item less any discounts you receive from the supplier. Purchasing cost also includes the cost of shipping the item to your location. This category is likely to be your largest cost.

- **Ordering costs:** This is the cost you incur for the process of approving, ordering, and receiving the order.

- **Carrying costs:** This is the cost of holding an inventory item and includes the opportunity cost of using assets to buy inventory. If you use assets to buy inventory, you give up the chance to use the assets to do something else. That's an opportunity cost. Head over to Chapter 11 for more.

- **Stockout costs:** An additional cost occurs each time you order an item for a customer when you are out of inventory. This category includes the opportunity cost of losing a customer order due to a stockout.

- **Quality costs:** This is the cost of selling an item that doesn't conform to the customer's needs (which generally means it's broken). Quality costs also include the cost of making sure the item is conforming to your quality standards. Head to Chapter 19 for a detailed analysis of quality costs.

Note that the list includes opportunity costs in two forms. Using cash to buy inventory, rather than for some other purpose, is a *carrying cost.* The cost (in lost revenue) of losing an order because the inventory is not available is a *stockout cost.*

Going through the ordering sequence

Take a walk through the typical ordering process. Say you own a clothing store. You need to order scarves for the upcoming fall season. A supervisor fills out a *purchase order* (PO). The form lists the amount, style, size, and unit cost of the items requested.

A manager must approve the order. He or she reviews it and verifies that the order is in the budget. The manager initials the order (by hand or electronically), which confirms approval.

The purchase order goes to the vendor (the scarf manufacturer or distributor). The vendor fills the order and ships the merchandise. When the shipping/receiving clerk opens the box, he or she finds two documents: a *packing receipt* and an *invoice.* (**Note:** Sometimes the invoice arrives by mail.)

The packing receipt confirms what's in the box — the items that were actually shipped. The manager needs to agree that the items on the packing receipt match the purchase order. This step verifies that the vendor sent what you ordered. If not, it may mean that some items are back-ordered. Perhaps the vendor can't fill the full order, and you have to wait. Generally, this is not a good thing. If the items on the receipt don't match the purchase order, it also may simply be a mistake. Call the vendor, and ask about the discrepancy.

The invoice is the bill. The store manager should verify that the invoice matches the purchase order and the shipping receipt. The manager should initial each document to confirm that they all agree.

Unless you, the owner, are also the manager (as is likely in smaller stores), all three documents (purchase order, shipping receipt, and invoice) now go to you. If you're the manager, you've already seen them. You review the documents to authorize payment, so you initial the documents and send them to the accounting department. An accounts payable clerk (AP clerk) generates a check, which comes back to you for signature. Finally, the check and a copy of the invoice are sent to the vendor.

If you're placing a lot of orders with a vendor every month, expect to see a *statement,* a summary of individual invoices. The process is the same; the owner authorizes payments only if all the invoices shown on the statement match individual invoices.

Your company incurs costs for all of the people involved with the order. The owner, manager, supervisor, and accounting clerk all spend time on orders. The *cost* of that time (salary, benefits, and so forth) amounts to ordering costs.

Carrying costs include your cost to store your inventory. You might store some inventory on the shelves at your clothing store, but what about the rest? You need a stockroom or a warehouse, and that costs money.

Taking a closer look at stockout costs

Stockout costs represent what you lose when an item is out of stock. You need to consider both the short-term and the long-term impacts of a stock-out. Assume someone sees a black-and-orange scarf on your shop's website. (Black and orange? They were my high school's uniform colors.) When he or she stops by the store, that scarf is out of stock.

Consider the impact on your business. Maybe you get lucky, and the customer is willing to wait a little for the item. You still get the sale, but you may incur a higher cost for the inventory item because you're placing a small order at the last minute. The purchasing cost might be higher, and you might incur a cost to get the item shipped overnight. So you "saved the sale" but certainly have a lower level of profit.

The lower level of profit in this case means a lower contribution margin (sales less variable costs) for one scarf. For stockout costs, focus on direct costs. You don't consider fixed costs like the lease payment on your building, or indirect costs, like utility costs for the shop. Bear in mind that if you lose sales, you have to spread your costs over fewer units sold. That increases your cost per unit.

You have two types of opportunity costs if an item is out of stock. First, there's *reduced contribution margin* if you fill the order. But there's *lost contribution margin* if you lose the sale. You also risk lost contribution margin on *future orders*. Because the item wasn't in stock, maybe the customer decides to do future business somewhere else. That's why for many stores, customer loyalty is important — the customer will stick with you. It also explains why on the Internet, when a sale is lost, the customer is at another website in an instant.

Bear in mind that opportunity costs aren't posted to your financial statements. That's because the dollar amount of the impact is hard to quantify. You can't put a dollar amount on the amount of business you lose due to items that are out of stock. (However, those losses may trouble you when you go home at night.)

Calculating Inventory Quantity with the Economic Order Quantity Formula

Economic order quantity (EOQ) is a decision tool. It's a formula that allows you to calculate the ideal quantity of inventory to order for a given product. The calculation is designed to minimize ordering and carrying costs. It goes back to 1913, when Ford W. Harris wrote an article called "How Many Parts to Make at Once."

EOQ is based on the following set of assumptions:

- **Reorder point:** The *reorder point* is the time when the next order should be placed. EOQ assumes that you order the same quantity at each reorder point.

- **Demand, relevant ordering cost, and relevant carrying cost:** Customer demand for the product is known. Also, the ordering and carrying costs are certain. A *relevant cost* refers to a cost you need to consider when you make a decision. The term is used throughout this book.

- **Purchase order lead time:** The lead time is the time period from placing the order to order delivery. EOQ assumes that the lead time is known.

- **Purchasing cost per unit:** The cost per unit doesn't change with the amount ordered. This removes any consideration of quantity discounts. Assume you'll pay the same amount per unit, regardless of the order size.

- **Stockouts:** No stockouts occur. You maintain enough inventory to avoid a stockout cost. That means you monitor your customer demand and inventory levels carefully.

- **Quality costs:** EOQ generally ignores quality costs. There's a discussion of quality issues in Chapter 19.

Economic order quantity uses three variables: demand, relevant ordering cost, and relevant carrying cost. Use them to set up an EOQ formula:

- **Demand:** The demand, in units, for the product for a specific time period.

- **Relevant ordering cost:** Ordering cost per purchase order.

- **Relevant carrying cost:** Carrying costs for one unit. Assume the unit is in stock for the time period used for demand.

Note that the ordering cost is calculated per *order*. The carrying costs are calculated per *unit*. Here's the formula for economic order quantity:

Economic order quantity = square root of [(2 × demand × ordering costs) ÷ carrying costs]

That's easier to visualize as a regular formula:

$$Q = \sqrt{\frac{2DS}{H}}$$

Q is the economic order quantity (units). *D* is demand (units, often annual), *S* is ordering cost (per purchase order), and *H* is carrying cost per unit.

Don't try this at home. You can research this formula, if you like, but be prepared to find the minimum point of the total cost curve by partially differentiating the total cost with respect to Q.

Say your clothing shop also sells men's hiking shoes. The model you sell costs $45 per pair. You sell 100 pairs of hiking boots a month, or 1,200 per year.

Your ordering cost is $50 per order. You added up the total time spent by everyone who's involved in the ordering process, and you figure that the combined time to process each order is one hour. Based on average salary and benefit costs, you assign a $50 cost per order.

The carrying cost per unit is $3. That rate covers the occupancy costs and insurance where the inventory is stored. The amount also accounts for the opportunity cost of carrying the inventory.

Based on the data for the hiking boots, here's your economic order quantity:

Economic order quantity = square root of [(2 × demand × ordering costs) ÷ carrying costs]

Economic order quantity = square root of [(2 × 1,200 × ($50)) ÷ $3]

Economic order quantity = square root of [$120,000 ÷ $3]

Economic order quantity = square root of 40,000

Economic order quantity = 200

You just determined that the ideal order level is 200 units. At that level, you minimize ordering and carrying costs.

Figuring a Favorable Reorder Point

The *reorder point* is the time when you should place your next order. You use reorder point to avoid running out of inventory — a stockout situation. Lots of bad things can happen if there's a stockout.

To keep life simple, assume that the demand level is known — you know how much product you're likely to sell. You also know the order lead time.

The reorder point formula requires a unit of time. That time period can be a week, a month, or a year. The choice is up to you.

Here's the formula for reorder point:

Reorder point = number of units sold per unit of time × order lead time

Say you manage a hardware store. One of your products is a 20-ounce straight claw hammer. You decide to use one week as your unit of time. Your weekly demand level is 70 hammers. Your purchase order lead time is three weeks. Here is your reorder point for hammers:

Reorder point = 70 units × 3 weeks

Reorder point = 210 units

When your inventory level falls to 210 units, you order more hammers. You want to make sure that you don't run out before your next order arrives. Now consider *how many* more hammers. The number you order is the economic order quantity (EOQ).

Introducing safety stock: Creating a cushion

Safety stock (also known as *reserve inventory*) is the amount of inventory held at all times. You maintain the safety stock inventory, regardless of the purchases you make using EOQ. This inventory serves as a buffer against stockouts.

You maintain a safety stock to address uncertainty in the ordering process. There are several uncertainties related to purchases and inventory levels:

- ✔ **Demand:** If actual demand is higher than planned, you can sell your safety stock and avoid a stockout.

- ✔ **Purchase order lead time:** You might have a longer lead time than planned. Maybe your order takes four weeks to be delivered, rather than three weeks. If the increased lead time sharply reduces your inventory levels, you can sell your safety stock.

- ✔ **Suppliers:** Safety stock can help you meet demand if a supplier can't deliver your required purchase. A supplier may run short of product. An unusual situation (weather, or material shortage, for example) may prevent the supplier from making or shipping your product in a timely manner.

Computing safety stock

Safety stock is computed as

Safety stock = excess demand expected × purchase order lead time

Say you manage a discount store. As you prepare for the back-to-school season, you need to stock backpacks. The red mountain backpack has always been a big seller. You already determined demand for the backpack and other factors, including the economic order quantity.

As you set up your back-to-school store displays, you mull over creating a safety stock. You start by checking weekly sales from previous years, and you notice that the higher sales level has happened several times; sales have been 100 units higher than your weekly planned sales. You determine that safety stock should be 100 backpacks.

The purchase order lead time for the red mountain backpack is three weeks. Based on the data, here's your safety stock:

Safety stock = 100 backpacks per week × 3 week lead time

Safety stock = 300 backpacks

You plan to hold 300 backpacks in stock *in addition to* your regular inventory level. The 300 units are your hedge against a spike in demand or a supplier's delay in shipping product to you. If something unusual happens, you're still able to fill orders. Note that your safety stock is a separate calculation from economic order quantity.

Evaluating Prediction Error

A *prediction error* occurs when actual costs differ from your estimates. You've seen the concept of *variance* throughout the book — a variance being a difference between planned results and actual results.

You calculate the cost of a prediction error in these steps:

1. Compute economic order quantity (EOQ).

2. Calculate the relevant total cost based on your planned amounts.

3. Because you determined that your estimate is incorrect, plug in the actual data and recalculate relevant total cost.

4. Compare the relevant total cost you planned with the relevant total cost using actual data.

Calculating relevant total costs

Say you manage a large chain of sporting-goods stores that sells a light windbreaker. The jacket is popular with runners and bikers.

Here are your planned estimates for the month: Monthly demand is 10,000 jackets. The ordering cost is $70 per order. Carrying costs total $3 per unit. You calculate an economic order quantity (EOQ) of 683.13 units.

Here's the formula for relevant total cost:

Relevant total cost = [(demand × ordering cost) ÷ EOQ] + [(EOQ × carrying cost per unit) ÷ 2]

The calculation is in the form of two fractions. Compute one fraction at a time and then add them to get relevant total cost. Here's the monthly relevant total cost for the windbreaker:

Relevant total cost = [(demand × ordering cost) ÷ EOQ] + [(EOQ × carrying cost per unit) ÷ 2]

Relevant total cost = (10,000 × $70 ordering cost) ÷ 683.13 + (683.13 × $3) ÷ 2)

Relevant total cost = ($700,000 ÷ 683.13) + (2049.39 ÷ 2)

Relevant total cost = $1,024.70 + $1,024.70

Relevant total cost = $2,049.40

The relevant total cost for the windbreakers is $2,049.40 for the month. You can't purchase a fractional unit, so you round down to from 683.13 to 683 units.

Note that you can simplify calculating relevant total cost. You get to the same total cost amount by multiplying EOQ by the carrying cost (with a slight rounding difference):

Relevant total cost = EOQ × carrying costs

Relevant total cost = 683.13 units × $3 carrying cost per unit

Relevant total cost = 683.13 × $3

Relevant total cost = $2,049.39

This version of the formula is easier, so consider using it. I provide the more complex formula earlier in this section so you can see how more components for relevant total costs fit together. This version of the formula simplifies the calculation for you.

But then you learn that there's a prediction error. You determine that your actual ordering cost is $85. The cost is higher than the $70 in your plan. All of the other assumptions are correct. Your new relevant total cost is $2,258.32. That actual amount is $208.93 higher than the amount using the planned ordering amount ($2,049.39). The impact of the higher ordering cost is $208.93 for the month.

You could plug in actual results for any of the variables in the relevant total cost formula. When you recalculate the relevant total cost, you see the dollar impact of your prediction error.

Acting on a prediction error

When you find a prediction error, you need to consider whether or not to take action. If your actual results differ from your plan, it may not be that big of a deal. You need to consider the size of the difference and how you use the data. Consider the relevant total cost explanation in this section.

When the actual ordering cost is plugged into the formula, the prediction error is $208.93. Well, consider how large that difference is as a percentage of the original relevant total cost:

Prediction error as a percentage of relevant total cost = $208.93 ÷ $2,049.40

Prediction error as a percentage of relevant total cost = 10.19 percent

Most accountants would consider a 10 percent change to be meaningful. That means that difference should be investigated. If you can determine why the difference occurred, you may be able to reduce your costs and increase profit. At the least, you can use the new figure of $85 in future planning.

You need to find out why the ordering costs increased. Maybe you have a new person processing orders. Because that person is still learning his or her job, orders may be processed more slowly. When the new employee learns the process, he or she should work faster. Your ordering cost should go back down.

Consider the *total dollar amount* of the change as well as the percentage change. You might conclude that a $208 difference isn't worth taking the time to investigate. The dollar amount is too small, regardless of the percentage change.

This analysis requires judgment. When you meet with other managers in planning, consider a *scope amount.* Auditors use the term *scope* to mean the dollar amount above which a difference must be investigated. Differences or exceptions below that amount won't be analyzed.

Scope is usually based on a percentage of some total. If, for example, you're analyzing accounts receivable, you might investigate any difference greater than 5 percent of the total receivable balance. If your receivables total $500,000, you investigate any exception over $25,000 (5 percent of $500,000).

Buying more and ignoring EOQ

Your purchasing manager may buy more inventory than the economic order quantity amount. That's because the manager's performance criteria are different from the company-wide goals and criteria. The manager and the company's goals aren't aligned. This situation is referred to as a lack of goal congruence.

Goal congruence is defined as consistency or agreement of individual goals with company goals. Everyone in the organization needs to be rowing in the same direction. That process gets tough when you start to set up evaluation criteria for employees. Your staff members have different jobs with different levels and kinds of responsibility. As you set up goals for everyone, the company-wide goals can get lost.

Say preventing stockouts rewards the purchasing manager. The manager avoids stockouts by — you guessed it — buying more inventory than the company really needs. So the manager's order size is higher than the economic order quantity (EOQ).

As the old saying goes, "It's no skin off his nose." The opportunity cost of tying up more dollars in inventory isn't posted to the financial statements. The manager buys more than enough inventory, so that he or she avoids a stockout. Bottom line: The purchasing manager gets a good job evaluation (an important goal for him or her) because stockouts never happen.

If the manager buys more inventory than the EOQ, there are impacts at the company-wide level: carrying costs, ordering costs, and opportunity cost.

The carrying cost is higher. If you buy more inventory than needed, you need to store it, insure it, and protect it against theft.

Also, if the purchasing manager panics every time inventory levels decline, he or she may place frequent orders. That activity increases total ordering costs. The whole point of calculating EOQ is to *minimize* carrying costs and ordering costs. The purchasing manager's actions don't allow the company to benefit from using EOQ.

Finally, larger purchases use up more cash. As a result, the opportunity cost is higher. The more you spend on inventory, the less cash you have for other purposes. You pass up other business opportunities. The company is paying more carrying cost and has less cash for other business purposes.

The solution is to evaluate the purchasing manager using multiple criteria. For example, you may want to evaluate the manager on the company's required rate of return on investment (ROI) as well as the "no stockouts" criterion. Return on investment is addressed in Chapter 12.

A required rate of return is used to calculate opportunity costs. The extra dollars that the manager is using to buy inventory *has a cost.* Required rate of return computes a cost for the money used by the purchasing manager.

When you raise money to run your business, investors who provide the funds to you have an expectation about what they will earn on those funds. Slide on over to Chapter 1 for more on rates of return.

If the purchasing manager is evaluated on stockouts *and* required rate of return, he or she has to strike a balance. The manager wants to avoid stockouts. However, he or she doesn't want to overspend on inventory. If you explain things to the manager, he or she will probably see the benefit of EOQ and use it. Later, you evaluate the manager using both criteria.

Practicing Just-In-Time Purchasing

Just-in-time purchasing (JIT purchasing) is the strategy of purchasing goods so that they're delivered just as they're needed to meet customer demand. With JIT, when you get customer orders, you plan purchases. You purchase the minimum number of items to meet customer demand. JIT purchasing typically results in more smaller orders and frequent deliveries.

The goal of JIT purchasing is to reduce the carrying cost of inventory. Less inventory on hand means you pay less in storage and insurance costs. JIT also requires less cash in the short term.

 Operating cycle is the average period of time from when you purchase inventory to when you collect cash for the sale. Say your operating cycle is 75 days. With JIT purchasing, you're buying less inventory, and therefore you're using less cash. As a result, you're not under as much pressure to collect cash.

Kicking around JIT benefits and risks

There are several benefits to JIT purchasing, but there are risks, too. You need to manage the process carefully. If you don't, you may have stockouts. Stockouts can lead to lost business — both short-term and long-term.

Two big factors can drive down the cost of your inventory: technology and long-term contracts. That's a benefit.

Using technology can sharply reduce your ordering and carrying costs. Technology allows you to create and approve purchase orders, update your inventory records, and pay for inventory electronically. Technology also allows many firms to have access to real-time inventory quantities. This change reduces the number of hours your staff spends on inventory. Fewer staff hours mean less expense.

Another big factor is long-term contracts. If you contract long-term with a supplier, you lock in an inventory price and the amounts to be purchased over time. You eliminate price fluctuations, which makes planning easier. You may also be able to secure discounts by entering into a long-term contract. Other benefits, such as superior quality expectation and on-time delivery, are expected with a long-term contract.

Of course, it's important that the long-term contract provides enough inventory to meet your needs. If you need to buy more product over and above the supplier contract, you'll probably pay higher unit costs. That's because you may be buying at the last minute, and you'll also be buying a much smaller amount than what's in the contract. A supplier, therefore, is likely to demand a higher price for these "extra" orders.

Here are two risk factors to consider before implementing JIT purchasing:

- **Carrying costs:** JIT purchasing allows you to carry fewer inventory items. Some of your carrying costs may be fixed — at least in the short term. If you carry less inventory, you won't need as much storage. But if you have a lease on storage space, you're paying the same amount for storage until the lease ends. JIT purchasing means that you spread the same lease cost over *fewer* units in inventory. The carrying cost per unit *increases.*

- **Ordering costs:** With JIT purchasing, you place smaller orders more frequently. Your supplier may need to *increase* the cost per order to cover their costs. For example, if you change from 10 orders a month to 100, the supplier may need to add some fixed costs. The fixed cost might include more staff or an upgraded computer system to process so many more orders.

JIT purchasing works, not only for retailers, but also for manufacturers. Toyota implemented *Kanban,* which (generally speaking) is a scheduling system for JIT production. It applies to the purchasing of materials that flow into the factory and incidentally to the flow of work-in-process from one department to the next.

Putting in a JIT purchasing system

Okay, say you decide to approach your supplier about moving to a JIT purchasing arrangement. The supplier needs to deliver smaller shipments more frequently. You request a price quote based on new, different levels of purchasing activity. This section compares the financial impact of your current purchasing system with a JIT purchasing system.

Laying out purchasing costs

Say you manage a large chain of sporting-goods stores. You're considering the impact of JIT purchasing for many products. At the moment, you're evaluating baseball bats.

Here's some information regarding baseball bat purchases:

- **Purchasing costs:** The cost per baseball bat is $100 for both your current purchasing method and JIT purchasing.

- **Ordering costs:** The cost per order is $150 for both purchasing methods.

- **Opportunity costs:** Company management has decided on an 8 percent required rate of return on investment. That 8 percent rate applies to any use of capital, including inventory purchases. This is the minimum return that the company expects from the money it has invested. If this return is not achieved, there are likely better alternatives for the company's cash.

✔ **Average inventory:** *Average inventory* is defined as the average value of inventory during a certain time period. Average inventory is (beginning inventory + ending inventory) ÷ 2. Currently, your average inventory is 10 percent of annual sales, or 2,000 bats. Under JIT, your average inventory will decline to 200 units.

✔ **Carrying costs:** You also incur costs for insurance and storage. Carrying costs total $15 per unit.

Table 18-1 compares your current purchasing costs with JIT purchasing costs.

Table 18-1 Current Purchasing Costs versus JIT Purchasing Costs

Total Costs			Current	JIT
Purchasing costs	Cost	Units		
	$100/unit	20,000	$2,000,000	$2,000,000
Ordering costs	Cost	Orders		
	$150/order	20	$3,000	
	$150/order	200		$30,000
Opportunity costs	Cost	Inventory		
8% rate	$100/unit	2,000	$16,000	
8% rate	$100/unit	200		$1,600
Other carry costs	Cost	Inventory		
	$15/unit	2,000	$30,000	
	$15/unit	200		$3,000
Total costs			$2,049,000	$2,034,600

JIT purchasing saves you $14,400 in costs ($2,049,000 current costs less $2,034,600 JIT purchasing costs).

Using JIT purchasing, the number of orders increases from 20 to 200. Purchase ordering costs increase from $3,000 to $30,000.

The opportunity cost multiplies the 8 percent rate × $100 unit cost × the average inventory. Note that the average inventory for your current process is 2,000 units; so, the opportunity cost for your current purchasing system is much higher than with JIT ($16,000 versus $1,600).

Carrying costs are $15 per unit. When you cut the average inventory with JIT, you also reduce carrying costs ($30,000 current versus $3,000 JIT).

Pinning down stockout costs

Before you decide on JIT purchasing, consider other costs. Stockout costs weren't included in Table 18-1. Those costs are more difficult to quantify.

The financial impact of a stockout is hard to pin down, but you can develop some data. You can probably identify *individual* stockout situations. Your store managers can track customers who ask for out-of-stock items. The total stockout cost would be the number of customers requesting an out-of-stock product multiplied by the cost you incur to get them the product.

Table 18-1 shows that the ordering cost is $150 per order. All suppliers give their clients a cost quote for placing small, last-minute orders. Now this is a different cost for a different service.

Say that the minimum cost for *any* order is $30. As stockouts occur, you place last-minute orders for small amounts — sometimes two bats, sometimes ten. You estimate a stockout cost per item of $5 per bat.

You forecast 50 customer orders placed when bats are out of stock. The total stockout cost would be $5 per unit × 50 orders = $250.

You can't quantify the opportunity cost of future lost business due to stockouts. Sure, you may be able to "save the order" by ordering the product when it's out of stock. The customer gets the product, but not as soon as he or she wanted it. That experience may mean that he or she will do business somewhere else going forward.

Turning to customer returns

Customer returns are another cost that you should include in your JIT purchasing cost decision. A *return* happens when a customer buys a product and isn't satisfied with the product's performance.

At that point, the customer may check to see whether the product is under warranty. Recall that a *warranty* is a commitment by the seller of a product (well, often the manufacturer, not the retailer) to repair an item at no cost to the buyer. Some products are covered under warranty and some are not; others have limited warranties. You find a super-cool discussion of warranties in Chapter 19.

You've probably purchased a product with paperwork explaining the warranty. If you buy a car, a refrigerator, or a new computer, the product comes with written warranty information. You know how long the warranty lasts and what repairs are covered.

Warranties are often touted in marketing a product. The best example is car commercials. Maybe you're told that the car has a "100,000-mile power train limited warranty." The car company is selling peace of mind: "We'll fix the car if it breaks, Mr. or Ms. Customer." (Note that an automobile dealership is a peculiar combination of retailer and manufacturer's representative. The auto-maker warranties the work, but the local dealer does the repair.)

A chain of car dealerships in my area uses a great tag line in its commercials. It ends each commercial with "If your car isn't right, we'll make it right — free." That simple line says a lot about quality and service. The car dealers might make a mistake, but they will do everything they can to fix it. The correction won't cost the customer a dime. That's what you want to hear from a supplier.

There are other warranties that are less formal. Instead of a detailed written agreement, warranties are assumed or implied. Say you pay $15 for a pair of reading glasses. You go out to your car and notice that the nosepiece on one side of the glasses is broken. So you go back into the drugstore and exchange them. (That just happened to me yesterday, so I thought it would make a good example.)

As a customer, you assume that *any* item you buy (for any dollar amount) should operate as it should for a reasonable period of time. If a business isn't willing to fix or replace all items when they don't work, it loses current and future business. And dissatisfied customers often tell others. (Groan! That, unfortunately, is "the kind of advertising that money just can't buy.")

Say your bats have a one-year warranty for any defects. That warranty assumes normal use of the bat. If a customer slams a bat against a tree 1,000 times, that's probably not considered normal use. Aside from that, you recognize that some bats can be defective in materials or workmanship. At this point you judge (based on experience) how many bats will be returned under warranty and how much it will cost to repair them or replace them.

You project that 2 percent of the 20,000 bats in Table 18-1 will be returned under warranty (2 percent × 20,000 = 400 bats). Each returned bat is estimated to cost you $40. Your cost for the customer return is 400 bats × $40 = $16,000.

Now, a $40 repair on a $100 retail item seems unreasonable. As the manufacturer, you need to consider changing your bat design or production. That's because the warranty repair cost is pretty large compared with the retail price of the item.

The repair scenario holds true for many small retailers. Sewing machine centers and vacuum cleaner stores come to mind. They have their own repair facilities "in the back." For other items, the customer usually sends the broken item to a regional repair facility or the manufacturer.

Adjusting total purchasing cost

As seen in Table 18-1, average inventory for the current purchasing system is 2,000 units. The current system assumes that you place 20 orders per year. That's one order every two or three weeks. You don't incur any stockout costs.

Your supplier has time to carefully inspect each item before it ships to you. As a result, all the products you receive work properly. All products you sell under the current purchasing system operate properly, so you don't incur any costs for customer returns.

 In reality, no purchasing system can eliminate the issue of a product breaking *after* the customer buys it. Hey, stuff just happens. You'll deal with customer returns using any purchasing system. Now, for a moment, focus only on customer returns due to product defects that were there *before* the customer received the item.

The JIT purchasing system requires that you place smaller orders more often. With JIT purchasing, your supplier ends up sending many more orders. You should plan for some errors in inspection. The more orders you place, the greater chance that some items weren't inspected carefully.

You may be able to require the supplier to cover the customer return costs, if the return is due to their inspection error. This example assumes that you (the seller) cover the cost.

Take a look at Table 18-2, which shows your JIT purchasing costs (from Table 18-1) with stockout costs and customer return costs thrown in.

Table 18-2	JIT Purchasing Costs with Stockouts and Returns
Type of Cost	*Amount*
Subtotal — JIT purchasing cost	$2,034,600
Stockout costs	$250
Customer returns costs	$16,000
JIT purchasing cost	**$2,050,850**
Current purchasing costs	$2,049,000
Total JIT less current cost	**$1,850**

Now that you've added stockout and customer return costs, total JIT purchasing cost is now *higher* than your current system's cost. At this point, you probably shouldn't move to JIT purchasing because "There ain't no money in it."

SCM and Customer Demand Issues

Supply chain management (SCM) is a management tool you can use to improve your ordering, manufacturing, and inventory processes.

Supply chain management is the technique of analyzing and monitoring the movement of raw materials, work-in-process, and finished goods — from origin to the final consumer.

As you implement SCM, consider how and when your customers order products. After all, customer demand determines when to make something (if you're a manufacturer) or order something (if you're a retailer). Customer demand starts the process. SCM helps you make the process more efficient.

Pulling apart the supply chain

The *supply chain* is the group of companies that contribute to the flow of goods from a product's creation to the end customer. Every company in the supply chain can help the overall process. When that happens, you might save money, improve products, or increase sales — all of which are the equivalent of making money. Do an Internet search on "supply chain management" to learn a lot.

When more companies than just your company are involved, as is usually the case, you're dealing with "the extended enterprise." It makes sense, because everything affects everything else. Many different people "touch" a product before it reaches the customer.

A principal concept of supply chain management (SCM) is that companies in a supply chain exchange information about fluctuations. The fluctuations include availability, timing, shipping, and seasonal variability.

With supply chain management, you try to manage all activities that affect you. This could include sourcing (materials for manufacturing or finished goods for retailing), production (improving efficiency, eliminating bottlenecks, or increasing capacity), and logistics management (usually shipping, but also inventory management for both manufacturers and retailers). Check the table of contents of this book to find various chapters on these topics.

Analyzing demand

You no doubt already know that demand varies. The world has uncertainties. Whereas some demand changes are predictable, others may come as a surprise.

You need to get the best handle possible on when customers buy your products and even *why* they do. That knowledge lets you plan your inventory levels more effectively.

Here are some possible sources of demand variation:

- ✔ **Variable customer demand, seasonal:** Demand predictability varies by season. Summer and the holiday season, for example, show predictable increases in customer demand for swimsuits and toys, respectively. You need to stock up before the season.

- ✔ **Variable customer demand, based on a product:** You may be surprised at high demand for a single product. For example, envision a retail clothing store that sells jeans — and men's jeans in certain styles in particular. Say you notice that men's prewashed, straight-legged jeans in size 32-34 *always* sell out. You can't sell more of what you don't have. The demand for jeans may be generally predictable, but the demand for a single style/size is a surprise. You need to compensate to take advantage of the popularity of this style/size.

- ✔ **Variable purchasing patterns:** There are many products that customers use steadily, maybe every day or week. But for whatever reason, the customers seem to buy the product randomly. So the customer *uses* the product steadily but doesn't *buy* it steadily. Consider giant packages of toilet paper or paper towels.

- ✔ **Variable demand affecting suppliers:** A material supplier may have a reduced supply of what you need because of demand from your *competitors*. Say you were the first to manufacture motorcycle jackets from rip-stop nylon, but now all your competitors are using the material. The material may become less available. You need to compensate by increasing your orders or finding additional suppliers.

When you combine the concepts of supply chain management with your customer demand patterns, your operate more efficiently — and meet the needs of your customers.

Chapter 19

Quality: Building a Better Mousetrap

*Y*ou can use cost accounting to improve your performance in delivering a quality product in a timely manner. Quality is a necessity — not a luxury — as technology now allows customers to research online how companies perform. They can post complaints, too. If your product is defective, word will get around. Also, customers don't like to wait. If you don't get your product to the client quickly enough, the client might tell his or her friends about the negative experience (or, for that matter, post the complaint on Amazon or Facebook).

This chapter addresses quality issues in a business. Assume that you manage a business — and you're concerned about quality. You consider how to measure quality. You look at how your business operates from the time you get an order until you ship your product to the client. In this chapter, you also assess customer satisfaction to see if your efforts to improve your processes are making a difference.

Your goals are to consistently deliver a quality product and improve your response time. If you accomplish these two goals, you can count on growing your business and earning a reasonable profit.

Considering Quality Benefits and Costs

Quality is defined as the features and benefits of a product, based on customer expectations. Customers have expectations about a product when they buy it and use it. When you meet or exceed customer expectations, that's quality.

Many companies (Xerox Corporation, for example) emphasized this concept in the 1980s. Quality is *not* about "goodness." Quality is *not* about providing extra features (fine as they may be) that customers don't want. Quality is about fully meeting customer expectations.

Listing the benefits of quality

Obviously, quality benefits a business. If you deliver a quality product, satisfied customers will come back. This is super, as all business owners should love repeat business.

Achieving customer satisfaction costs money, but it's far less expensive than spending marketing dollars to find *new* clients. You don't pay nearly as much in marketing and sales costs for repeat clients.

Producing a quality product may actually *lower* your costs. When you focus on quality in production, you pay more attention to your production process. You're likely to figure out how to work smarter. As you gain knowledge about production, you can remove unnecessary costs *without compromising quality*. You also are able to make products with fewer defects.

A friend of mine owns a landscaping company. He works hard and does quality work. I referred a neighbor to him, and then I ran into my neighbor a few days later. She had checked a consumer website, and the site listed several negative comments about the landscaping company. Ouch! It turns out that my friend wasn't following up with customers in a timely manner. Although not everything posted on this website was true, there were a number of comments that talked about the lack of follow-up. As a result, my neighbor hired *another landscaper*. Be careful. This is the age of "review sites," such as Yelp! (for restaurants) and Angie's List (for everything else).

Quality (meaning features and benefits of a product) is made up of more than just form, fit, and finish. To meet customer expectations, you must also be extraordinary in *timeliness* and *follow-up*.

Listing the costs of quality

Obviously, quality costs a business. The *cost of quality* is defined as anything related to creating, maintaining, and improving a product's quality. The definition also includes anything related to negative consequences of not producing a quality product.

The cost of quality includes the cost to prevent defective products in your production system, the costs of providing superior design, timely delivery, and customer follow-up. It also includes defective products and even lost customers if quality is poor.

Also included in cost of quality is the cost is buying (for retailers) or holding (for manufacturers) inventory to meet the needs of customers. After all, you want enough product on the shelf when customers show up to buy. If your shelves have "voids," or your finished goods inventory is empty, you will fail on timely delivery.

Consider the full production/delivery process. First, you perform market research to find out what customers want and need. You then design a product that meets those wants and needs. The design is the "recipe" for making your product.

Retailers have a similar task, as selecting well-designed products is the recipe for stocking what the customer wants and needs.

Of course, there are design compromises, except famously in the case of Apple products, which have a reputation for uncompromised design. Apple can afford it; it has big margins because of high prices, low manufacturing costs, and fanatic buyers.

Now comes the hard part. Your production department has to make a product that *conforms* to the design — every time. Customers expect not only a superior product design, but one that works, too! If your product doesn't conform to the design, you end up with a defective product. Cost accountants call defective products *spoilage*.

Here are four specific costs related to quality. Several of these topics relate to the spoilage, scrap, and rework discussion in Chapter 17:

> ✔ **Prevention costs:** The cost to prevent *nonconforming items* from being produced. Prevention cost also includes the cost of designing a quality product. Materials and workmanship have to be "to spec," following specifications. This isn't quite the same as appraisal costs (explained in the following bullet point). Prevention costs occur *before* the product begins assembly or manufacturing. Prevention costs include verifying that materials are as ordered and that machines are producing parts within the correct tolerances.

You find plenty of examples of conformation in real life. For example, the City of Los Angeles maintains a lab that tests asphalt for the streets to make sure it meets the city's specifications. Inspectors check out the material, not the finished road. The asphalt needs to hold up to heavy street traffic and changes in temperature.

✔ **Appraisal costs:** *Appraisal costs* are the costs of the inspection process. You inspect products during production to determine if they're defective. A variant of inspection is the work of the quality engineering department (also known as the shake-and-bake department). In some companies, the products are stressed and strained. Tests include subjecting them to heat, cold, shock, water, humidity, and the famous drop test. That's where a fully loaded pallet of cartons is dropped from about 12 feet to hit the concrete below.

✔ **Internal failure costs:** When a unit is found to be defective, you incur costs to repair *(rework)* it *before* you ship it to a client. You may actually have to dispose of the product if it can't be repaired. Ultimately, one of your goals is to reduce or eliminate failures.

✔ **External failure costs:** *External failure costs* are costs you incur *after* you ship a defective product to a client. *Warranty work* or *replacement* is no fun. Obviously, you prefer to recognize and repair a defective product before it gets in the hands of a customer. External failure costs can also include the cost of a lawsuit from a customer or even the cost of a losing a customer. These are often the most costly costs of quality and the most difficult to quantify.

Taking steps to ensure quality

You can take steps to produce a quality product. They are simple but not necessarily easy.

Start with a good product design. Plan a product with fewer moving parts, for example. The product is easier to build, and there is less chance for human error in production.

Perform scheduled maintenance on your machinery and equipment so tolerances are maintained and breakdowns are rare. These costs are prevention costs.

Verify that the product operates properly in testing. Product testing should start before production and continue throughout the manufacturing process. Say you're producing yo-yos. During product testing, you notice that the string knots up when the yo-yo is used. So you change the type of string. Based on additional testing, the change fixes the knotting problem. When you start production, you won't produce defective yo-yos. Product testing is a prevention cost.

Get a handle on defective products. Internal failures are due to something that created a defect in production. You find that something didn't go as planned; maybe there was a machine malfunction, or there was an employee error. When you find defects, take steps to reduce them. If possible, rework the defective units.

 Complex products require more thorough testing. For example, do you know who some of the best saxophonists in the world are? The men and women at Conn-Selmer band instruments in Elkhart, Indiana. A sax has many tight-fitting parts and a complex array of valves and levers. The testers play each new horn like mad, and they do a thorough job. I know this because I saw the video on *Sesame Street*.

Compiling a Cost of Quality Report

A *cost of quality report* lists your costs related to quality. Your goal is to list all of the costs of quality, both direct and indirect costs, and *allocate* those indirect costs to each unit produced. The direct costs, by definition, are traced to your product. (Note that a cost accountant isn't having a good day unless he or she is listing and allocating something.)

Assume your product is a ten-speed adult road bike. Here are the costs related to quality again, but this time they are specific to your bike production:

- ✔ **Prevention costs:** Your design team improves the bike's ability to shift from one gear to the next. This smoother shifting puts less strain on the bike chain. As a result, the chains last longer and don't break as easily.

- ✔ **Appraisal costs:** Each bike is inspected before it leaves your factory. An inspector shifts through all of the gears on the bike. He or she checks the ease of adjusting the height of the seat and verifies that each wheel can be removed and locked back into place.

- ✔ **Internal failure costs:** You find an internal failure with some of the metal bike wheels you just produced. A small piece of metal was left exposed on the inside of the wheel. When you insert and pump up a rubber tire tube, the metal piece punctures the inner tube. Your staff is able to remove the piece before bikes are shipped to customers. However, there's a labor cost.

- ✔ **External failure costs:** Your bike's frame and parts have a limited warranty. A production run of bikes has chains that are breaking (good bike design but bad sourcing of the chain). It turns out that the master link holding the chain together is failing. Because the bikes are already in customer hands, you issue a *recall,* and each customer takes the bike to the local bike shop for repairs. You must reimburse the bike shops for repairs and pay them a fee.

Taken together, individual findings constitute a *cost of quality report*. Because all of these costs are indirect, you will *allocate* costs to each bike. So you must come up with a cost allocation base. You need some level of activity you can use to allocate the costs to each bike. There's a crystal-clear discussion about cost allocation in Chapter 5, if you need more in this topic.

You can use hours worked to allocate all four of the costs covered earlier in this chapter. In each case, someone needs to *do something* to prevent a defect or to repair a defect. Yes, there are some material costs involved (that new master link for example). The activity that's driving the indirect cost is labor hours.

Use bike inspections as a cost allocation example. Your latest production run is for 2,000 bikes. The inspection requires 15 minutes (one quarter of an hour) of labor per bike. Your labor rate for inspectors is $30 per hour. Here's your cost allocation rate for each bike:

cost allocation rate = 0.25 hours per bike × $30 per hour labor rate

cost allocation rate = $7.50 per bike

This cost ultimately is built back into the total cost of each bike and affects the product's profitability.

Go on to compute a cost allocation rate for each of the other indirect costs related to quality. You spread the costs over the total production, which works the costs into your product pricing and profit calculations.

Putting Quality Practices in Place

I recently worked with a food distributor. When a food company wants to get a product on the shelves at grocery stores, it calls the food distributor. It's a business with heavy competition and small profit margins.

The owner noticed that one of the local grocers stopped placing orders for a type of salad dressing. In fact, the orders had stopped months earlier. Because the food distributor works with hundreds of products, he didn't notice right away.

When he followed up, he found out that a competitor offered a slightly lower price. Price isn't part of quality, *but service is*. The competitor's sales/delivery people also visited the grocery store more often. They made sure that the product was in stock and properly displayed on the shelf.

The lesson: Pay attention! If you don't constantly pay attention to your customer's needs, your customer may very well do business with someone else. You lose the revenue and profits from the business. When the customer leaves, it is very difficult to get the business back. The local grocer got what it wanted and needed from the competitor. "But I didn't know" should never be an excuse.

Grocery stores love it when a vendor checks stock and restocks as needed. You see this mainly with the bread delivery person. A *vendor* is a company that supplies a product or service to another company. In this case, the vendor is a food distributor to grocery stores. The store saves on labor, and a specialist handles the work. Can you apply this to your operation?

Companies that grow over the long term put quality into every part of their business. Put simply, quality represents doing things the right way — nearly every time you do them.

Quality in job costing

There's a quality component to job costing. Many tradespeople (plumbers, carpenters, and roofers, for example) use job costing. These are typically smaller companies with lots of competitors. Delivering a quality product can make the difference between keeping a client and losing the client to a competitor.

In many cases, companies use job costing to provide the customer a cost estimate (a detailed listing of all work needed on a project). Each job is assigned estimated costs for labor, materials, and overhead.

Here's where quality comes in: Smart companies like yours invest time to generate an accurate job estimate. The number of labor hours is well thought out (no wild ballpark estimates). The cost of materials is based on current prices and industry knowledge.

The result: The project's actual costs should be close to the estimated costs. That shows the customer that you know what you're doing. By the way, preparing a quality estimate tends to ensure the right profit margin for you. Investing the time to create an accurate estimate allows you to deliver a quality product — with a cost that is close to your estimate.

Taking a spin through inventory

Your product needs to meet your client's expectations. Yes, of course. A customer should feel that the product's price is reasonable. Yes, of course. But the first thing about a product is that there *is* a product. Your product has to be in your inventory. This section looks at the concept of inventory and quality.

The main points are obvious. Maintain inventory to supply your customers' needs. And maintain inventory with no defective products. It goes without saying, but I'll say it anyway: Inspect your products before they go into finished goods inventory. Ideally, no customer should ever receive a defective product.

Okay, it can happen: Even with the best intentions, a bad unit can slip into the finished goods inventory. Say the product stops working after the unit is shipped to a customer. Your company should have an excellent written policy for addressing this issue. To provide quality (after the fact), you should have a *limited warranty*. A *warranty* is a promise to repair or replace a product for a limited amount of time, assuming normal use. A real-life example is Amazon's Kindle, a very reliable e-book reader. A friend of mine received one that flat-out didn't work. Amazon replaced it instantly, no questions asked.

You want to see quality? I'll show you quality. At one time, the warranties for Magnalite cookware and Fenwick fishing rods were simple: *forever*. Times have changed, however. Fenwick seems to now have a limited warranty. Magnalite is now warrantied for only *50 years*.

You have some choices on how a repair is done. If a company local to the customer can repair the product, you can reimburse them for the cost and pay them a fee for their trouble. Another choice is for the customer to ship the item to you or to a repair vendor (sometimes called a regional service facility) that does the work. The item is shipped back to the customer after repair. Customers may prefer the local option; in that way, the item stays in town. They also have a local contact that can explain the repair. There's no shipping involved, either.

Customer Satisfaction: Measuring and Improving It

For a retailer, *customer satisfaction* is a measure of whether or not the customer has had a first-class buying experience (and why or why not). For a manufacturer, customer satisfaction is a measure of the customer's happiness with the product and maybe the buying experience. The measurement is your report card from the customer. So you're wise to ask your customers how things went. This section shows you how to measure customer satisfaction and suggests how you might improve it.

Satisfied customers tend to be repeat customers, whereas unsatisfied customers go elsewhere. Repeat customers can have a *huge positive impact* on your business. You save time and money when you sell to them, because you're not investing as much in marketing and sales costs to find *new* customers.

In more personal lines of manufacturing, retailing, or service, if you've worked with a client before, you understand what he or she wants. Maybe a client prefers a phone call rather than an email. The customer might prefer ordering on a certain day of the week. Your experience with the customer means you can improve your level of service. This is easy, not hard.

The road to getting repeat business starts with offering quality. That should be reflected in your advertising, website design, and live customer service. Of course, the product itself should be well designed, well made, and delivered in a timely manner. You can try to beat your breast about quality while delivering a shoddy product (as, frankly, some of the largest corporations have been seen to do), but don't fool yourself. Smart customers usually see through phonies in an instant.

Customer satisfaction's non-financial measurements

Non-financial measurements of customer satisfaction don't make it into your financial statements, but the information is critically important. The measurements help you to continue producing products that customers buy over and over, long-term.

Here are some examples of non-financial measurements that reflect customer satisfaction. A couple of them reflect product quality before the item leaves the plant.

- ✔ **Market research:** Research gives you information about customer tastes, preferences, and satisfaction with your product. You are likely to see comments about changes or updates your clients want. You can use surveys, watch Amazon ratings, conduct focus groups, establish email dialogues, or conduct personal interviews. To find out how you're doing, just *ask* your customers.

- ✔ **Defective units:** A listing of the types of product defects and how often they occur. Information about the number of defective products you catch before shipping shows an internal problem. Information about the number of defective products that are shipped to customers suggests that there's a customer satisfaction problem and/or an external failure problem with the product.

- ✔ **Customer complaints:** This report might include information about slow delivery, orders damaged in shipping, or poor customer service. Be *especially sensitive* to complaints about poor customer service. Some companies have abused customers so much that (and I'm not making this up) the customers create websites and Facebook pages such as "I hate ACME Corporation."

✔ **Timely delivery data:** This report contains information about the percentage of deliveries considered to be on time. It should show the average number of days or hours to deliver a product to the customer.

✔ **Process yield:** The *process yield* is defined as the percentage of good units produced (good units produced ÷ total units produced × 100). Good units, of course, are units you can sell to customers.

If you stay sensitive to non-financial measurements of customer satisfaction or quality and make changes, there are several benefits:

✔ The measurements are easier to understand than financial measurements. You also find that explaining non-financial measurements to other people is easier.

✔ Customer feedback is very easy to understand and is your *most critical short-term quality concern.* Trust me, you sometimes see and hear shocking stories. Think "Your product arrived in a crushed carton!" "Your customer service agent was extremely rude." "Your rep never called back, as promised." "I had to call six times to get someone to talk to me." You need to fix the problem for the individual customer and to make some aggressive changes in the area causing the problem.

✔ The quality measures identify weaknesses in your production system. Non-financial weaknesses are easier to identify than plowing through financial data. If the report says that production line 3 is producing the most defects, you shoot for improvements in line 3. Taking action is easier because the reports are clear.

✔ Non-financial measurements of quality make it easier to monitor the results of your production changes. It's simple to do some before-and-after analysis. Say that production line 3 had 100 defects per month before production changes. You can count the defects after the change and determine if the defects decreased. Pretty clear.

There's great value in internal reports. Say you make automobile tires and get a report showing defects found during the final inspection of the tires. The data divides the defects by type (steel belt defect, tire tread defect, and so forth). You use that report to change your production process. The information never makes it to your financial statements. The "outside world" (shareholders, creditors, and so forth) never sees the report, but the report helps you create a better product. Selling a better product likely leads to better results on your financial statements.

Also, keep in mind that a company's *annual report* includes the financial statements and other information. Many times, the "other" information includes a letter from the chief executive officer (CEO). That letter might include comments on internal reporting issues. Say the firm had a large issue with a defective product. The cost of the defect was significant. The CEO might explain that the defect has been addressed and is not expected to cause problems going forward.

The CEO letter appears in the annual report, but it's not part of the financial statements. The *cost* of the defect would certainly get posted to the financial statements. Take a spin through Chapter 17 for more on accounting for defects.

Is measuring customer satisfaction worth the effort?

All this customer satisfaction, quality, and defect information is great, but you need to consider the cost of gathering it and compare that to the benefit of having it. Do the benefits justify the costs?

The benefit could be that you will likely find improvements you can make in your business. The improvements could lower costs and increase customer satisfaction.

Say you're able to change your production to reduce the number of defects per production run. The changes cuts the number of defects from 2 percent of production to 1 percent. That also means that the process yield becomes 99 percent of production, so 99 of every 100 units produced are good units.

Sounds awesome, but consider the costs of those changes. Assume that a 1 percent increase in good units means that $10,000 worth of additional good units are available for sale. Super! Assume the cost to improve your production of good units is $50,000. Not so super. So $10,000 in additional good units has an initial cost of $50,000. Now mull over whether the additional cost is worth the additional good production. Bear in mind that the $50,000 cost may generate more good units for several years, or it may make it easier to retain customers in the long run. That's the thought process on costs and benefits.

Doing More in Less Time

Many companies use time as a competitive strategy. Those companies shorten length of time from the customer order to product delivery. Imagine "squeezing" the process into a shorter time period. The faster response time may become a big selling point. "You can get that product from us sooner, Mr. or Ms. Customer."

Producing products in less time may cost more, but it may also produce cost savings. There's the possibility, too, of increasing revenue through repeat business from satisfied customers.

This section takes a look at several issues related to company performance and the concept of time.

In the high-tech pharmaceutical world, the time problem begins with design, not manufacturing. The cliché is "time to market is *everything*." Whereas the approach can enhance competitiveness, it can occasionally produce disastrous results.

Analyzing performance related to time

Customer response time or *lead-time* is the period between when a customer places an order and when you deliver the product. A shorter response is generally a good idea, but a time driver may delay your process.

A *time driver* is any factor that changes the speed of an activity. These are the factors that speed up your response time or slow it down. Speeding up is no problem, but slowing down can be a big problem. Here are some time drivers:

- **Customer specifications:** It may take time to determine exactly what your clients want. The more complex the product, the longer this may take. Often, a sales or marketing department tells a production department about customer specifications. That's a good start, but it takes more effort to develop detailed specifications.

- **Waiting for parts or supplies:** You may have a delay in getting a part or specific material to produce the product. This is where having a good supplier is invaluable. If your supplier gets you the things you need in a timely manner, you can avoid this type of delay. Some corporations mandate that parts will be dual sourced, just in case one supplier runs into unexpected trouble.

- **Bottlenecks:** When your workload exceeds your production capacity, you have a *bottleneck*. Capacity means having available labor, machines, and factory space to make the product. If you're operating at capacity, in theory, you can't handle one more order until you clear out current orders. And *special orders* can't be processed, either. You can't take on special orders unless you have excess capacity. See Chapter 11. Operating at capacity will lengthen the customer response time for new orders.

- **Uncertainty about total customer orders:** If you have customers that come back and order regularly, great! But sometimes, you're unsure whether a customer will reorder, but you want to have available capacity and product in case the customer *does* reorder. Uncertainty makes it difficult to plan production and inventory requirements. You may need to delay production until you get the issues figured out.

"We have clearance, Clarence." "Roger, Roger." "What's our vector, Victor?"

Those are lines from the outrageously funny film *Airplane*. If you've never seen the movie, consider buying or renting it. Now back to our regularly scheduled program. Commercial airline flight times are a great example of companies using time as a competitive strategy. Airlines are very sensitive to their on-time performance results. Airlines compete with one another based on performance numbers. One way to perform well is for the airline to set flight departure and arrival times that it can meet easily. But there needs to be some balance, because people like to have a lot of flights to choose among.

A typical flight from St. Louis to Chicago is about 50 minutes. It's an important route for St. Louis. Many longer flights (international flights, for example) out of St. Louis connect through Chicago.

Now, if a fly-by-night airline (no pun intended) offers a flight time of 2 hours, the airline will always make it to Chicago with time to spare. However, the airline is likely to lose business. Its competitors will list a flight time that's much shorter. The competitors may occasionally be late, but customers are probably far more satisfied.

A business traveler might be okay with a late arrival once every ten flights for a 50-minute flight. That's much more attractive than 100 percent on-time record for a 2-hour flight to the same destination.

On-time performance is a how-often measurement, a metric that shows how often your product or service was delivered *when it was promised*. On-time performance results in more satisfied customers. Even if your delivery times are relatively long, good on-time performance removes any uncertainty from the customer's mind.

 In business as in life, it's better to promise only what you can deliver. You need enough time to produce, test, and ship what the customer wants. That means that your delivery dates and times should be reasonable. Try to avoid asking for a redo. Keep in mind that delays in delivery times frustrate your customers and make you look a little silly.

Calculating average waiting time

Average waiting time is defined as the average amount of time before an order is processed. Here are the factors you use to compute average waiting time:

- Average number of orders waiting to be processed
- Manufacturing time per order
- Machine capacity

Say you manage an oil-change shop. Your basic service is an oil- and fluid-change service for cars. During the process, you also check on other maintenance items, such as a clean air filter. The typical customer requires 20 minutes to service the vehicle.

You use three garage bays to work on cars — that's your order (machine) capacity. You can work on three cars at a time. On average, you have two cars waiting to be serviced. You can perform a simple calculation of average waiting time:

> average waiting time= (orders waiting to be processed × time per order) ÷ (order capacity)
>
> average waiting time = (two orders waiting × 20 minutes per order) ÷ (3 order capacity)
>
> average waiting time = 40 minutes ÷ three orders
>
> average waiting time = 13.3 minutes per order

Now, keep in mind that this is a simplified version of the concept. The formula is something you may be able to do in your head. The calculation should be simple, so you can recalculate the numbers as things change. There are more complex versions, but they aren't very useful for this book.

Adding in manufacturing lead-time

Adding a new product will add revenue and costs. To analyze a decision to add a new product, you calculate *manufacturing lead-time*. The lead-time is the average waiting time plus the manufacturing time. The term represents the time from order placement until the product is complete.

Here's the formula for manufacturing lead-time:

> manufacturing lead-time = average waiting time + manufacturing time

Consider the relevant cost and revenue when the new product is added. Say you own a pastry company. Here are some issues to consider when you add your new line of customized cookies:

- ✔ **Revenue:** Revenue increases based on sales of the new product. The revenue is relevant revenue.

- ✔ **Variable costs:** Consider the amount of material (flour, sugar, and so on) required for the cookies. You also incur labor costs. Material and labor costs are relevant because total variable costs change when you add the new product.

> ✔ **Carrying cost of inventory:** Assume that the customized cookies are delivered quickly, usually the day they're made. You pay a driver to make deliveries, so there's no need to store cookies anywhere. If you have to store the new product somewhere for a short time, you incur a *carrying cost.* Head on over to Chapter 9 to find out more about carrying cost.
>
> ✔ **Capacity costs:** If you bake more pastries and don't add any baking capacity (number of baking ovens, for example), you have a longer waiting time to start each batch of cookies or cakes. So the added waiting time is a relevant issue. The waiting time is a cost, in the sense that you risk losing business if customers consider the wait to be too long. Tough to figure!

Eliminating the Constraint of the Bottleneck

The *theory of constraints* (TOC) essentially says that a chain is no stronger than its weakest link. A production bottleneck is a weak link. You can apply the theory of constraints to maximize income by eliminating *bottlenecks* in production.

One simple definition is that a bottleneck occurs when your workload exceeds your production capacity. But there are many ways a bottleneck can happen.

Imagine that you're a highway planner. You forecast traffic flow, and you may plan more lanes on some stretches of highway to reduce bottlenecks and congestion. In your business, TOC applies to your forecasting and planning production processes.

To literally see a bottleneck in action, open a bottle of ketchup and turn it upside down. The bottle's narrow neck prevents the ketchup from flowing. But never fear! Food processors have answered the call by moving to wide-mouth containers and squeeze bottles. You can do the same (metaphorically speaking) with your business.

Fewer bottlenecks mean increased contribution margin

It's hard enough to make an honest buck; don't let bottlenecks hold you back. If you can eliminate bottlenecks and operate more efficiently, you generate contribution margin dollars faster. (Recall that *contribution margin* is sales less variable costs. See Chapter 3). Assuming that demand is available for your product, the faster you are able to produce goods, the more sales you can make and, hence, the greater contribution margin. A bottleneck is something that prevents you from producing the product more quickly. The converse, of course, is also true: More bottlenecks mean decreased contribution margin.

The more production you can push through your system, the more items you have to sell. Production also increases your variable costs (direct materials and direct labor), but that's okay; those increases are to be expected.

Your goal is to produce efficiently so you make as many sellable units as possible. Here's how you accomplish this:

1. Find the biggest bottleneck, the part of the production process that holds up producing a product. When you need the production line for multiple products, the bottleneck can hold up *all* production. Look for the stage of the production process with the most work in process (partially completed units) waiting for further processing. (Stroll over to Chapter 4 for a work in process explanation.)

2. Eliminate the bottleneck. Make clearing the bottleneck your first priority. Getting product through the bottleneck is job one.

3. Find the next biggest bottleneck. Repeat as needed.

You clear the bottleneck by increasing efficiency, but how you do that varies depending on the situation. The next section has several examples.

The Businessperson's Dream is to manufacture and sell products so well the market is *saturated*. Every unit is sold. Additional units go unsold until the marketing department finds a way to increase demand.

Clearing bottlenecks

Obviously, bottlenecks slow down production, or they wouldn't be called bottlenecks. Here are some ways to clear them:

- **Look for inefficiencies in the bottlenecked department.** You may have a capacity problem. Maybe there's too little labor, or the machines are too slow. Maybe machines are breaking down too frequently. Consider upgrading machines or hiring more employees.

- **Increase incoming units from other departments.** Say you have too few work-in-process units (partially completed units) coming in from another department. Fix the situation, and the bottlenecked department runs more efficiently. This means that you have to look at that other department to see why its outputs are inadequate.

- **Decrease incoming units from other departments.** Slowing production in the non-bottlenecked departments supplying the bottlenecked department may help. The bottlenecked department won't be overwhelmed by work in process units. The goal is to give the bottlenecked area enough, but not too much, work in process.

Stay with me on this reasoning. It seems counterintuitive to ask a department to produce less, but if your sales projections are accurate, you don't need too much product. Further, your sales projections determined how much material to buy. Ah, so the non-bottlenecked department is making the right quantity of product. However, it's delivering it *too fast*. Now you can't make money by asking that department to slow down. Consider alternative uses of labor and machines in the non-bottlenecked department to divert some of the productivity.

✔ **Eliminate idle time in the bottleneck.** *Idle time* is when production slows or stops. You're paying salaries and other costs, but you're not getting the production you expect. Remember that an absent employee can make a machine idle, and a broken machine can make an employee idle.

✔ **Reduce setup time.** Any production area spends time on setup and then production. Any other time is probably idle time. If setup time is taking longer than expected, consider spending resources to reduce the time. For example, maybe you make improvements to a machine, so setup is faster — or you buy a new machine. If the cost savings (long-term) from reduced setup time is more than the cost of the machine, the purchase makes sense.

✔ **Consider outsourcing.** When you hire someone else to perform a task, you are *outsourcing*. Mull over whether or not you can shift production to another department (or, in some cases, another line in the same department). You may also consider outsourcing the bottlenecked product. Step on over to Chapter 11 for more on outsourcing.

You need to perform some analysis to determine if outsourcing makes economic sense. Consider whether the cost paid to the outsourcing company is more or less than the cost of fixing the bottleneck. Consider whether the bottleneck is a short-term or a long-term problem. If outsourcing is cheaper, the decision makes long-term sense. If outsourcing is more expensive, that's another story.

Although you can outsource in the short run to get rid of the bottleneck, it's probably not the right decision over the long term. Keep in mind that outsourcing has non-financial considerations, such as employee morale and productivity.

✔ **Eliminate defective products.** Ensure that you're producing as many good units as you can. Defective products require reworking, with the dubious benefits of slowing production and increasing costs.

Prioritize which units you produce first. Fill your customer orders first by producing the units they ordered. Your customer orders produce immediate revenue, and revenue is part of the contribution margin formula.

You can still make some allowance for ending inventory, but produce it last. Of course, ending inventory doesn't generate immediate revenue, but when you open the doors on the first day of the next month, you have some inventory to sell. That way, customer orders coming early in the month are filled early in the month without waiting for new production.

There may be a workaround that's superior to outsourcing. Call it *insourcing*. Say you're a garment manufacturer, and you have a bottleneck in the shirt-sewing department due to an issue with a machine. You also manufacture cargo pants, and a sewing machine in the cargo-pants department performs a similar task.

If the pants machine can be set up to handle the shirts, that machine can be a short-term solution for your shirt bottleneck. That assumes, of course, that pants department can do without that machine for a short time.

Using equipment or staff from other departments isn't a long-term solution to the bottleneck. Those departments have their own production needs. They can't afford to do without their resources for very long. At some point, their own productivity will suffer.

You should inspect work in process *before* you start production in the bottle-necked department. An inspection allows you to remove defective units from production. (They're defective, so why spend the effort on finishing them? They'll only get rejected later.) Fewer units in production reduce the size of the bottleneck. In Chapter 17, the inspection point is usually at the *end* of production. In this case, an extra inspection up front likely reduces the number of goods in production.

The long-term solution to a bottleneck is analysis using activity-based costing (ABC; see Chapter 5). Consider the activities related to the costs you incur. That analysis includes a review of how efficiently your departments work. The process considers whether costs (labor, machine, and so on) are used to produce the maximum number of goods possible. ABC analysis can help resolve the bottleneck problem long-term.

Part VI

The Part of Tens

In this part . . .

Forget the loss, but don't forget the lesson. The chapters in this part are brief and filled with useful information . . . lessons learned by managers using cost accounting. Chapter 20 walks you through the ten mistakes that can lead to losses in your business. Chapter 21 lists ten improvements you can make to improve the profit level in your business. This wisdom makes the cost accounting process easier.

Chapter 20

Ten Common Costing Mistakes and How to Avoid Them

In This Chapter

▶ Allocating product costs more accurately

▶ Understanding types of costs

▶ Following up on variances

▶ Planning when costs will be incurred

T his chapter covers the most common mistakes related to costs. Reducing your costs can lead to a higher profit — without the need to raise your product price. Unfortunately, making costing mistakes can lead to lower profit (or losses). As an accountant, you can make a big impact on your company's bottom line by addressing these mistakes.

Pricing a Product Incorrectly

Overhead is the most commonly mishandled cost. Overhead should be allocated based on an activity level (labor hours and machine hours, for example). If a business owner doesn't understand cost accounting, the overhead costs may not be allocated at all, or too much or too little cost may be allocated to the product. As a result, the full product cost isn't accurate, so the product price also isn't set accurately.

Listing Fixed Costs As Variable Costs

Accountants must price a product to cover all costs and generate a profit. Because total fixed costs are difficult to change, it's particularly important to focus on them. You can't reduce or eliminate fixed costs easily in the short term. So make sure you sell enough to cover those expenses.

You should analyze fixed costs in total dollars, not fixed cost *per unit.* Using a per-unit calculation implies that every unit sold generates more fixed costs. In reality, you may cover all of your fixed costs with only a portion of your total sales.

You need to spend enough on fixed costs to have enough capacity to produce. When you analyze fixed costs, however, focus on total dollars, not a per-unit calculation. See Chapter 8 for more on fixed and variable costs.

Labeling Period Costs As Product Costs

Period costs are incurred with the passage of time. For example, you incur interest costs on a loan each month. Product costs are incurred when you make your product or deliver your service.

It's critical that you define period costs correctly for two reasons. You must do so to be in compliance with financial reporting standards. And if you incorrectly label a period cost as a product cost or vice versa, the profit you show on your income statement may be incorrect.

If you reduce your production by 50 percent during the month, your product costs (material and labor costs, for example) also decline by 50 percent. Your period costs *are still incurred,* regardless of your level of production.

If you label a period cost as a product cost, those costs may not be recognized as expenses until the product is sold. If they are truly period costs, they should be expensed every month or year. The mistake leads to errors in your product costing.

Misusing Target Net Income

Target net income is the goal a business owner sets for his or her profit. After you set target net income, you can adjust the variables in the formula to reach your profit goal. For example, you might change the number of units sold, and that affects sales and profit.

Business owners often make the mistake of projecting an unrealistic target net income — either too high or too low. As an accountant, you can help the owner address this issue.

Target net income may be too high if your *actual* results come in lower than planned and generate a loss. Because the target is an estimate, actual results may vary. You want your target net income to be some amount above the break-even point (greater than zero), but you want to make a conservative estimate so that you leave some room for error.

Your target net income's level of sales may also be unrealistic. There's no point in selecting an income target using a units sold number that's unreachable. Also, don't project net income with a sale price that's so high no customer will pay it.

Forgetting About Taxes

After-tax income is your profit after paying taxes. Think of your take-home pay. The income that matters to you is the money you keep after deductions for taxes — what you take home. When computing profit, don't forget to allow for taxes.

When you know your tax rate, you can compute your after-tax income. Say your target net income is $10,000. If your tax rate is 30 percent, your profit after paying taxes is 70 percent (100 percent less the 30 percent tax rate). So your net income after tax is $10,000 × 70 percent, or $7,000.

Assigning Costs to the Wrong Product

You may identify all of your costs, but assign costs to the wrong product. This means that the full costs of *individual products* are wrong. The situation can cause serious problems with your sales mix.

Sales mix is the proportion of your total sales that any one product represents. Assume you sell two sweaters — a rock-climber model and an ocean-surf model. Maybe the sales mix is 40 percent rock-climber sweaters and 60 percent ocean-surf sweaters.

Each sweater has a different profit margin. You plan your total sweater profit by adding the profits from both lines of sweaters.

If you don't assign costs correctly, your product cost and your profit calculations won't be accurate. As a result, your sales mix won't generate the profit you expect. Unfortunately, you may not catch the error until the month or year is over. At that point, it's usually too late to make corrections.

Not Reviewing Variances Correctly

A variance is defined as a difference between actual and budgeted (standard) costs. If a variance is unfavorable, you should analyze the variance and consider taking action to improve your results going forward. Understanding whether or not a variance is unfavorable can be a challenge.

If actual costs are higher than budgeted, the variance is unfavorable. You spent more than you planned. If actual revenue is higher than standard (budgeted), the variance is *favorable*. Keep in mind that higher actual costs are a problem, but higher actual sales are a good result. Higher costs are a warning that you need to make changes. That's not the case with higher sales.

If you notice a large favorable variance, analyze those variances, too. Sure, a favorable variance is a good thing. But you need to know why your actual results were so different from your plan.

Redlining: Pushing Production Activity Above Relevant Range

If you don't have sufficient capacity, you may not be able to deliver your product or service. To ensure that you have enough capacity, you need to know the relevant range of your assets (machinery, equipment, and staff).

Sometimes, business owners operate at the top end of their relevant range for too long. If you push too hard, your assets eventually lose some productivity. The situation is similar to pushing your car's engine too hard for too long. *Redlining* the engine causes it to break down.

A better choice is to add capacity. Rather than run your machinery at 100 percent capacity, consider investing in another machine. You can spread production across two machines.

Note, however, that you need to analyze the cost versus benefit of adding another machine. If the second machine is only used at 10 percent capacity, it probably won't be worth it. This strategy reduces the risk of a breakdown due to overuse.

Ignoring the Timing of Costs

When you analyze costs, you should consider timing. Although the amount of cost is important, it's just as critical to know *when* you will incur the cost.

A common business mistake is not planning your cash needs for production. When you collect cash from clients, you need to budget some of that cash for future material and labor costs. If you don't have sufficient cash, you can't make your product.

Not Implementing Activity-Based Costing

Activity-based costing (ABC) is a method of analysis that allows you to assign costs more accurately. You should consider implementing ABC. If you don't, you're spreading costs across all of your products evenly. Your costs won't be assigned to individual products accurately. Check out Chapter 5 for more on activity-based costing.

Chapter 21

Ten Ways to Increase Profits Using Costing

In This Chapter

▶ Selling the most profitable products

▶ Forecasting a reasonable profit

▶ Planning to identify more costs

▶ Training to improve performance

Cost accounting's big payoff is making improvements to a business. This chapter covers some of those improvements. You can use cost accounting to identify costs and reduce them. Better cost control results in a lower total product cost — and a higher profit. As an accountant, you can apply these ideas to the business and be a hero.

Selling More Of The Right Products

Your company wants to sell more of the most profitable products because those sales increase the company's overall profit. You can compare profit levels using cost accounting. When you know the correct full cost of a product, you can compare it to the sales price. The difference between the two is the profit for the product.

Compare the profit generated by each product. To make a fair comparison, compute profit as a percentage of sales, or profit ÷ sale price. The products with the highest percentages are the most profitable.

Implementing Sales Mix Analysis to Increase Total Profits

After you determine which products are the most profitable, you're ready to use sales mix analysis to increase total profits.

You can compute the percentage of total sales any one product represents. That percentage is the sales mix percentage. The idea is to sell more of your most profitable product and shift sales away from other products.

Change the focus of your marketing and sales efforts to move sales to more profitable products. If your efforts generate more interest in those products, sales and, more important, profits will increase.

Building a Higher Margin of Safety

A higher margin of safety means that your company can remain profitable even if actual results differ from your plan. *Margin of safety* is the difference between your planned level of sales and your breakeven level of sales.

Say your planned sales level is $1,000,000, and your breakeven point is $700,000. If actual sales come in at $800,000, you're still profitable. Always include a margin of safety in your plan for sales.

Deciding How Much You Need: Production and Scheduling Issues

Accountants can make improvements to the production process to reduce costs. If you move products between departments, make sure that each department is ready for production and has work in process available from the previous department. This planning helps avoid costs for downtime.

Plan purchases so that materials are available for production when you need them. Schedule enough labor hours to meet your needs. All of these efforts will ensure smoother production and help minimize your costs.

Who Does What: Handling Costs and Employee Issues

If your company manages employees effectively, those efforts can have a tremendous positive impact on costs and generate more profit.

Each worker should have a written job description. The staff must receive clear instructions about what needs to be done and when. These steps minimize labor costs; otherwise, you pay for worker time that isn't productive.

Reducing and Managing Scrap

If your production process generates scrap, consider how you can reduce it. This requires an analysis of your entire production process. Assume you make cotton shirts, for example. If you use machines to cut the cotton fabric, mull over whether or not the machine's setup can be changed to reduce the amount of material wasted.

Maybe the machine can be reset to cut fabric more precisely, which would reduce scrap. Better employee training may result in more careful use of materials. Take a look at the whole process. If you can reduce the amount of scrap, it's worth it. For more info on scrap, see Chapter 17.

But sometimes, scrap is inevitable, and you may end up with unused materials. Keep in mind that scrap is a cost, but your decisions about scrap can reduce your costs.

Consider creating a list of other companies that could use your scrap in their product. The more companies you identify, the more likely you are to find a buyer for your scrap. Also, think about whether or not you can use your scrap to produce another product.

Moving It off the Shelf: Inventory Issues

Inventory is often the largest cost for a business, particularly for a retailer. Perform an analysis to compute your economic order quantity (EOQ). The EOQ formula is designed to minimize your ordering cost and carrying costs for inventory.

Make sure that you take advantage of purchase discounts, whenever possible. Finally, consider how frequently you have to restock your shelves with inventory (inventory turnover). Try to balance the costs of ordering and carrying inventory with the need to fill customer orders in a timely manner. Check out Chapter 9 for more on inventory.

Effectively Taking Special Orders

A special order allows you to use excess production capacity to generate revenue. Use your cost accounting skills to determine a unit sale price that makes the order profitable. Keep in mind that fixed costs are irrelevant to your special-order decision.

Be proactive about special orders. If you have excess capacity, tell your customers. If they place a special order, the extra business generates more revenue.

Making Accurate Cost Allocations

When you allocate indirect costs to your product, you need an accurate allocation method. Make sure that the costs you allocate are closely related to the *driver* of the costs. If the cost and the cost driver are closely related, the cost allocation is more accurate.

Say you're allocating cost for machine setup. That cost can be allocated using the number of setups. In that way, the setup cost is connected to the activity that causes the cost to occur — setups. This process generates a reasonable cost allocation.

Addressing the Issue of Spoilage

There's nothing worse than producing a product that can't be sold to a client. You can take some steps to prevent spoilage before units start rolling off the assembly line. Consider whether the production department understands the product design.

Your production staff should be able to understand the design and produce the product without complications. Your design staff should be able to design products that are easier to manufacture. A good example is a product design that minimizes the number of moving parts. The more streamlined the production process, the less likely there are to be spoiled units.

If spoiled units are a problem, beef up your employee training. Maybe your staff is making production errors because they aren't properly trained to use your machinery.

Most important, if you do have spoilage, strive to rework every spoiled unit. If you spend money to make a product, make sure that you can sell it to someone. See Chapter 17 for more on spoilage.

Index

• *J* •

Notes

Notes

le & Mac

d 2 For Dummies,
Edition
-1-118-17679-5

one 4S For Dummies,
Edition
-1-118-03671-6

d touch For Dummies,
Edition
-1-118-12960-9

c OS X Lion
Dummies
-1-118-02205-4

gging & Social Media

yVille For Dummies
-1-118-08337-6

cebook For Dummies,
Edition
-1-118-09562-1

m Blogging
r Dummies
-1-118-03843-7

itter For Dummies,
d Edition
-0-470-76879-2

rdPress For Dummies,
Edition
-1-118-07342-1

usiness

sh Flow For Dummies
-1-118-01850-7

vesting For Dummies,
Edition
-0-470-90545-6

Job Searching with Social
Media For Dummies
978-0-470-93072-4

QuickBooks 2012
For Dummies
978-1-118-09120-3

Resumes For Dummies,
6th Edition
978-0-470-87361-8

Starting an Etsy Business
For Dummies
978-0-470-93067-0

Cooking & Entertaining

Cooking Basics
For Dummies, 4th Edition
978-0-470-91388-8

Wine For Dummies,
4th Edition
978-0-470-04579-4

Diet & Nutrition

Kettlebells For Dummies
978-0-470-59929-7

Nutrition For Dummies,
5th Edition
978-0-470-93231-5

Restaurant Calorie Counter
For Dummies,
2nd Edition
978-0-470-64405-8

Digital Photography

Digital SLR Cameras &
Photography For Dummies,
4th Edition
978-1-118-14489-3

Digital SLR Settings
& Shortcuts
For Dummies
978-0-470-91763-3

Photoshop Elements 10
For Dummies
978-1-118-10742-3

Gardening

Gardening Basics
For Dummies
978-0-470-03749-2

Vegetable Gardening
For Dummies,
2nd Edition
978-0-470-49870-5

Green/Sustainable

Raising Chickens
For Dummies
978-0-470-46544-8

Green Cleaning
For Dummies
978-0-470-39106-8

Health

Diabetes For Dummies,
3rd Edition
978-0-470-27086-8

Food Allergies
For Dummies
978-0-470-09584-3

Living Gluten-Free
For Dummies,
2nd Edition
978-0-470-58589-4

Hobbies

Beekeeping
For Dummies,
2nd Edition
978-0-470-43065-1

Chess For Dummies,
3rd Edition
978-1-118-01695-4

Drawing For Dummies,
2nd Edition
978-0-470-61842-4

eBay For Dummies,
7th Edition
978-1-118-09806-6

Knitting For Dummies,
2nd Edition
978-0-470-28747-7

Language &
Foreign Language

English Grammar
For Dummies,
2nd Edition
978-0-470-54664-2

French For Dummies,
2nd Edition
978-1-118-00464-7

German For Dummies,
2nd Edition
978-0-470-90101-4

Spanish Essentials
For Dummies
978-0-470-63751-7

Spanish For Dummies,
2nd Edition
978-0-470-87855-2

Math & Science

Algebra I For Dummies,
2nd Edition
978-0-470-55964-2

Biology For Dummies,
2nd Edition
978-0-470-59875-7

Chemistry For Dummies,
2nd Edition
978-1-1180-0730-3

Geometry For Dummies,
2nd Edition
978-0-470-08946-0

Pre-Algebra Essentials
For Dummies
978-0-470-61838-7

Microsoft Office

Excel 2010 For Dummies
978-0-470-48953-6

Office 2010 All-in-One
For Dummies
978-0-470-49748-7

Office 2011 for Mac
For Dummies
978-0-470-87869-9

Word 2010
For Dummies
978-0-470-48772-3

Music

Guitar For Dummies,
2nd Edition
978-0-7645-9904-0

Clarinet For Dummies
978-0-470-58477-4

iPod & iTunes
For Dummies,
9th Edition
978-1-118-13060-5

Pets

Cats For Dummies,
2nd Edition
978-0-7645-5275-5

Dogs All-in One
For Dummies
978-0470-52978-2

Saltwater Aquariums
For Dummies
978-0-470-06805-2

Religion & Inspiration

The Bible For Dummies
978-0-7645-5296-0

Catholicism For Dummies,
2nd Edition
978-1-118-07778-8

Spirituality For Dummies,
2nd Edition
978-0-470-19142-2

Self-Help & Relationships

Happiness For Dummies
978-0-470-28171-0

Overcoming Anxiety
For Dummies,
2nd Edition
978-0-470-57441-6

Seniors

Crosswords For Seniors
For Dummies
978-0-470-49157-7

iPad 2 For Seniors
For Dummies, 3rd Edition
978-1-118-17678-8

Laptops & Tablets
For Seniors For Dummies,
2nd Edition
978-1-118-09596-6

Smartphones & Tablets

BlackBerry For Dummies,
5th Edition
978-1-118-10035-6

Droid X2 For Dummies
978-1-118-14864-8

HTC ThunderBolt
For Dummies
978-1-118-07601-9

MOTOROLA XOOM
For Dummies
978-1-118-08835-7

Sports

Basketball For Dummies,
3rd Edition
978-1-118-07374-2

Football For Dummies,
2nd Edition
978-1-118-01261-1

Golf For Dummies,
4th Edition
978-0-470-88279-5

Test Prep

ACT For Dummies,
5th Edition
978-1-118-01259-8

ASVAB For Dummies,
3rd Edition
978-0-470-63760-9

The GRE Test For
Dummies, 7th Edition
978-0-470-00919-2

Police Officer Exam
For Dummies
978-0-470-88724-0

Series 7 Exam
For Dummies
978-0-470-09932-2

Web Development

HTML, CSS, & XHTML
For Dummies, 7th Editio
978-0-470-91659-9

Drupal For Dummies,
2nd Edition
978-1-118-08348-2

Windows 7

Windows 7
For Dummies
978-0-470-49743-2

Windows 7
For Dummies,
Book + DVD Bundle
978-0-470-52398-8

Windows 7 All-in-One
For Dummies
978-0-470-48763-1

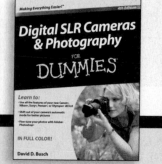

Available wherever books are sold. For more information or to order direct: U.S. customers visit www.dummies.com or call 1-877-762-29
U.K. customers visit www.wileyeurope.com or call (0) 1243 843291. Canadian customers visit www.wiley.ca or call 1-800-567-4797.

Connect with us online at www.facebook.com/fordummies or @fordummies

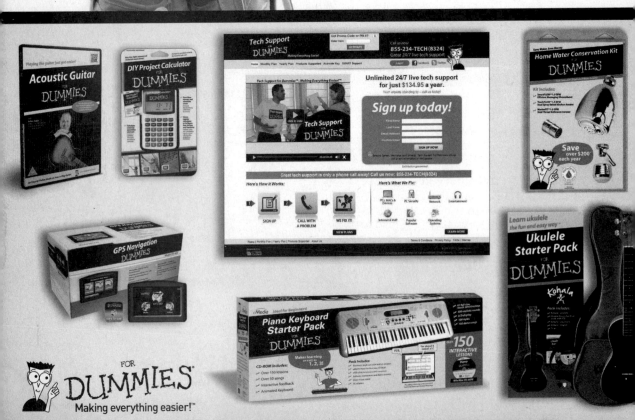